B.D. Pande (Bhairab Datt Pande) w[as the first person from Kumaon] and Garhwal division to pass the India[n Civil Service examination] from London in 1938. In his thirty-[nine years of civil service, he] held many important offices in the [country.]
He served as finance secretary, development commissioner and food commissioner in Bihar; chairman of LIC at then Bombay; and finally cabinet secretary to the Government of India from 1972 to 1977. Pande was also the first person from Uttarakhand to be appointed the governor of West Bengal and later Punjab. In 2000, then President K.R. Narayanan conferred on him the Padma Vibhushan for his meritorious service to the nation. He was also honoured with a DLitt (*honoris causa*) by the Kumaon University in 2006. He passed away peacefully on 2 April 2009.

In the
SERVICE of
FREE INDIA

Memoir of a Civil Servant

B. D. Pande

SPEAKING TIGER

SPEAKING TIGER BOOKS LLP
125A, Ground Floor, Shahpur Jat, near Asiad Village,
New Delhi 110049

Published by Speaking Tiger Books 2021

Copyright © Ratna Sudarshan 2021

ISBN: 978-93-5447-158-2
eISBN: 978-93-5447-153-7

10 9 8 7 6 5 4 3 2 1

All rights reserved.
No part of this publication may be reproduced, transmitted, or stored in a retrieval system, in any form or by any means, electronic, mechanical, photocopying, recording or otherwise, without the prior permission of the publisher.

This book is sold subject to the condition that it shall not, by way of trade or otherwise, be lent, resold, hired out, or otherwise circulated, without the publisher's prior consent, in any form of binding or cover other than that in which it is published.

In memory of Vimla Pande

CONTENTS

	Introduction	ix
	Preface	xv
1.	My Family, Childhood and Education	1
2.	Cambridge and the Civil Service Examination	16
3.	The Bihar Years: District Postings	39
4.	The Bihar Years: Patna	55
5.	Delhi and Bombay: 1960–66	80
6.	Patna, 1967 and Delhi, 1967–72	105
7.	Delhi: Cabinet Secretary (1972–77)	131
8.	Post-Retirement Years: 1977–81	154
9.	Governor, West Bengal: 1981–83	163
10.	Punjab: The Sikhs and the Hindus	185
11.	Punjab: The Anandpur Sahib Resolution	211
12.	Governor, Punjab: 1983–84	238
13.	Punjab: 1984	265
14.	Punjab: 1984 and After	295

Annexure I: Epilogue—20 April 1994, Ram Navami Day	308
Annexure II: Uttarakhand Paryavaran Shiksha Kendra	314
Annexure III: Epilogue: September 1999	317
Timeline	319

Introduction

This book will come as a surprise to those who knew my father.

After leaving Punjab in the wake of Operation Bluestar in 1984, my father came away to Almora deeply burdened. He started writing, penning down what he had understood and experienced in Punjab. He recalled the days of his childhood and schooling, his career as an Indian Civil Service (ICS) officer that began under the British and through the early years of Independence, his years spent in Bihar and later Delhi, ending with governorships in West Bengal and then Punjab. He was awarded the Padma Vibhushan in 2000. Having been cabinet secretary during the Emergency, there was never a shortage of journalists wanting his opinions then and later. However, he chose never to talk about these events in his lifetime, not even in private.

These memoirs were handwritten and filled two blank diaries, with a third short addendum. As he says very clearly in his opening paragraphs, they were written out of memory and were not based on any written notes or records. The bulk of it was completed in 1986, a short epilogue was added in 1994 along with photocopies of some old documents he had come across in the library and found to be of interest; and a second briefer one in 1999. His instructions, pasted on each diary, were that the diaries were not to be opened 'until five years after my death or 1 January 2001, whichever is later'. He passed away in 2009 at the age of ninety-two. It is now more than ten years since his death and more than thirty years since the events of 1984.

The sections on Punjab are contained in later chapters of this book. They were written in April and May 1986, a couple of years after Operation Bluestar. The whole manuscript is written in a sort of stream of consciousness style. To make it easier for the reader, I have taken the liberty of placing what was written in roughly chronological order and divided it into chapters. I have only slightly edited the manuscript; the language has not been tampered with, and nothing has been added into the manuscript. The style remains conversational and there are some digressions, given his writing style. A few explanatory footnotes have been provided. The handwriting is mostly clear and legible, although a few words took some effort to decipher. I have not tried to verify anything written here, except to check some places and names where possible, and to give the correct reference to one of C.P. Snow's books that he mentions.

Born into a fairly conservative Kumaoni community, education—as it so often has in India—lifted my father into the world of the civil service. He was the first Kumaoni to join the ICS, and the first to become a governor. He always retained a strong attachment to the community and kept in touch with close relatives. Family, in many ways, remained an anchor. He grew up under the care of a devoted father who was ambitious about his son's career. My father set off to England in 1936, at the age of nineteen, with the intention of appearing for the ICS exam, which required two years of study at an English University. He qualified on his first attempt in 1938. He would have been among the last few recruits into the service, what with the disruption of the Second World War. In today's world, international travel is commonplace. In 1936, being an Indian in England would have been a very different experience from what it is today, and we get a glimpse of what it might have been like. Moreover, the war clouds were already gathering. He qualified for the ICS just as the Second World War broke out and he returned to India as an ICS officer in 1939, on a ship under complete black out due to the war. Thus began his long career of thirty-nine years as a civil servant wherein he witnessed and partook in the building of a nation.

The ICS has been described (as my father quotes in these notes) as 'neither Indian, nor civil, nor a service'. It is equally known for values of integrity, impartiality and merit. The Indian ICS officers, by covenant, owed loyalty to the British Government. With Independence, the same officers became an integral part of the project of building a nation. After Independence, the ICS was replaced by the Indian Administrative Service (IAS). My father describes his own career as a movement along 'the bureaucratic escalator', that is, progression based on seniority and merit. His memories of the years spent in Bihar, and later Delhi, provide vivid descriptions of the civil service life.

Altogether, he held a very large number of positions which are briefly summarized in the timeline at the end of this book. The first twenty years of his career were spent in Bihar—a time of hardwork, optimism, friendships and a young family. The next nineteen years in Delhi were far more stressful. He was appointed cabinet secretary in 1972 and retired from this post in 1977, making his tenure one of the longest of any cabinet secretary in sovereign India. He was therefore in this position when the Emergency was declared by then Prime Minister Indira Gandhi. In 1981, he went as governor to West Bengal, and in 1983 as governor to Punjab. He remained in Punjab during Operation Bluestar—a military operation carried out in June 1984 at the order of the Prime Minister to establish control over the Harmandir Sahib Complex in Amritsar and to capture armed followers of the religious leader Bhindranwale. Immediately after, he resigned and left for Almora. The events leading up to the Emergency and Operation Bluestar are presented herein from a very unique perspective.

Although my father had studied in Almora as a child, his links with the place grew more tenuous. He had not made any particular plans for his retirement (such as building a house in Delhi) and so when he resigned from the post of governor, Punjab, he took the one option that was immediately available—of returning to live in Almora in the old family house, which had been vacant for several decades then. As he points out, this was neither planned nor anticipated. Perhaps he initially thought of it as a temporary residence. But various factors contributed to keep my parents there for the rest of their lives. They made of this old house a warm and welcoming home which became a necessary stop for many visitors and was much enjoyed by their grandchildren. Once again, without any conscious effort on his part, he became chairperson of an NGO and got involved with an environmental education programme, and with the life of the hills in a very new and different way. Although only briefly discussed in the annexures, this work has left an important legacy.

The annexures also include some details relating to his family history in Almora, based on old documents, including the schism that developed in the community around various social matters.

In publishing these memoirs, I hope they would be of interest as they bring out some of the challenges that faced civil servants, and the commitment with which these were resolved, in the years following Independence. The experience of the Community Development programme still has important lessons for today's Panchayati Raj institutions. The Emergency and Operation Bluestar remain important for our understanding of Indian history, and perhaps some details might be of value to historians of modern India.

An old Sufi saying that is used at several points in the manuscript is 'This too shall pass', emphasizes the ephemeral nature of all situations in human life. Towards the end of his life, my father asked me more than once to suggest a good book on the social history of India to him. Having lived a long life, he had experienced some major and dramatic changes at a professional level—through the political life of the nation, the economic development of the country, social norms and values; and at a personal level—with sons and daughter whose lives and choices meandered into unexpected trajectories. In a small way, these writings contribute to understanding the values with which an earlier generation of bureaucrats had contributed to nation building, and at a more personal level, the mixture of modernity and tradition that (still) characterizes Indian lives, as well as the necessity of having the ability to cope with change.

In conclusion, it needs to be said that no attempt has been made to ensure political correctness or to change the tenor of what was written, recognizing that we all speak the language of our own times, and also to remain faithful to what was written down. Some words used here have a rather different meaning now. For example, 'terrorism' today has very specific international connotations. It is used in a more general sense here. While all opinions expressed here are personal opinions of my father, I take responsibility for editorial decisions.

In putting this manuscript together, my brother Lalit has helped me in more ways than one, for example, getting the old papers referred to in the annexures translated into Hindi and locating old photographs. I am grateful for the sage advice from Aditya; and support of different kinds from Arvind and Mrinal; Anant and Diva; Anuradha, Abhishek and Ashish. I am grateful to Preeti Gill and Ravi Singh for making this publication possible, and to Shreya Gupta for ensuring that it is presentable.

In the memoirs that follow, while there is much personal information in the first two chapters, very little follows subsequently, barring a hint here and there. My mother, Vimla Pande, who married my father at a very young age, came from a similar family background; but in contrast to his lonely and disciplined life, she was the eldest daughter with nine siblings and had grown up with companionship and laughter. In a different time, she might have been a writer—instead many generations of children were kept entranced with her stories—unfortunately never recorded. Their different personalities shaped a marriage that was strong and a home that was always open to the wider family. This book is dedicated to her memory, to her courage, and her compassion.

Ratna M. Sudarshan
New Delhi, India
March 2021

Preface

Om Namah Shivaya

Today is Saturday, 8 March 1986—Maha Shivratri. I have started writing what may be called my reminiscences, recollections, memoirs—the name will emerge; however, it is not an autobiography.

Ever since I retired in 1977, people have been asking me to write my memoirs, even more so after I resigned as governor of Punjab in July 1984. I have also been approached by some publishers. But I always refused on the grounds that I have no talent for writing. I was a student of science and writing was never my forte. During my service, I did not write notes exceeding a page or page-and-a-half, no matter how intricate the subject. And more importantly, I kept no notes during my service or lifetime, kept no copies of important papers, letters or memos and therefore my recollections will tend to be biased. With the passage of years, one's memory tends to play tricks and I might even get facts wrong. Furthermore, I did not possess any means of rechecking what I have written from contemporary accounts or official records. For these reasons I never took up pen to write.

Recently, my wife, Vimla, went to Delhi for a fortnight or so to be with our eldest son Raja (Arvind), his wife Minu (Mrinal), their daughters Radhika and Rohini, our daughter Ratna, her (then) husband Sudarshan and sons Anant and Aditya. She recounted how Ratna said that I must write my memoirs, and that for historical and other significance my account of what transpired in Punjab during Operation Bluestar in June 1984 must be narrated. What is important are my memories and recollections. I could also lay down that what I write now should not be published for some years.

So I have decided to write. However, these memoirs are not to be published or read by anyone till 1 January 2001. Not all the actors in the scene will have departed from this world by then, but in any case, it will be almost sixteen years after the incident. I have no intention of writing what may be called 'instant history' nor do I wish to see the book published in my lifetime. What I am going to write need not even be published.

CHAPTER ONE

My Family, Childhood and Education

I think I should go back to the very beginning and say something about myself, my family and my early life. I was born on 17 March 1917, at Haldwani (District Nainital). My full name is Bhairab Datt Pande, but I came to be known by my initials only—B.D. Pande. I was the youngest of five children. My two eldest brothers would have been fifteen years or so older than me. Both died very young—of measles followed by pneumonia. I had two sisters—eight and six years older than me. My father was almost forty when I was born. My mother, who came from the Jhijhar family of Joshi's, died when I was only six or seven years of age. By that time both my sisters were married. I grew up as a lonely child and was brought up by my father who was intensely devoted to me.

My earliest childhood memory is that of the marriage of my eldest sister in Lucknow, in a red brick house, when I was about four years old. I do not remember the marriage of my second sister which took place a few years later at Almora.

Another memory I recall is of the night before my mother died. My father was then posted at Meerut as superintendent of post offices. One evening, I had an intense longing to be with my mother and to be fed by her but was told that she was not feeling well and so I should not disturb her. I was persuaded to go to sleep. Very early the next morning, at about four, while it was still dark and cold, I was suddenly woken up. I was told that my mother was dying and I should go and see her. By the time I reached her room, she was no more. This was the only time that I saw my father weeping, as he told me that my mother was no more.

*

My father, Chandra Datt Pande, was the youngest of six or seven children, of whom four were boys. He was born on 15 July 1878, and lived to the ripe old age of eighty-two. He died on 23 December 1960 in New Delhi. My grandfather, Manorath Pande, died when my father was only four years old. My grandmother also died at about the same time. So my father was orphaned at a very young age and brought up by my eldest uncle, Jai Datt Pande. My other uncles were Hari Datt and Jwala Datt. Jwala Datt also died young and was survived by one son, Padma Datt, who later became a district judge and built a house at Kailash Colony in New Delhi. The two other older uncles, Jai Datt and Hari Datt, had no children.

My father was one of the first young men of Almora to pass the MA examination from the Allahabad University—or the Muir Central College—as it was then called. In 1898, he obtained a BA and in 1900, an MA in history. After passing the MA exam he joined the Indian Posts and Telegraphs Department. He retired in 1933 as deputy director general, Posts and Telegraphs (Postal Services) at New Delhi.

My father moved back to Lucknow soon after my mother's death. We stayed in a yellow painted house with columns at 11 Station Road. I do not think this house exists anymore. I attended my first school here in Lucknow. I was enrolled in second grade at St Agnes Loreto Day Convent which was located at the end of the road towards the Lucknow Charbagh Railway Station.

I must have been seven or eight years old then. Until then I had studied at home. A lady living across the road, one of two Indian Christian sisters, gave me lessons in English and piano. In a year's time, I was given a double promotion at school and joined the fourth grade. My father then shifted to New Delhi as the assistant director general, Posts and Telegraphs. For a few months I studied at the Philander Smith College in Nainital. This building now houses the Birla Vidya Mandir. My eldest sister's father-in-law was living in a house called 'The Towers' quite close to the school and was thus my local guardian. It was mainly sons of Anglo-Indian parents who attended this school, which was run on the lines of an English public school.

I then came to Delhi to be with my father. For a short while, I was admitted to one of the Convent schools, either Jesus and Mary or St Columba's. Soon after, I joined the Modern School, in late 1927 or 1928, which had just started in Daryaganj. At this time, my cousin, Keshav of Grand Hotel Nainital, came to live with us, so I had some company at home also. I still remember my school friends of the Modern School days. They included Balwant Nehru (Balloo, as we called him)—younger brother of B.K. Nehru (ICS), Bharat Ram and Charat Ram—sons of Lala Shri Ram, Khushwant Singh and his future wife, Pratap Singh, Brij Mohan Soi, and Atul Kumar Mukarji (elder brother of Nirmal Kumar Mukarji who was the last of the ICS, and succeeded me as cabinet secretary in 1977). Atul got into Customs Service but died young. We used to go to school at about seven or eight in the morning and return at five or six in the evening. We had breakfast, lunch and tea in school. It was intended to be an all-round schooling. Apart from the usual lessons, we learnt music, carpentry, painting, riding and games like hockey and football. This period of my schooling was a happy one.

But two incidents come back clearly. We used to be taught

both vocal and instrumental music. The instrumental music began with 'dilruba'. The music teacher soon found that I was always out of tune. So he decided that it would be better if I devoted my time to gardening instead of disturbing the rest of the class. My class report of that time read, 'He has no ear for music'. Later during physics experiments I found that I could not detect 'beats' with my ear. Still later, in England, I tried to learn dancing. My teacher said that I had no ear for rhythm and could not get my steps right, so she told me to give up ballroom dancing. I was equally bad at painting. I could not get my perspectives right, even though we had a famous artist Sarada Ukil as our teacher. I remember doing a decent job painting a lotus. It was to be hung up in class, but before that could happen I managed to smudge it with black paint.

During this period in Delhi we moved two or three houses, and finally lived at 10 Ashoka Road, where my father stayed until his retirement. Perhaps in 1928, I think, I had my yagyopavit* ceremony. Many relatives came to attend it and the house was very crowded for several days. In 1928 or early 1929, we—that is my father, Keshav and I, along with a driver and cook— went to Kashmir by car. My father had the famous T-model Chevrolet of this period. It was summer, April or May. I met my wife-to-be in Srinagar, though I had no idea at all at that time. My future father-in-law, Pitambar Datt Pande, was then posted as accountant general, Jammu and Kashmir. He was the first Kumaoni to get into an All India Class I service, the Indian Audit and Accounts Service. My wife-to-be was then very young. She is eight years younger than me.

I still remember the enormous amount of cherries we ate. They cost 4 annas a seer in those days†. We lived in houseboats

---

*Sacred thread ceremony

†Anna—former currency, equal to one-sixteenth of a rupee; seer is a measure of weight, approximately one and a quarter kilograms.

and travelled all over the valley—Wular Lake, Gulmarg, Pahalgaon, Martand—but not Amarnath caves as it was too early in the year. At Martand, where the Pandas—priests for the Amarnath pilgrims—normally stay, my father made an entry of his visit in their books. When I visited the place again with my eldest son Raja in 1956 on the way to Amarnath, I found this entry. Our car broke down on our way back from the valley near Verinag, the source of the Jhelum river. The driver had to go to Srinagar to get it repaired. So we stayed in a small dharamshala in Verinag for a few days. I remember that the only food we had to eat all those days was coarse, hand-pounded, red-husked rice with karam ka saag. No pulses or any other vegetables were available there in those days. I took my first photographs during this trip and the album still survives in my collection. Some memories of the lovely landscape are still vivid—the poplar avenues near Baramula, the glades of Gulmarg, Banihal pass, Batote.

My school days in Delhi came to an end by June 1929. I then came to Almora to study at the Government Intermediate College (GIC). The reason for this shift was that the schools in Delhi in those days were affiliated to Punjab University and the standard of education therein was considered to be low compared to that of Uttar Pradesh. So my father thought that it would be much better if I was educated in Almora. My uncle, Hari Datt, and his wife were living in our ancestral house and became my local guardians. I was admitted to grade nine at the GIC. At the time of my admission the teachers said that while I was alright in English, history, geography, and science, I was very weak in mathematics and Hindi and would require special coaching in these subjects. My father arranged for that. While I acquired just enough proficiency to pass my high school Hindi examination with 44% marks, I did much better in mathematics. I owe this to my cousin, Harish Chandra Pant, who was our mathematics teacher. His mother was my bua (aunt)—my father's elder sister. Harish was a very good teacher and the foundations that he laid helped me in securing a distinction in mathematics in the high school examination. I went on to get good marks in my Intermediate and BSc examinations, take the Part I exam in Mathematics Tripos at Cambridge, and also appear for two papers in Applied Mathematics for my ICS Examination.

I lived a very lonely life at Almora. My uncle and aunt used to live in what we called our 'old house'. This was the original home built by our forefathers when they came to Almora around 1750. I lived alone in what we call the 'new house'. It is across the courtyard and was built by my father's eldest brother, Jai Datt, in 1904. This is a big house by comparison. The rooms are large with a high ceiling and are built on modern lines. The house is spacious and airy and gets plenty of sunlight. Most of this house was locked up, except the north-east facing room in which I lived. In those days we had no electricity, no tap water, and no attached bathrooms in the house. A servant brought water in kerosene tins from the nearby natural spring reservoirs (called 'naulas' in our dialect). We had to go to especially constructed toilets in the fields quite far from the house to relieve ourselves. Although there was such a stark contrast between life in Almora and that in New Delhi, I apparently did not mind or think it unusual. We had to climb a steep way up to the main road in Almora—there are now 125 steps—and then walk about a kilometre to the college.

We got electricity in Almora only around 1950 and piped water came even later. Today these discomforts have disappeared. We have sanitary-fitted attached bathrooms, electric geysers for hot water, gas for cooking (in 1930 we used only firewood—kerosene stoves came later) and telephones. All this has made life here more comfortable.

I had the company of cousins and nephews. They were more or less my age but were several classes behind me in school. My class fellows were all at least two or three years older than me. I was the youngest and slightly built. I passed my high school examinations in 1931 when I was just fourteen years old. I grew up to only 5'3" in height, so back then I must have been even shorter. I did well in my school exams. I stood first in Kumaon and also secured a merit position in Uttar Pradesh. When I got to the Intermediate science class, I was ahead of other boys and the teachers would ask me no questions; I was also the butt of teasing by other boys. All this made me unhappy. The schooling, as I said, was good. We had a very good principal—Thakur Netrpal Singh of the Indian Education Service (IES). I think we had two other teachers also belonging to All India Service. Then we had senior State Education Service teachers. One of them, Padma Datt Pant, was our neighbour in Champanaula. He used to teach us physics and we called him 'Pope Sahib'. He cultivated my interest in physics which continued to be my subject of study at the Allahabad University and even later at Cambridge.

Towards the end of 1931 or so, I told my father that I was lonely and unhappy in Almora. He then decided to shift me to Allahabad. At this time, he opted for premature retirement from his service and moved to Allahabad for the sake of my studies. I was admitted to the GIC at Allahabad. For the next four years my father lived with me in Allahabad, except during the summer vacations that we spent in Almora. The GIC at Allahabad was at that time the most prestigious Intermediate college in Uttar Pradesh. The best students from all over the state (or province, as it was then called) came to study here. There was very keen competition among the students. When the Intermediate exam results of 1933 were announced, I passed in the first division with distinction in physics, chemistry and mathematics. I was also third in order of merit in the list of successful candidates of Uttar Pradesh, thus winning a merit scholarship for my BSc studies. Many of my colleagues at the Allahabad Intermediate College later qualified for the prestigious All India Services, like Anand Swarup Gupta for the Indian Police Service (IPS), and Govind Narain and Satish Chandra for the ICS.

After passing the Intermediate exam, I joined the BSc (Pass) course at Allahabad University in July 1933. At that time, Allahabad University had a very high reputation with distinguished teachers like Dr Meghnad Saha FRS for physics, Dr Nil Ratan Dhar for chemistry, Dr A.C. Banerji for mathematics, Dr Amarnath Jha for English, Prof Ranade for philosophy, and so on. The university also produced students who were outstanding in their field of work and did particularly well in competitive exams. I passed the BSc examination in 1935 securing a first class with distinction in physics, chemistry and mathematics. This time my merit position was either second or third in the university. I played tennis and joined the UTC* and, without any special distinction thereafter, joined the MSc in Physics course and passed the MSc Previous (the first year of MSc) in March 1936, standing first. The three years in Allahabad University were pleasant enough wherein I made a number of lifelong friends. In my first year, I remained a 'delegacy' student attached to the Muir Hostel. This was later known as the Amarnath Jha Hostel. Dr Jha was the warden of the hostel in my time and continued as such for years thereafter. Later, he became the vice-chancellor of Allahabad University and chairman of the Bihar Public Service Commission at Patna. During my second year I went to live at the hostel while my father lived alone in a rented house. This arrangement continued

---

*University Training Corps, predecessor of the National Cadet Corps (NCC)

for another two years. I particularly remember our house on Park Road, and later on Hamilton and Malviya Road in George Town.

Throughout this period, my father was working towards getting me admitted to Cambridge. He was in correspondence with Sir Hubert Sams, ICS, who had earlier been his director general, Posts and Telegraphs while he was in Delhi and had joined Peterhouse College in Cambridge as Bursar after his retirement, I think. However, I could not secure admission for the academic year beginning 1935. My father also approached the Indian High Commission in London and their Education Advisor to Indian students, but they were not at all helpful. Sir Hubert Sams, however, was able to get me admission to Christ's College, Cambridge for the academic year 1936. Before that I had to take a special matriculation examination in Sanskrit because a certificate in one of the classical languages was a must for admission to Oxford or Cambridge even if one was going to study natural sciences. The recognized classical languages for this purpose were Latin, Greek, Sanskrit, Arabic or Persian. It was thus that my studies at Allahabad finished around March of 1936. Thereafter preparations for going to England began, as did a wholly new chapter in my life.

*

I set sail from Bombay in July 1936, aboard a Lloyd Triestino boat. This was an Italian liner that Indians preferred over the British P&O vessels, since they always experienced discrimination aboard the latter. One was better treated aboard the Italian ships. The student concession fares in the Italian liner were also cheaper, at only £24 in the tourist class. July was perhaps the worst possible time to set sail for Europe. We were hardly out of sight of land at Bombay when I began to feel sick and had to take to my bunk. I could not get up from my bed all through the four days and nights that it took us to reach Massawa, in Italian Somaliland opposite Aden. Even going to the bathroom was a torture, the sight of food most nauseating and the cabin was hot and damp. I lived on an occasional Californian orange, which felt cool when held against the cheeks. I had to eat it without lifting my head from the pillow.

It got better after Massawa. Although the journey through the Red Sea was very hot, I could go on the deck and walk about. There was almost no breath of wind inside. My fellow passengers included a Bengali student from Calcutta—a Ghosh—who was planning to go to London just like me. I got down at Port Said along with a party of tourists as the ship was going through the Suez Canal and went to Cairo. We saw the Pyramids and the Sphinx and joined the ship again at Port Suez. There were popular shops on the sea front, with streams of people selling trinkets. But a new experience for me was a horde of people selling dirty postcards and whispering into people's ears asking 'you want boy or girl'.

It was on board the ship at this time that I began eating non-vegetarian food. A popular conception in those days was that one could not live as a vegetarian in England and that eating meat was necessary. My own experience was that although one could live as a vegetarian, it was very difficult. I was told that it was easy to start with fish, then go on to chicken, and try red meat last of all. Until then I had been a vegetarian. I think my father gave up eating meat after my mother's death. There was a custom in our family that forbade one from eating meat until one had made the pilgrimage to Punyagiri Devi temple in Champawat. Punyagiri was our Ista-devi, our family goddess. One was supposed to make the pilgrimage after every major event in the family, like the birth of a son, the yagyopavit ceremony, a marriage, etc. My father took me to Punyagiri after my yagyopavit ceremony. I have no recollections of the journey which was considered very difficult even in those days. Punyagiri is considered as one of the important Devi temples where the navel of Sati is said to have fallen when Shiva was dancing the Tandava nritya or the cosmic dance of death carrying her corpse. In those days, at the end of this pilgrimage, a goat had to be sacrificed and its meat consumed thereafter as prasad or offering made to God. So on completion of the journey we had to eat goat meat thus cooked. I remember my father saying that I should not think of it as eating meat or flesh but just prasad. After this pilgrimage, there would be no objection if I ate meat in the future.

I could not revisit Punyagiri for many years. The opportunity came last year in April 1985 when my wife, our son Lalit and I went from Almora to Tanakpur, via Lohaghat and Champawat. Nowadays, a coconut is offered by most people as prasad instead of a goat. What however surprised us was the very large number of devotees making this pilgrimage: young and old, men and women with babes in arm. On some days over a lakh people visited.

New tastes are difficult to acquire. Although I started eating non-vegetarian food and began to relish fish and chicken, I could not reconcile myself with consuming crabs and lobsters. They used to be displayed on the glass windows of the bigger restaurants of London and I always wondered how one could eat them. But in August 1939, my friend Balloo and I were on a holiday in Norway and found ourselves in a small village in the countryside. There was only one small restaurant and we were famished. The only thing available to eat was lobster. So we ordered lobsters that arrived with special forks that have only two prongs and are slightly turned up at the end. The lobsters were delightful and we both felt as if we had missed out all this time. Thereafter, whenever there was lobster or crab on the menu of a restaurant I visited, it was my first choice. I did not consciously though ever eat beef, veal or ox (tongue). One could not say about the cooking fat. I have never been able to reconcile with those who eat beef to show off, as if they have emancipated themselves from the orthodox and meaningless rules of Hinduism that taboos beef because the cow is seen as a sacred animal and referred to as a mother. In England, many told me that even if I objected to Indian beef, I should have no objection to English beef. We have a constant barrage of propaganda decrying the Indian-Hindu belief in the preservation of cattle—they give all kinds of arguments—economic, social, and so on. It is even referred to as a panacea for our economic difficulties. If only we would agree to kill off our cattle—specially those that give inadequate milk. But while all this propaganda is directed against us Hindus, no one in the West tells the Jews or Muslims to consume pork in any form. People belonging to these two communities consider pig to be an unclean animal and its meat is therefore taboo. I have always considered this as a typical hypocritical attitude especially towards Hindus.

We disembarked at the port of Brindisi in Southern Italy. From Brindisi we travelled overland by rail, to the beautiful bay of Naples: as they say, 'see Naples and die'. We could not visit Pompeii or the famous Isle of Capri. We then went on to Rome. These were the days when Mussolini was in power and the Fascists were ruling. I remember attending an open-air opera where thousands of people were present. It was summer and the setting was lovely. We then travelled to Venice, another beautiful city. From there via Milan to Lake Lucerne, through the Simplon tunnel, I think. Lake Lucerne is very beautiful indeed. Then via Paris to London where Narendra Nath Pant met us. This was a journey of discovery—new places, new sites, new languages.

Narendra Nath Pant, one of our distant relatives, had gone to England the previous year and joined King's College, London, where he was preparing for the ICS examination. He had passed his MSc in Chemistry from Allahabad University. Since my father felt that there would be at least one person whom I would know on reaching England, I stayed in the same boarding house as Narendra. I remember the address as 21 Stanhope Road, Highgate London N6. Brijnandan Singh Sahi was another Indian staying there. Both he and Narendra went ahead to appear for the ICS exam. Sahi returned to join the Provincial Civil Service while Narendra completed his PhD from Allahabad University in Chemistry and joined the Defence Research Organisation. Even after Narendra returned to India, I continued to stay at this place whenever I had to spend a week or more in London during my vacations. I was here when I later appeared for my ICS examination. It was a nice house with a garden at the back. The charges were £2 a week, which included breakfast, dinner on weekdays and a hot lunch on Sundays followed by a cold supper. Today this sounds fantastic.

As I had reached England in July and college was not scheduled to open till the first week of October, we had a lot of time on hand, especially after Pant and Sahi had finished their competitive examinations. We decided to go on a tour of Europe, travelling by the cheapest class. Our itinerary from England included Ostend in Belgium, through Brussels to Cologne, up the Rhine by steamer, through the Black Forest, Heidelberg, with its famous university. The only German which I still remember is *'Ich habe mein herz in Heidelberg verloren, in einer lauen Sommernacht'* (I lost my heart in Heidelberg, on a mild summer night).

We then visited Munchen or Munich. This had become famous as Hitler and his brown shirts, the Nazi SS, had seized power. A popular place to visit was the memorial where twelve members of the earliest group of Nazis had been killed by the police when they had attempted to create local problems. Another famous place to visit was the Hofbrâuhaus, the famous beer cellar of Munich where Hitler used to meet with his followers and speeches were written. On our way by train to Munich we were in a railway compartment with one or two Germans. We started talking but our German and English were weak and inadequate. The Germans told us when we said we were on our way to Munich, that there was very good beer available in Munich. We said that we did not drink beer. I was, until then, a teetotallar and so were the other two. He asked what did we drink then. We said water—*Wasser*.

'*Wasser!*' he exclaimed. Then proceeded to say who ever drank water, and by the movement of his hands explained that water was only for washing one's face and swimming.

Then on to Vienna, which was somewhat of a disappointment. The great capital of the Austria-Hapsburg empire had been reduced to a provincial capital. There were signs of poverty and great unemployment among the youth. Students continued to be in universities for seven or eight years as they could not get any jobs.

From Vienna or Wien, as it is called in Austrian-German, we went to Budapest. We found this to be a most beautiful city—we had not anticipated it. Situated on both banks of the Danube, full of gay Gypsy music, our stay was memorable. Then through Bratislava to Prague—'Praha' in Czechoslovak—with its beautiful churches and the famous bridge with the crucified figure of Christ, and the tower clock where people appear whenever an hour is struck. From Prague via Dresden to Berlin—then an important and bustling city—and shall I say 'recovering' from the very permissive period during the Weimar republic. This was the cleanest city we had seen. One could not even drop a matchstick on the road. In the streets, in the parks, in fact nowhere, did one see any litter.

We then travelled from Berlin to Amsterdam and the Hague and finally back to England. We visited most of the important art galleries, historic places, operas and gardens. I carried a pocket dictionary of English-German-English and English-French-English with me. I had passed a diploma examination while at Allahabad University in both German and French and although I could not speak much or understand very well, this smattering helped in finding our way about, ordering food in restaurants, etc.

We also spent several days sightseeing through London and visited the Tower of London and Hampton Court among others. I did not explore London for almost the next three years as I kept putting it off. I did see the Westminster Abbey just before finally leaving London in September 1939.

CHAPTER TWO

Cambridge and the Civil Service Examination

*

I lived in Cambridge from October 1936 to September 1939. Let me divide it roughly in three parts—the first deals with my life and academics in Cambridge, the second with how I spent my holidays, and finally some reflections and impressions of my overall stay in England.

*

I joined the BA Part I Tripos in Mathematics in my first year. My aim was to prepare and appear for the ICS examination. A rule had been introduced for those wishing to appear for the 1938 exam: a two-year stay at a British University was a must. From 1939 onwards, a degree would also be essential. Since the first time I could take the exam would be in 1938, when I would be twenty-one (which was also the required minimum age), I decided to take the Part I Tripos in Mathematics. This was a years' course. I then planned to take my Part II in Natural Sciences (Physics) in the remaining two years if I did not succeed in my first attempt in 1938.

I found the teaching methodology in Cambridge in great contrast to that at Allahabad University. I still remember the first lecture we had. The professor said that the teachers would not cover the course in the lectures. The course was given in detail in the University Calendar and we were expected to study it ourselves. The teachers would only cover and give lectures on some important mathematical principles and we were expected to understand and apply them to solve problems ourselves. We were supposed to consult our supervisor or tutor in the college in case we faced any difficulty. We were assigned to a tutor whom we usually met with alone, or sometimes in groups of two, once a week for an hour in the evening. The schedule of examinations was such that at the end of the academic term, while lectures continued till May 29, the exams were held on three consecutive days—May 30 & 31 and June 1, with two papers a day, so six in all. The final results would be declared on June 10 before the summer vacation. My first year's result was a disappointment—I secured third division in the Part I of the Maths Tripos. And Part I was considered easy! The brighter lot went straight to Part II and if they secured a first division they were called 'wranglers'. The very best went on to Part III of the Maths Tripos. This was the only subject in which there was a Part III. The papers had several questions with the stipulation 'answer as many as you can'. It was generally asserted that questions which professors themselves could not solve or which were subjects of research were put therein.

My tutor at Christ's College, Cambridge, was C.P. Snow—a physics man. Later he became Lord Snow, a member of the first post-World War II Labour Government. He was also the author of several books, including *The Masters* and *The Two Cultures*. He was a member of the British Public Service Commission. In one of his books—*The Affair*—he has an Indian student as a character named 'Pande'. I had a separate supervisor for mathematics. As my English was weak and I needed to prepare for the ICS compulsory papers, I took lessons in English language from a young tutor, mainly on essay writing, precis and correct and idiomatic English.

In my first year, I also joined some clubs—the Cambridge Union and the Rifle Club. I used to play tennis and squash. Because I was very light in weight I was selected to be a cox (coxswain) for the College Boat Race Club. But I gave this up after a term as it took too much of my time. I could never become a speaker or debater which was what the Cambridge Union was about. I also joined the Indian Majlis, a society of Indian students in Cambridge. However, in none of them was I an outstanding or prominent member nor an office bearer of any kind. Perhaps I was too shy.

In my very first term, I remember, I had problems with the cost of boarding and lodging. To begin with, I looked for lodgings with a bath. Being an Indian I could not contemplate starting the day without an early-morning bath. For this, hot water was essential, and was very expensive. It used to cost sixpence per bath. Moreover, the water would take time to heat, and one had little time in the mornings. There were no showers in the lodging houses. We had no central heating either. In the evenings, a coal fire was lighted after one came back from the classes at about 3 p.m. or so. Lectures started at 9 a.m. and the winter days were dark throughout. The first months' bill that my landlady handed me was beyond my means. The charges for bath, a bag of coal a week, tea, toast, porridge in the morning was also far too much. I showed the bill to C.P. Snow. He agreed that it was too high but said that nothing could be done. He suggested that I look around for another lodging from the following term and buy my own stores for breakfast, etc. The first lodging was in a place called Christ's Pieces, quite close to the college. For the second I had to go out to Newmarket Road which was somewhat farther. I later learnt the reason for the high bills—most landladies thought that the Indian students who came to study at Cambridge were rich sons of rajas, maharajas, or business magnates. They were not very wrong because several were very well-to-do. They had their own cars, went racing, etc. People like me who came from ordinary middle-class families had to feel their way about.

In the second year, I got a room in college. This was a pleasant change even though the rooms were very old. In Cambridge, both at college and in private lodgings, we were given a set of two rooms—a sitting room-cum-study and a bedroom. The sitting room had a fireplace and we could entertain our friends to meals, breakfast, lunch or tea, usually prepared in the room by ourselves. The bedrooms were cold and not heated. In my last year, I moved into a lodging just behind the college in Christ's Lane. The wing in the college where I stayed, as also the Christ's Lane buildings, have both since been demolished to make way for a modern set of rooms.

Christ's, though a small college compared with Trinity or St John's, was a famous one. It boasted of Milton and Charles Darwin as its alumni and was located in the centre of town as well.

In my second year, I joined Part II of the Natural Sciences Tripos in Physics. I still remember that before I could join the class, I was asked to explain the 'physics' of the Second Law of Thermodynamics. Everyone was familiar with the mathematical equation which was used for this law, but its physics was difficult to explain in plain English. I was apparently able to do so, and joined the Cavendish Laboratory—as the Physics department was called. It was in a very old building, dark, with winding and irregular staircases, but it was the mecca of physics in those days. The Cavendish professors at Cambridge apart from Lord Cavendish himself, had been Clerk Maxwell who propounded the electromagnetic theory of light, then Sir J.J. Thomson, the discoverer of the electron and in my time Professor Emeritus and Master of Trinity. We had Lord Rutherford as the Cavendish Professor—he was the father, or shall I say the grandfather, of the atom bomb. He had studied the disintegration of radioactive substances like uranium and had developed the theory which later was utilized for the atom bomb in World War II. At that time, Cambridge boasted of names like De Broghe, Aston, Kapitza, Max Planck and so on. So many Nobel laureates, such names to conjecture with!

The students could choose which lectures they would or would not attend. Most selected lectures with more direct relevance to the examinations. However, because of the fame of the professors and because I had studied their work while I was in Allahabad, I decided to attend a few extra lectures. One of them was a series of lectures by Lord Rutherford. He was a very difficult professor to follow. He would come to class and not look around at the dozen or so students, of whom usually there were only a dozen or so, all seated in the first row. He would go to the blackboard, continue giving his lecture and writing the equations, and as soon as thirty-forty minutes were over he would go away. No questions could be asked and no one dared either. If we had any difficulty we would consult our tutors later. The other series of lectures I remember were by Lord Aston. To begin with, there were about twenty students in his class, but soon these numbers dropped drastically and one day it was only I who was present. After the lecture, he said that since I was the only one present and interested, I could go over to his room and complete the subject.

I have some memorable recollections of my time in the Cavendish Laboratory. I was once working on sodium rings in spectroscopy and despite all my care I could not see the rings. I could detect no fault in my arrangements of the experiment. So, I went to the demonstrator, who made a very minor adjustment and said that it was alright and I could take the readings. When I looked again, I could not see the rings. I approached him again. After some thought he said that I may be colour blind in the red and should try with a filter. This turned out to be perfect. Later, when I was taking my medical exam after passing the ICS exam, I was found to be colour blind in the red and green.

Meeting Sir J.J. Thomson is yet another memorable recollection. I first saw him once in the library. He was then well over eighty and was trying to retrieve a book from one of the shelves. I got up to help him. 'Thank you, my boy, thank you,' were his words. On another occasion, some few of us went to meet him at Trinity and just being in his presence is an experience I have not forgotten.

The third incident relates to the installation of a cyclotron. The first cyclotron in the world was being set up, or programmed, for the California Institute of Technology. There were many people who were keen that Cambridge should also have a cyclotron. Sir J.J. Thomson and Lord Rutherford opposed this. Sir J.J. Thomson said that all his experiments relating to the discovery of the electron had been performed in apparatuses constructed by him out of simple test tubes and glass tubes. Lord Rutherford's experiments on radioactivity were carried out in a gold leaf electroscope which had hardly cost 2 shillings and sixpence. So where was the need to install a cyclotron at a cost of £250,000. The proposition was then dropped. It was only after the War, sometime in the 1950s, that Cambridge got its first cyclotron.

At about this time, Kapitza went to Russia from where he never returned. There were all kinds of rumours, but later it transpired that he had been appointed head of a vast research organization and later helped to develop Russia's atomic capability.

I passed the preliminary to Part II of the Natural Sciences Tripos without difficulty and this time I secured a much better position. I also applied to appear for the ICS exam which was due to be held in July 1938. My tutor, C.P. Snow, said that I should really not feel disappointed if I did not get through, because most of the candidates would have already acquired their degrees and would be a few years older. However, it would still be an experience for me. I sat for the ICS exam with that resolve and planned to spend the summer vacations at home. I had been away for two years and thought that I would have to spend another two in England if I had to appear for the ICS exam again in 1939.

The Secretary of State in India would not permit me to appear for the final in physics just to complete the academic part of my third year at Cambridge, after I had passed the ICS exam. They said that physics was of no use in my further official life. They might have agreed to a subject like politics or economics or even history. This left me with the prospect of returning from Cambridge without a degree at all. At this stage C.P. Snow helped me. He wrote to the senior tutor at Christ's following which they both wrote to the University authorities. They said that since students who qualify for the ICS or the Home Civil Service are all students who have passed their Honours or Masters exam, I should be deemed to have attained that standard. The University agreed, but desired that I should sit and appear in some other papers. In May 1939, I appeared for some papers in French and world history, and the University conferred a Pass BA degree on me. Since I was not going on for any further studies this was alright by me.

*

Now for the holidays. It was not generally possible for undergraduates to stay at their 'digs', as the lodgings were called, during the vacations. The landladies liked to go on a holiday themselves or they had cleaning and repairs to do. All my holidays were spent out of Cambridge. One winter I spent in London, others on the sea coast of Brighton, Bournemouth, and Torquay. I liked Torquay best and stayed in a small village nearby. I once motored through Devon, Cornwall, to Land's End through Wales and the Lake district, where I spent two holidays. One of these holidays was spent at Keswick and another at Windermere, then on to Glasgow, Edinburgh, York and finally London. I could not visit the real Highlands, Inverness or Ireland. Thus I saw quite a bit of England.

I spent some holidays in Europe. It was usually cheaper and better to go on a conducted tour arranged by the National Union of Students. One summer, I went to Geneva as part of a special programme for the League of Nations. I remember having a conversation with a waiter at an open-air restaurant in Geneva who spoke very good English. He told me that he had picked it up while working at the Piccadilly Hotel in London for two years. I asked him why he left, as he must have been earning more there, to which he responded, 'How can you live in a place if you can't see the mountains from there'. I have always been reminded of this remark and that is one of the reasons I came to live in Almora after my retirement. The view of the Himalayas, the magnificent snowy peaks, the lovely sunsets, the brilliantly lit starry skies at night and the deep azure blue sky of the morning. These are things which one does not get to see in the plains, there is too much dust and smoke there. Years later at Rashtrapati Bhavan, while sitting down to a banquet for a visiting dignitary, I often faced a large portrait of Dr S Radhakrishnan painted by the famous painter Roerich. He is especially known for his Himalayan landscapes. The background colour in Dr Radhakrishnan's portrait is a very deep blue. It looked unnatural and I always wondered why Roerich had chosen this colour. Then while living in Almora I saw the deep blue skies and witnessed just how really blue they could be. This is something which is so satisfying to one's consciousness.

I spent two winters in the Alps, one in Switzerland—in the Bernese Oberland, and the other in the Austrian tyrol. I became very fond of skiing but unfortunately, I could never partake in it again. During the Swiss holiday there was an interesting episode. A young medical student was visiting with his fiancée and the couple was enjoying themselves. The young man asked a friend of his in London to join them. He came and then began the case of the eternal love triangle: this boy from London and the girl fell in love, the two friends fell apart, there was an exchange of blows and black eyes—a real drama in actual life. In the Austrian Tyrol, we met some Austrian boys who were experts in skiing, just as our instructors and guides. One day an English girl fell down while skiing and cut her face, and some blood gushed out. The Austrian boy remarked, 'Your face is bloody'. At first there was consternation all round and the girl got red in the face. Then they all realized that what the Austrian had meant was that her face was bleeding and had not meant to hurl an abuse at her. Later in the evening when we were all sitting down to dinner, this incident was again narrated by someone. The Austrian then insisted 'it *was* bloody'. This incident taught me a lesson for my later life: how inadequate knowledge of a language, or wrong use thereof, often leads to quarrels and riots. Back home I found that quarrels arose in the office because people did not speak correct English or did not understand it properly. This applied to all other languages also. A misuse or misunderstanding thereof has been the cause of numerous estrangements. At this moment I am reminded of a meeting that S.V. Sohoni, then irrigation secretary, and I, as famine secretary and food commissioner, had in 1951 with then minister for irrigation and electricity, Ramcharitra Singh. He came from the Beghusarai sub-division in North Monghyr. He told us that relief works in North Bihar should be stepped up to provide employment. Sohoni said they had taken up a big programme of canal construction and this had been done 'to whip up the enthusiasm of the people'. Ramcharitra Singh flew into a rage and started banging the table. We were both bewildered. Then he said 'people are starving and you want to whip them!'

My last summer holiday was spent in Norway and Sweden. I had thus travelled quite a bit in Europe. I could not visit Spain or Portugal as I had hoped to because of the Spanish Civil War. The trip to Norway and Sweden in August 1939 was really nice. Balloo and I went to Bergen, Oslo, Trondheim, to the Lofoten Islands and then Narvik inside the Arctic Circle, to Abisko in Lapland where the sun set at 11 p.m. and rose again at 1 a.m. It was light enough to read at midnight. The dense forests and lakes housed the biggest mosquitos I had ever seen. I liked Norway better than Sweden and even felt that if I had to choose a country to live in other than my own, I would vote for Norway. We were once travelling in a small boat on one of the lakes in Norway, in the company of a boy and his sister whom we had met in Cambridge. They had come to study English. Their father was the headmaster of a village school and they had invited us to stay with them. While we were boating around, a lone fisherman came up and asked where we had come from. We said India. 'Ah India—Gandhi, Nehru,' he replied. These names were known the world over. Then he asked us how we liked Norway and what we thought of the people. We said we were very happy and enjoying ourselves. He then made a remark which I have always considered to have been very profound. He said all over the world, the language of sorrow and happiness is the same!

From Abisko we travelled to Stockholm via Güllivare and Östersund. When we reached Güllivare the station master said that he had heard over the radio that Hitler and Stalin had signed a no-war pact. We said we could not believe it, but if it were true then war was imminent. On our journey from Güllivare to

Stockholm, the conductor came to ask if we would have lunch, but we could not understand each other. On the adjoining seat sat a gentleman with two dogs. He had a gun with him for bird-shooting. He turned around and interpreted what the conductor said for us in English. We said no to lunch as we were getting down at Östersund. We got into a conversation with this gentleman, who asked where we came from and what we did. My friend Balloo said he was an engineer and was keen to visit some factories in Stockholm. This gentleman said there would be no difficulty, and we should get in touch with him when we got to Stockholm. He gave us his card. And to our consternation—the card read 'ADC to HRH Gustavus Adolphus, the Crown Prince of Sweden'! We could not believe that such an eminent person could be travelling like an ordinary citizen, that too without a guard or companion! The crown prince's aide-de-camp asked us where we would be staying in Stockholm. We had not decided so he suggested that the only place to stay was the Grand Hotel. When we reached Stockholm we did not dare go to the Grand Hotel for fear that we would not be able to spare the charges. So we waited for Thomas Cook's office to open and enquired from them. We found that if we shared a room in the attic and had no meals in the hotel, we could be able to cover the expenses. That's what we did, and Balloo was able to visit some factories.

At Stockholm we had a letter waiting from Balloo's father, who was then in London, hoping that we were following international developments and would return to England if things got worse. So we started reading the newspapers and became aware of the gathering war clouds. On 1 September 1939, we returned to London, arriving at a deserted Croydon airport. Blackout had been enforced from that night. On 3 September 1939, war was declared. I remember we were all given gas masks, as it was feared that one of the first things that Germany would do was to throw poison gas bombs. However, that did not happen. Then everyone who had no business in London was asked to leave the city. I went to Windermere in the Lake District to await further instructions from the India Office. By then I had signed my covenant as a member of the ICS, having completed my probation. It was in late September that we were all told to gather in London to return to India in a convoy. We set sail from Southampton and were escorted by a couple of destroyers to guard against the German submarines. Thus ended my three-year stay in England.

*

And now for some reflections and impressions of my stay in England and Europe. The first is about an incident on Guy Fawkes Night, 5 November 1936. It is a boisterous kind of celebration, somewhat reminiscent of Diwali at home. On this particular night, some students outside our college smashed a street lamp and knocked off a police constables's hat. This happened around 11 p.m. The next morning the boys had been summoned to appear before the magistrate and by 11 a.m. they had been let off after paying a fine of £5 each. This was the British administration of justice and method of maintaining law and order. We in India say that we have adopted the British system of jurisprudence and that our system of administration of justice is also modelled on their system. And what a contrast! Cases here do not come up for trial for years on end, the cases drag on further and judgements are passed after further delays.

When I was leaving India in July 1936, I met an American scholar who was then living in Almora, Dr Eraus-Wertz. He had lived in Tibet for seven years and was a great scholar of Buddhism, having translated Tibetan scriptures and writing on the Mahayan school of Buddhism. He warned me against getting de-nationalized on going to England. He said I would see great prosperity, a lot of money, things would be different and attractive, but I must remember that India is a very great country with a great culture and philosophy. The West should not be allowed to dazzle my sight. In my time, I found that we Indians became more intensely nationalistic when we saw the freedom enjoyed by the people there. Things are so different now. Whoever can do so, wants to leave and settle in England, Europe, or America, even if it be as a second-class citizen. Gone is the pride of one's country, of the motherland, of our national heritage and our religion. This is yet another profound difference between then and now.

Yet another experience in London was that of loneliness. One day all my friends were out and so I could not contact them. I went to the cinema by myself. I remember spending the entire day going from one cinema hall to another. There were millions of people in London, but not one person to talk to. This intense loneliness is something that I have never felt in India. Perhaps the biggest punishment that a criminal is given is solitary confinement. Here in England or elsewhere, the same sense of loneliness can be felt without the jail walls.

The last experience that I wish to mention is that of being a minority. Sometimes, as I walked down the streets, children would run behind me shouting 'nigger'. I had always thought that Indians could not be classed as 'niggers', but then people called us so. Sometimes girls in Hyde Park would call out 'Indian dogs'. You saw a flat advertising rooms to let. You knocked: the landlady saw you were an Indian, said that there was no room available, it had been let out, the signboard had been left on by mistake. Once I made a reservation at a private hotel in a small seaside town from my Cambridge address. Upon reaching the place, and them discovering that I was an Indian, they apologized, informing me that the room had been taken and only regretted I could not be informed earlier. It was the cumulative result of such small but hurtful incidents that taught me what it felt like to be a minority and to be rejected or not accepted by the majority. So in a way I learnt what a minority would feel in India, be they people belonging to Scheduled Castes, Tribes, language or religious minorities. No member of a majority, and especially a high-caste person, can feel what the minorities do. I felt that my experience in England gave me some inkling of this.

But on the whole, life in Cambridge was very pleasant and I have very beautiful memories. Cambridge is tradition-bound. Every time I asked a friend why a certain thing, whose rationale I could not understand, was done, I was told that in England certain things are just done! Women would attend university classes, pass examinations but would not be conferred degrees; there was a debate in the Cambridge Union: should women be admitted as members? The motion was lost. Sundays were terribly dull days in Cambridge, everything was closed, there was hardly any traffic on the roads. A motion in the Cambridge Union that this house would rather spend Sundays in Paris was passed by an overwhelming majority. But all of that—the beautiful city, the university, the library—are, at my age, only pleasant journeys down memory lane. Things have changed greatly in the last half century and that is only natural.

*

Let me now come to the ICS examination that I took in July 1938.

Besides the compulsory papers, I had opted for Lower Applied Mathematics and Lower and Higher Physics as my optional subjects for the examination. The exams began with a paper on Applied Mathematics. I was hoping to do very well in this and score almost full marks. When the paper was handed over to us, I thought it was easy. There were six questions in all and we had to answer them in full. I started on the first question which I hoped I would finish in ten minutes. However, forty minutes later I was still struggling. Thereafter, I could solve only half of another question and all others remained more or less partly attempted. I felt very disappointed at such a bad start. However, I hoped that the second paper in the afternoon would make up for this loss. Four of us had lunch together and then sat for the afternoon paper. Unfortunately, it was a repetition of the morning—I could solve only one-and-a-half questions out of six. I felt sorely disappointed and thought of not giving the rest of the exams as I felt I stood no chance, whatsoever, of being successful. But then I recalled my tutor's advice to attempt this exam for the experience of it. I also did not know how I would tell my father that I had given up. And further, my date for sailing back home was just a few days away. So I decided to appear for the remaining papers, but in a wholly different mood. I closed and packed all my books on physics in a box and spent my time reading novels—I remember reading Swift's *Gulliver's Travels* at this time—and visiting the theatre and cinema.

The rest of the examinations were uneventful. The four papers in physics went off well as did the compulsory subjects. The interview, or viva voce as it was called, was interesting. I had arrived half an hour before the scheduled time. I found that I was the only candidate in the waiting room. Before I had even settled down, the previous candidate came out and I was summoned in. It was a forbidding sight—a big table with five or so examiners sitting on one side and the candidate all by himself on the other. The room was also quite big. They fired questions at me and I kept on replying. I had decided to admit ignorance in case I did not know something instead of guessing an answer and getting it wrong. I remember two questions in particular. The first was that even though I was a science student, had I read any English literature, especially poetry. I replied that my acquaintance with English poetry was confined to Palgrave's *Golden Treasury* and that I always carried a copy with me whenever I went on a holiday. The second was about the English press and my impressions thereof. I said that my view was that in order to get at the truth of any event or development, one had to read the news and comments thereon in at least five or six papers, ranging from the extreme right, the Beaverbrook papers—like the *Daily Telegraph*, to the conservative papers—like *The Times* to the Labour paper—like the *Daily Herald* and even the communist—such as *New Age*. Each gave a different version, sometimes even the narration of events differed. After being in England, I had also formed the impression that one should not take everything appearing in print as the gospel truth. We in India even now seem to think that whatever is printed must be correct—what naivete! The interview lasted some twenty minutes and I came away quite happy.

Thereafter, I made speedy arrangements to return home. This time, too, I travelled by the Italian liner Lloyd Triestino. I remember seeing the famous leaning tower of Pisa on this occasion. The return journey was uneventful. From Bombay, I came straight to Almora where my father was then living for the summer. During this absence of two years, my eldest sister had passed away. She was not even thirty. My uncle, Hari Datt, and my aunt, with whom I had lived during my school days at Almora, were also no more. They were of course advanced in age, my uncle must have been in his late seventies, as was my aunt who had not been well even while I was studying at Almora. A close school and college friend of mine, Lalit Mohan Joshi, had also died during this period. There was a curious incident connected with his death. While in England, one night I had seen him rather vividly in my dreams. The next morning,

I wrote to my father telling him about this and enquiring how Lalit Mohan was since he had not been keeping well. My father wrote back that Lalit Mohan was no more, in fact he had passed away the very night I had dreamt of him. He also wrote that in the Indian tradition there was a belief that on death the soul went to visit the near and dear ones and hovered around the earth for a few days. It was only thereafter that the soul rested till it was reborn.

Throughout the two years that I had been away in England, my father had lived alone, spending summers in Almora and winters in Allahabad. He would cook his own food in an 'ic-mic-cooker'.* This was an interesting contraption—charcoal fire had to be lit at the bottom. The cooker had three compartments for rice, dal and vegetables, water was placed in an outer case. The food got cooked in about two hours. My father would start the day early with a cold water bath and take only one meal a day, at about midday. After his bath, he would sit down to offer his prayers. People here at Almora still remember him for this routine and his devotions. While at Almora he lived in our ancestral house, at Allahabad, he had taken a small two bedroom house on rent. It was near my younger sister's place so he had some company. He also devoted himself to Harijan welfare work along with Munshi Ishwar Saran of Allahabad. Although an orthodox person himself, who would not eat food cooked by anyone or at any time or place and avoided certain foods altogether like meat, eggs, garlic, onion, and devoted himself to our traditional prayers; he was totally opposed to the practice of untouchability. He was an outspoken person and often upset people by his plain speaking. (Lalit, my son, has inherited the features and some of the characteristics of his grandfather.) My success in the ICS exam, subsequent progression in life

---

*An older version of the modern rice cooker.

and even my appointment as Governor long after his death, all attributed to his austerities, prayers and blessings. His sacrifices for my welfare cannot be put into a few words.

*

When I returned in July 1938 the only subject of discussion at home was whether I would get through the ICS examination. So far, no other people from the community had been successful.

My father believed in astrology and would often consult well known astrologers and pandits regarding my future. At the time I appeared for the ICS exam, one pandit (I forget his full name), generally known as 'Touch Panditji' used to visit my father. He would predict events and answer questions relating to the future not so much by reading horoscopes as by asking the questioner to pluck any flower that he liked. He would smell the flower and give his answers or predictions. My father consulted him about my success in the ICS exam on the day I sat for the maths paper in London. Touch Panditji said that I would get through, even though I had not done my papers well. I would get only four annas in the rupee—25% marks. My father wrote to me about this prediction. I got the letter just as I was leaving London to come home.

My sister and her children were also staying in Almora in the summer of 1938 with my father. The ICS results were usually announced on the first Saturday of September. It passed, as did the next three days, but no results were announced. Touch Panditji used to come almost every day to tell us that I would get through. The following Saturday evening, we received a cablegram from Sir Hubert Sams from London that read, 'Congratulations, successful'. Touch Panditji's predictions were correct. Later I found that I had been successful because I had scored well in my physics papers and had done particularly well in the viva voce. This enabled me to pass and qualify though I was somewhat lower down in the list.

Hectic preparations were then made for my return to England. There was not enough time to return by sea and reach by the date of the medical examination. So I travelled by air. This was a very exciting event in those days. I went by a KLM plane from Allahabad. The fare was £101 (the £ sterling was then equal to Rs 13 and 6 annas). That first afternoon we flew directly from Allahabad to Jodhpur with a halt at the Maharaja's palace in Jodhpur. We went around visiting the city at night and saw the famous fort where we were told that some people had been buried alive in the foundation! We left at 4 a.m. the next morning. This plane had fourteen passengers, travelled at a height of 5000 ft with a speed of about 120 miles an hour. Perhaps it was a version of the Dakota. From Jodhpur we reached Karachi, where we had breakfast, then to a Gulf airfield, Bahrain, and a night halt at Basra. Basra was dreadfully hot— 120º F in the late evening—lots of dates, flies and a bustling bazaar. Because of the heat one could not sleep at night in the hotel, which although new, had no air conditioning arrangement then. People lay on the grass outside.

Next morning, we left at about 4 a.m. before sunrise. The sunrise over Baghdad was a beautiful scene. We then headed to Tel Aviv in Palestine then on to Athens for the afternoon and night stay. We were put up at the Hotel Grand Bretagne and went around seeing the sights of Athens. We were put up at the best hotels. We were served meals at the various airports where we landed. The next morning we left Athens early in the morning, flew to Budapest and had an excellent breakfast. We then reached Frankfurt. An eerie feeling descended for the first time. There was a tension in the air, that of approaching war, with pictures of Hitler everywhere as people greeted each other with a click of the heels, a raise of the right hand, and a 'Heil Hitler'. A change of plane took us from Frankfurt to Amsterdam, and then to London, where we reached by late evening—just in time for dinner. The journey had been quite pleasant and only three-and-a-half days long as opposed to a fortnight that it would have taken by ship and rail. I was also in time for the medical examination which was a few days ahead. I remember the porter on duty giving us a tip before the medical exam—that of drinking a lot of water so the urine sample would be free of sugar or albumen. I passed the medical test though it was found that I had flat feet and was colour blind in the red and green. However, neither of these were grounds for a disqualification from the ICS.

Thereafter, we had a one-year probation period and I continued to stay at Cambridge. We were paid an allowance of £300 per annum. This relieved my father of having to meet my expenses in England. Academically, this was now an easy year. We had to study Indian History, the Indian Penal Code, the Criminal Procedure Code, and the Indian Evidence Act. Horseriding was compulsory and I acquired a special art of falling. But it was fun. The hardest test involved clearing a three-and-a-half-feet high hedge without stirrups and reins. They were both folded up so one had to have a firm knee grip and balance. We were not allowed to use spurs. We had to also learn an Indian language depending on the province to which we were allotted. I was to go to Bihar and as Hindi—the first language of Bihar—was my mother tongue, I had to learn Bengali. Our seniority was decided on the basis of the final examination at the end of the probation period and not on the basis of the qualifying examination. I stood first among all the probationers in Cambridge and was awarded the Bhavnagar gold medal. However, the war intervened and by the time the medal reached me some two or three years later, it had turned bronze.

Our date of commencement of the service would count

from the day we signed our covenant with the Secretary of State for India. This was in September 1939. The full length of service was thirty-five years or until sixty years of age, at the end of which we technically resigned from the service and got an annuity. However, when the Indian Administrative Service was formed after Independence, the members of the old ICS became its initial members. In case of the IAS, the length of service began the year one passed the qualifying exam. The period of training was also counted as part of the service, though termed as probation, so we were given the benefit of one year when figuring our seniority. So in the later civil lists my service allotment year was 1938. And yet again, in 1972 or 1973, the so-called privileges of the ICS were abolished by an Act of Parliament which in effect meant that the retiring age for all of us became fifty-eight years of age. The annuity was changed to pension. In my case, however, I would have originally retired on completion of thirty-five years of service but then I would have been only fifty-seven-and-a-half years of age—so I got a benefit of another six months of service. Later I got an extension of service of another two years—so I actually retired on completing sixty years of age, and counting four months of leave thereafter, I actually served a month less than thirty-nine years in the ICS—that is from September 1938 to August 1977.

The final year in Cambridge was a pleasant one, especially as there was no worry regarding a degree-qualifying examination. I think life was generally uneventful.

A few recollections here. In 1936, I remember we were at the cinema when an announcement came on that King Edward VIII had abdicated the throne. His famous speech was relayed over the sound system in the cinema hall. There was great excitement about this. Then I remember how we queued up overnight on a pavement in Hyde Park to see the Coronation procession of King George VI. Since it was summer, we were able to spend the whole afternoon, night and the next day sitting on a pavement—but then one was young and it was possible to do all this.

I must reproduce a quotation that I found in some travel tourist literature while we were in Abisko, in Swedish Lapland, in August 1939. The pamphlet read, 'Hospitality, that sweet barbaric virtue, is to be found more in the wilds of Lapland than in the streets of Paris!' And how true. I have repeatedly experienced this in life and travels. And I quote this sentence ever so often as it has a great appeal to me.

Towards the end of the period of my ICS probation, I think sometime in September 1939, a tea reception was held by the Secretary of State for India, then Marquess of Zetland. This was after we had all signed our covenants and had become members of what was then called 'the heaven born service' or by the Indians as 'neither Indian nor civil nor a service'. Present at the function was the Viceroy of India—Lord Linlithgow. Lord Zetland said that this would be the only time when we could meet the Viceroy at such close quarters, because once we reached India we would all be dispersed and occupy junior posts for some years.

We had all been asked to evacuate London after the declaration of the War. I was spending time with a couple of friends at a hotel in Windermere in the Lake District. We were awaiting instructions for sailing home. Eventually we were all asked to report to London. From here, we travelled by train to Southampton and thereafter embarked on a P&O liner. Four ships sailed together in a convoy escorted by two destroyers. There was complete blackout ordered on board and even lighting a match outside was a most serious offence. There was nothing to do on board. This journey was not like the normal peacetime journey that had entertainment available. All I did during the fifteen days that we were on board was play bridge from about 8 or 8.30 a.m. till about midnight with breaks for meals and some exercise on deck. The sea journey was long. We almost went up to the American coast, then came to Gibraltar through the Mediterranean and Red Seas, and finally to Bombay. Later, ships were ordered to sail round the Cape of Good Hope. I think the blackout ended only after we got past the Red Sea into the Arabian Sea.

At Bombay, my father had come to receive me. We stayed at Pitamber Datt Pande's place—my future father-in-law. He was then posted at Bombay as accountant general, I think, in the railways. It was here that I again met Vimla. My father had written to me earlier that there was a proposal of my marriage with her. She was then fourteen-and-a-half and I was twenty-two-and-a-half. I had just come from England and in contrast with the girls I had met there, I thought she was too young for marriage. I remember we went out walking in the evening. My father and Pitamber Datt ji contrived to walk ahead leaving Vimla and me to walk behind together so we could talk to each other. She was very shy then. I liked her well enough. She was naturally good looking and of a pleasant temperament, and although the idea of marriage had already been planted, I wanted to wait for a couple of years before marrying her. I wanted to see what life in the service was like. Soon after this, we dispersed. I had received orders to report to the Chief Secretary of Bihar in Patna, with an indication that I would be posted to Bhagalpur as assistant magistrate. This was sometime in October 1939. My father and I travelled together to Allahabad and then I went on alone to Patna. A new life had begun.

CHAPTER THREE

The Bihar Years: District Postings

In October 1939, on reaching Patna Railway Station in the morning, I found out that H.C. Sarin had been travelling in the adjoining compartment. At Patna Junction, both of us were met by S. Jagannathan, then undersecretary, Appointments Department. I had been invited by Justice S.B. Dhande to stay with him. He was a senior member of the ICS and a judge of the Patna High Court. When I went to see the Chief Secretary, I was told that instead of Bhagalpur, I was to go to Gaya. The explanation I received was that there was a more experienced deputy collector at Gaya, a Rai Bahadur B.N. Singh, and that he would be able to train me better, while the Collector at Bhagalpur was a junior English ICS officer with only seven or eight years of service. I took this change at its face value, although I realized much later that the change had been made in order to post an English probationer under an English Collector as opposed to an Indian one.

Till then, I had never been east of Benares. The new capital area and the Secretariate in Patna were impressive, as were the houses and lawns. Next in importance came the mosquitoes. One had to carry a flit pump if one went to the cinema, even in the highest class!

The first popular Congress Ministry formed under the 1935 Government of India Act had resigned and already political tension was mounting. Soon a proclamation was issued under Section 93 of the Act, as per which the Governor took over the formation of the entire ministry himself and assumed direct rule. This was to last till the end of the War in 1945.

After a week or so in Patna, I came to Gaya. Although a strict disciplinarian, the Collector was a very nice man. I rented a house that was bigger than the one that the earlier assistant magistrate had occupied as my father would be coming to stay with me. I remember that I had bought a bed for myself, with poles for a mosquito net, for Rs 10. This bed was with me for some thirty years of my service, or more. I also learnt to sleep under a mosquito net. We had to do this all through our stay in Bihar for the next twenty or so years. Babu (my father) came and joined me sometime thereafter. He found that I had no furniture, so he ordered some from Bareilly—then famous for its furniture made of Burma teak.

I used to go to office on a bicycle, which I had bought for about Rs 200. I thought of buying a second-hand car, however my father suggested that I should go in for a new car. The choice was then between an American car—a Ford or a Chevrolet, costing about Rs 3000 or an English car—an Austin or a Morris costing more or less the same. I said that an American car would be too big and more expensive to maintain. Petrol then was 15 annas a gallon, or less than Re 1 per five litres. So I bought a Hillman Minx saloon. Babu paid for it. This was to be with me for the next ten years. In 1949, I changed it for a Studebaker, which again was with me for ten years. In 1959, I bought an Ambassador which I sold in 1965 when I went to Bombay as chairman, Life Insurance Corporation (LIC). The last car I bought was in 1967—a Fiat which I sold in 1981 when I went to West Bengal as governor.

*

It was while I was in Gaya that I got married to Vimla on 19 May 1940. I had gone to Lahore, where Pitamber ji was then posted, during the Easter vacations of 1940. I had met and talked with Vimla again and liked her well enough. My only thought was to wait another year or two as she was just fifteen years old. While I was in London, my father had written to me about other proposals that he had received for my marriage, both from within and outside the community. However, I held the belief that I would rather marry someone from my community, unless there were no suitable girls available. Babu was very happy with this decision of mine. He preferred Vimla because her stars were most favourable. Her father was in an All India Class I Central Service. She was good looking and everyone spoke highly of her temperament. She was good at studies, although she had not been to a Convent School, and perhaps was not fluent in speaking English, but that could be easily rectified. After seeing Vimla at Lahore and talking to her I had agreed. Babu had then written to Babuji (Pitambarji) asking him to hire an English tutor for Vimla.

At the end of April 1940, Babu left for Almora. On the way, he halted at Dehradun for a few days where my first cousin, Padma Datt Pande, was posted as judge, Small Causes Court. While in Dehradun, Babu got a message from Pitamberji that the marriage should be performed early as the engagement had already been announced, and any delay would lead to unfavourable comments. My mother-in-law was keen that there be no postponement. And Vimla even wrote a letter to me saying that I was letting her down, that I should agree, and in case I did not want to live with her, I could leave her as other ICS officers are reported to do. So I had to agree. Babu had rented out Maharaja Nabha's house. We all stayed there and the barat party started from there. The marriage took place in Meerut. Although Pitambarji was at Lahore, the rest of his family was at Meerut. The barat travelled partly by bus and partly by a complicated rail route. It was very hot, being midsummer, and I had taken only a few days' casual leave. After a big reception at Dehradun, I returned to Gaya and Vimla to Meerut and eventually Lahore. Babu wrote to me at this time about the fact that things had happened too suddenly. When he had left Gaya at the end of April, he had not thought that the marriage would take place so soon. All these developments happened very suddenly despite Vimla's anger at the delay and even the thought that I may leave or divorce her! We have now been together for forty-six years. God's will. And we have been happy with each other. God has been kind to us.

*

I had the usual work to do as an assistant magistrate. I made my first acquaintance here with the performance of the Muharram by Shia Muslims, their heart-rending narration of the battles of Karbala, the beating of their breasts with iron chains and blood flowing out; the Gaya pilgrimage during the Pitra-paksh for shradh of the departed ancestors; the prevalence of filaria and malaria in the districts, with men and women developing inflamed feet—elephantiasis due to filaria, and children with distended stomachs and rickety legs and arms due to malaria. Gaya was famous for three things—macchar, mokhtar aur maalzadi—i.e. mosquitoes, pleaders and prostitutes. It was also famous for its smoking tobacco (hukkah) and pethas—a sweet.

I appeared for the departmental examinations while at Gaya and passed with high marks in subjects like revenue law, criminal law, accounts etc., but failed terribly in Hindi. This happened as I could not read the petition written in Kaithi script. In Kaithi, there are no matras, sanyukta akshar or compound words, or line at the top. It is a kind of shikast Hindi used by petition writers in court. I lost my increment and Rs 600 in all, until I passed the next examination held six months later. My collector was very angry with me for failing in Hindi. Incidentally, this was the only academic examination in my life which I had failed. I made up for this loss of Rs 600 later by passing in Mundari, a Tribal dialect of Ranchi and getting a reward of Rs 1000, and still later in 1944 by passing in Nepalese Paharia and getting Rs 500.

*

A new development began taking shape in the working of the administration around this time that is worth mentioning because, in retrospect, I think, it has had a profound negative impact. This was regarding collections for the war and war bonds. Initially it started as a purely voluntary effort with appeals made to people, but as more money was needed, more pressure was applied, like while issuing gun licenses, renewing any other licenses, giving permits, etc. In the beginning all money went to the government. But gradually, some unscrupulous officers and staff began keeping a portion of this amount to themselves. The Congress condemned it most strongly and vowed to stop this practice as soon as possible. However, nothing of the kind happened. It was found to be a very lucrative method of collecting money: for the party, for elections, and also for oneself. This led to a most unholy alliance between profit-seekers, that is, businessmen and industrialists, corrupt people, politicians and the bureaucracy. Today, it has transformed into a monster which is feeding at the whole social and political fabric. The rampant corruption that this has unleashed and the absolutely tremendous dimensions it has attained, its widespread nature, the generation of black money—of which this is the most potent source—is leading to a terrible disaster in the national body politic. Will it be arrested? And if so, how? At present there is no answer, and this is one single aspect of our national life today which causes the greatest discontent and forebodings of a calamity. But perhaps the good in human nature will triumph and this gangrenous growth will be cut off. It will require a surgical operation!

*

There was nothing much to do in the evenings, so I spent mine at the club, playing tennis and bridge till late hours. Gaya was very hot in summers with temperatures going up to 114 or 115º F and loo blowing all the twenty-four hours making even sleep at night impossible. But the days passed quickly enough. In October 1940, I received orders for my transfer to Aurangabad, a sub-division of Gaya, first as assistant magistrate and a short while later as sub divisional officer (SDO) taking over from H.R. Krishnan, also ICS, who was the SDO at the time and was to join as additional district and sessions judge somewhere. Right before joining, I went to Lahore and brought back Vimla to Aurangabad with me.

I stayed in Aurangabad for six or seven months, mainly in dak bungalows and tents. There were no houses available for an assistant magistrate. After a few months I had to let Vimla go back to Lahore. Life was dull and there was little work. As my orders to take over as SDO did not come, I went to Patna to meet the Chief Secretary to urge him to do something. Some alternatives were thought of and finally I got my orders to go to Khunti, a Munda sub-division in Ranchi district. I was happy to go—and as always happened, a fortnight after I had joined at Khunti, Krishnan was transferred from Aurangabad.

Khunti was a very nice but a very small place. The population of the sub-divisional town was then 2000. There was about a quarter mile of empty space between the SDO's house and the court, so we had no neighbours. However, the view over the Chhotanagpur plateau was beautiful. I had hoped that Ranchi would be a thickly wooded forest area, but that was not so. There were very few trees. This was also my first acquaintance with the tribal people of India and I got to like them immensely. They were simple, honest, truthful people with no guile about them and were hence exploited by the people from the plains (dikus). Their village life was a communal living, in the sense that land was held by the village as a whole and given out to individual families according to their needs. Life among the sexes was free and easy before marriage, but strict fidelity was enforced after marriage. Any illicit relationship with a non-tribal always ended in excommunication and being driven out of the village. Although their possessions were few, their villages, houses, and their bodies were extremely clean and well-cared for. The women had a flower stuck to their well-groomed hair and their sari was spotlessly clean and white. Thefts were unknown. One could almost call it an ideal state. In several respects, the tribals were more civilized than us.

Some incidents of that time come to mind. Once, a munda in possession of two bottles of wine was arrested by some excise people. Drinking, especially home-brewed rice beer, is common among the tribals and excise laws or prohibitions are not understood by them. Wine is offered in their religious ceremonies to the great God—Bonga. So this person was produced before me. He said he had the liquor. I fined him Rs 15. He said he had no money but would come and pay it in fifteen days' time. There was no one to pay for his bail. The excise people and my staff wanted me to send him to prison for a few days instead. However, seeing the man and his apparent honesty, I let him go on bail on a personal bond. All the while I kept thinking that if he did not come back, I would have to pay the fine by myself. Fifteen days later, he appeared, walked straight to my court and deposited the money.

Then there was the case of a young man who killed his uncle over a dispute concerning a chicken, which then cost 2 annas. After killing his uncle, this man went to the police station and reported the murder. The sub-inspector sent a village chowkidar to find out what had happened, who corroborated his plea. The case came to me for commitment to the sessions court and despite my warning, the man pleaded guilty. He did the same before the Sessions Judge who, while pronouncing the death sentence, recommended clemency to the high court, but before their orders could be received, the man died of remorse in prison.

Another similar incident ocurred during a loan recovery drive in 1951 or '52. A magistrate had gone to a village in Gumla sub-division, more than a hundred miles from Ranchi. Here, four Adivasis (Oraons) came to him and told him that they had taken a loan of Rs 10 each a few years back, but did not remember whom to repay. Now that the magistrate was here, they had come to him with the money. The magistrate checked but could not find any amount recorded against them. He even sent someone to the Ranchi Treasury to check up. The magistrate told these people to come meet him some four or five days later. They did so. Still, no amount was found due from them, but they insisted on paying, even though they were poor with small, rather tiny, holdings.

During my tours, I found a very big, double-storey, pucca brick house amidst a group of mud houses of the Adivasis in a remote village. I enquired about the owner of this house. He was a businessman (sahukar) from the plains. His main business had been to bring in salt in large quantities during the fair weather and store it in his godown. Later, during the rains, when all communications were cut off and the unbridged rivers and streams had turned unfordable, the salt was sold at exorbitantly high profits. And hence the house. There existed a deep resentment among the Adivasis against the exploiters from the plains. In the last century, this kind of situation had resulted in an uprising led by Birsa Munda—renamed Bhagwan in Munda terminology. Many Adivasis died as they fought with bow and arrow against rifles and guns and naturally lost. This undercurrent of hostility remains to this day and is at the bottom of the uprisings in the northeastern parts of India.

Many Adivasis were converted to Christianity by several missions, like the Roman Catholic, Church of England, Baptists, Seventh Day Adventists. Promise of education, jobs, and medical care was usually the method and inducement for conversion. Government schools were few and far between. These missions actually did some really good work for the Adivasis who were largely neglected by the Hindus.

My stay in Khunti was very short. At the end of December 1941, I was transferred to Bihar Sharif in Patna district. This was a very big sub-division and the work was very heavy. The area had just recovered from very serious Hindu-Muslim communal rioting. I was to stay in Bihar Sharif for nearly two years. They were very busy and eventful years.

During those days, practically all sub-divisions survived without electric lights or piped water supply. There were no telephones either. Several district headquarters were also in a similar position. So one had a host of servants, a pani-wallah to bring water from the nearest well, a sweeper, a cook, a mali, and a bearer. I still saved more per month then than I did as Secretary to the Government of India some twenty-five years later.

I think it was in early 1942, around January, that I joined at Bihar Sharif. It was such a contrast to Khunti. It was crowded, with a population of 50,000. My court was in front of the house not even a hundred yards away, dirty and full of problems. Bihar Sharif was famous for the three th's—turk, teli, and taar—i.e. Turks (Muslim), oil men and palm trees.

The early part of 1942 was spent in restoring normalcy after the communal riots of 1941. This meant ensuring the payment of compensation to victims and their rehabilitation alongside collection of fines imposed on villages. However, some tension remained which continued to be fanned by political parties. In 1946, there was again a recrudescence of the communal riots not only in Bihar Sharif but practically the whole of Patna and in other districts. This was, so to speak, in retaliation to the Great Calcutta Killings of 1945 and the subsequent Noakhali riots in East Bengal. The last riots in 1946 practically made Pakistan a certainty. We all felt it was inevitable and unavoidable, especially when the majority community, viz., the Hindus, hit back. This was tragic, as it made the minorities fear for their safety in a Hindu majority area. I experienced the same feeling in February 1984, when Sikhs were attacked by Hindu mobs in Hindu majority Haryana and more vividly in November 1984, when there was large-scale killing, arson and looting of Sikhs in almost the whole of Northern India. This has been a tragic turning point in Indian history. I have never understood why 85% of the population of India, namely the Hindus, should feel threatened by several communities which themselves constitute less than 15% of the population. This includes about 11% Muslims, 2% Christians, and some 2% Sikhs. Other minorities like Parsees and Budhists are very few in number. If centuries of Muslim and Christian rule could not destroy or convert the Hindu masses to any other religion, then why this ill-perceived threat to themselves? Why Hindu Suraksha Vahinis? Why Hindu communal chauvinistic militant organizations? The greatness of Hinduism and the reason for its survival is its catholicity, its large-heartedness in religious matters, its recognition of all faiths and the unity of mankind and Godhead.

The year 1942 was also a memorable one for us as our first son was born in Almora on September 7. I could not get leave at that time, so I managed to come to Almora only towards the end of October 1942. Vimla and the baby came to Bihar Sharif only at the beginning of 1943. We named the baby, Arvind. Later, my mother-in-law began to call the baby 'Raja'. And this name has also remained with him. Babu was especially happy and I was told that the chhatti and naamkaran were celebrated with great enthusiasm.

In August 1942, the Congress Working Committee passed the famous 'Quit India' resolution at Bombay. Early next morning, Mahatma Gandhi and all the members of the Congress Working Committee were arrested. This sent a tremendous shock wave throughout the country. In fact, I have personally not experienced anything like it in my later life. The future looked dark and there was great apprehension throughout. In the evenings, meetings were held everywhere to protest against these arrests. A few leading citizens of Bihar Sharif were also arrested. Later, I tried them in jail and sentenced them to six-months' simple imprisonment.

I got a message from my Collector and District Magistrate (DM) W.G. Archer to immediately come to Patna for discussions. I left on August 10 and reached Patna late at night. I went to see him next morning but was told to contact him later since he had gone to the Secretariat as a large mob had gathered there. In Patna, the Assembly building and the Secretariat are in the same compound and the said crowd was in front of the gates facing the Assembly. It consisted mainly of young students who were determined to hoist the Indian tricolour at the Assembly building. Armed police personnel were present to prevent them from doing so. Day long parleys were of no help and in the end the DM ordered the police to fire. Seven people were killed at the spot. The crowd dispersed but a fire had been kindled.

A famous martyr's memorial built by the famous sculptor Ray Chaudhuri stands here today.

I went to meet Archer late in the evening. He was visibly upset at the proceedings of the day and was also apprehending trouble elsewhere in the district. He asked me to go back to Bihar Sharif immediately. So next morning, on August 11, I left Patna by car. I had hardly got out of Patna city and not even reached Fatwah, when I found the road underwater. The Ganga was in high flood and the road and the track were wholly submerged for miles. I returned to Patna, left the car at S.V. Sohoni's place, who I was staying with at the time, and went to the railway station to catch a train. Sometime later, a train arrived and I entered the first-class compartment. The only occupant of this compartment was an Englishman. He was drunk and greatly excited and insisted on calling me 'Mr Bose'—Subhash Chandra Bose—throughout the journey. He said he had 'quit Burma' and now was 'quitting India'. He gave me a piece of a parachute string with which he had once bailed out in Burma. He would get down at every railway station and scatter coins all round saying, 'Here, I am quitting India'. At some stations, especially at Fatwah, a mob at the railway station became very menacing. I got down from the compartment and talked with the people. I said the Englishman was drunk, was going to Calcutta and then leaving India, and they should not harm him. They agreed, and let us go on. However, the very next train that came after ours was carrying four Canadian airmen who began to fire at the crowd with their revolvers. The mob killed all four of them on the spot.

I got down at the next junction, Bakhtiarpur, from where I had to take a light railway for Bihar Sharif. While I was waiting for the train to leave, a village chowkidar came running to the station saying that the police station was surrounded by a mob that was threatening to set fire to it. The sub-inspector (SI) and some constables were trapped inside. They were in need of help. Bakhtiarpur was not in my sub-division but, accompanied by my chaprasi, I went to the police station which was not far. As we approached, I saw that the thana had been set on fire but the crowd was melting away. The SI and others were rescued and I sent them to Patna as a train that was leaving just then. I, on the other hand, went to Bihar Sharif.

We kept receiving reports of dacoitees and attacks on police stations, post offices and railway stations from the interior and more inaccessible parts. The half of the sub-division which had better roads was more or less all right, as they could be patrolled, but the other half was totally inaccessible because of rains and lack of roads. One then realized how very important it was to have good roads for maintaining law and order and preventing crime. For example, even when we knew that a dacoity was likely to be committed in a particular village, the police could not go there as there was no road. One night at about 2 a.m., my second officer Satchidanand Singh came to me. He had received information that his first cousin, SDO Sitamarhi, had been attacked by a mob and killed. The armed police that had accompanied him had also been killed. Singh wanted to go to bring his sister-in-law and children from Sitamarhi to Patna. I said he could go. A conviction this incident left in my mind was that a person was safer without an armed guard or a weapon and so some time later, I began to tour my district without a guard, accompanied only by a chaprasi. I felt it was safer that way.

Bihar Sharif was completely cut off from Patna for six days. Some bridges and culverts had been broken, railway tracks uprooted, telegraph lines cut and big trees chopped and thrown across the roads. This kind of thing happened all over North and South Bihar. Six days later, British troops arrived from Ranchi—they shot and killed any group of people found on the roads without any hesitation—and road communication with

Patna was re-established. Peace was restored and an ominous silence descended on the countryside.

Life continued like this for sometime. The situation in Patna, except in Bihar Sharif, had greatly worsened especially in the Barh and Jehanabad sub-divisions. Archer was transferred to Santhal Parganas and a new DM, Hardman, came from New Delhi. He was soberer than Archer and helped in restoring order in the Patna district. Archer left the ICS in 1947 and joined the Victoria and Albert Museum in London as in-charge of the India section. He co-authored several books on Indian art and folklore with M.S. Randhawa, also of the ICS; but later committed suicide.

As things began to settle down in the early part of 1943, there was talk of my transfer to Patna as under secretary, Finance Department. But the impending Bengal famine began to cast its shadows. The Japanese occupation of Burma, the increasing intensity of the Second World War, the failure of the rice crop in India and a severe cyclone in Bengal, along with the denial policy and requisitioning of all modes of transport—especially boats—in East Bengal, contributed to the greatest Indian famine of the twentieth century. The food situation in Bihar also became grim. Prices began to rise steeply, 100-200% or more in a matter of weeks. The Government of Bihar, like other governments, constituted a new Department of Food and Civil Supplies. I was drafted to work therein. From September 1943, for the next six years, I remained in this new department in various capacities, first as regional grain supply officer (RGSO), Darbhanga, for a year, then as RGSO Monghyr, from where I came to Patna in December 1945 as food controller and deputy secretary, then joint secretary, and finally secretary to government in the Supply Department. I became almost an expert in food and civil supply matters. Towards the end, however, I became very bored with the work as it began to lack any novelty.

But a lot of things happened during these six eventful years. Let me try to recall them chronologically. At Darbhanga, we stayed in a private house at Laheriasarai, some five miles from the main Darbhanga town. Laheriasarai was the District Magistrate and Civil Headquarters. Darbhanga was where the Maharajadhiraj of Darbhanga stayed. He was the richest landlord of eastern India. Although he had no princely powers, his income from zamindari was over Rs 1 crore in those days. Bihar Government's annual budget was then less than Rs 5 crores. In this district and in Darbhanga, I witnessed the starkest poverty that I have ever seen in my life alongside the most staggering contrasts. We were once invited to a dinner with the Maharaja of Darbhanga. We were served in plates of solid gold in a most sumptuous dining hall. The whole palace compound was surrounded by high walls. And just outside, in houses of split bamboo, with hardly a piece of cloth as a covering, whether for men or women, children with distended bellies due to malaria and poverty hit one in the face. Over the last forty years, this has somewhat diminished. Zamindari and the house of Darbhanga are no more and such stark poverty is also no more.

War dislocated all transport, including LOC 101 (lines of communication 101), and as a result mangoes from Darbhanga could not be sent to Calcutta. So we got our hands on the best Langra mangoes—a hundred for a rupee. I ate them with such relish and in such quantities that the wife of the district judge, an Anglo-Indian lady, began to remark that I had grown fat as a tub. Breakfast consisted of dahi and chura, both of which Darbhanga was famous for. Buying rice and paddy, mostly from Nepal terai regions, was my main work. I visited Janakpuri in Nepal, some miles from the Madhubani sub-divisional border. This was said to be the capital of Raja Janak of Ramayana fame.

The year in Monghyr was a change. The climate of Monghyr was better and the touring was also better. I had a much bigger area in my charge—the whole of Monghyr district, Southern Bhagalpur, and Santhal Parganas—the last being the most interesting. I travelled extensively, buying and selling foodgrains from the surplus to the deficit areas. It was here we made our first acquaintance with L.P. Singh. He had been my senior in Allahabad by a few years and was posted to Monghyr as collector during this time in 1945. We got to know each other and have remained good friends since. We also made friends with Sahdeo and Santosh Gupta of the Indian Tobacco Company.

May 1945 saw the end of the war, first in the European sector, and then later in the East after the bombing at Nagasaki and Hiroshima. We duly celebrated the end of the war.

CHAPTER FOUR

The Bihar Years: Patna

I came to Patna in December 1945 and remained there for nearly fifteen years with a break from 1953–1954 when I was appointed commissioner, Tirhut Division in Muzaffarpur for nine months and then as commissioner, Bhagalpur for three months. During this period I held several jobs and changed several houses—the first was at 42 Hardinge Road, then 3 Strand Road, then 6 Circular Road, 9 Circular Road and finally 4 Strand Road. Life for us, for the next few years, proceeded more or less smoothly. As some would describe it, it was going up the 'bureaucratic escalator'. But great events were taking place in India and elsewhere.

I remember it was around this time, in 1946, that I was selected for the finance and commerce pool of the Government of India, along with H.C. Sarin. However, the state government refused to release me. I was called by the Chief Secretary Y.A. Godbole and told of this decision. Then he said let him (Sarin) 'drown in the pool', while I 'stick in the mud here'. So we remained stuck in the mud and, in retrospect, did not regret the decision. Once again, after Independence, when the Indian Foreign Service (IFS) was first formed, Vimla and I were, so to speak, 'interviewed' for this service. Again the Government selected us, but then Chief Secretary S.N. Mozoomdar said that the Chief Minister was not willing to release me.

In 1946, elections were held for the state legislatures and the Congress again came into power in Bihar. Shri Krishna Sinha stepped in as chief minister again, with Anugrah Narain Sinha as his number two and finance minister. At that time, the food situation had again become critical and the Government was contemplating a direct levy on the producers. This was a very important decision to take and would have evoked considerable opposition, such that popular support was most necessary for such an enactment and enforcement. As a popular ministry was about to take office, I was asked by the British Advisor to meet Shri Krishna Sinha and get his reaction, especially his support. I was the only Indian officer in the Department and the Englishmen—my seniors—were not keen on calling on 'Shri Babu'. So I went. This was my first ever meeting with him. He was occupying a room upstairs in a partly completed house. Downstairs housed a press, publishing a weekly and pamphlets for the Congress Party. The room upstairs was bare and divided into three parts. In the extreme end was a small space for prayers. Then a single bed—a takhat—for sleeping alongside a table with two chairs where he wrote and met visitors. I introduced myself and told him the purpose of my visit. He thought for some time, and then said that the food situation was bad, large cultivators were holding on to big stocks of foodgrains (and he himself was one of them) and it was necessary that hoarding be discouraged. He then said he was in favour of the levy order and that the government could go ahead with it. His party would support it and when his government took office they would continue with it. I reported this back and the order was issued.

Soon thereafter, Shri Babu took over as chief minister. There was no house vacant for him to occupy and all Indian officers were willing to vacate their house and move into the Circuit House, should the Chief Minister wish so. However, Shri Babu said he would not disturb any officer then as the government would soon be moving to Ranchi, and by the time they returned in October some houses would fall vacant because of transfers and he would then select a place. This brought forth a spontaneous expression of loyalty from us. However, as the years went by, the attitude of the Congress Party began to change. Not only the Chief Minister, but all ministers began to ask for bigger and bigger houses, displacing government servants and causing great inconvenience. This tendency has now gone to such an extent that houses for government servants, especially the better ones, are all occupied by ministers, ex-ministers, MLAs, ex-MLAs with no thought of paying rent or vacating the house. It has almost become a racket or 'privilege' of the party bosses.

*

One of our loveliest memories is of a holiday we took with the Singhs (L.P. Singh's family) in the autumn of 1946 in Mussoorie. We stayed at the Kashmir Hotel.

The year of the great divide—1947. We were in Ranchi during the summer. In those days, the state government used to move to Ranchi from April to October every year. We used to stay at the Doranda staff quarters. The time we spent there was very pleasant. The children had a lot of company, as did the ladies. We would frequently go out for picnics in the pleasant countryside. Sometime in the summer, perhaps in May, I got orders for my transfer to Dumka, Santhal Parganas, as deputy commissioner. We were very happy at the prospect. I bought a kerosene operated electrolux frigidaire in preparation of the transfer, as Dumka had no electricity. But just a few days later, in June, came the announcement of the impending Independence of the country accompanied by partition into India and Pakistan. As all Muslim officers opted to go to Pakistan, and the British had to leave India, a sudden vacuum was created in the bureaucratic hierarchy. My orders to go to Dumka were cancelled and I was asked to stay on in the Secretariat. In fact, thereafter I never went as a District officer.

The day of Independence, 15 August 1947, was one filled with excitement. All officers were in Patna for the main celebrations. There were flag hoisting ceremonies at several places. I remember that though it was very hot in Patna, the celebrations were joyous and spontaneous. The memory of that day remains fresh and invigorating. Soon it was marred by the trauma of Partition, especially the movement of populations in Punjab. Despite earlier violent communal clashes, Eastern India remained quiet and peaceful, though large numbers of Bihari Muslims migrated to Pakistan, the richer families to Karachi and Lahore and the poorer ones to East Bengal.

In December 1947, I went to Kathmandu, Nepal. The first ever delegation from independent India to Nepal was led by Anugrah Narain Sinha, the food and finance minister of Bihar. It was to discuss the supply of rice and paddy from Nepal to India. Babu was accompanying me. The journey was most interesting. We travelled from Patna to Raxaul (Champaran) by rail, then crossed over to Nepal and again took another train for some distance through very thick jungles. Then we changed over to buses and came to the end of the terai and the beginning of the Nepal hills. Our luggage was taken up on ropeways installed by the Nepal Government, while people had to go up on foot, horseback or dandi. There was no road worth the name. One had to climb up stone by stone, and big ones at that. The Nepal Government had deliberately retained the abyssmal road conditions to discourage visitors. I went up on foot though a horse was available if needed. Babu went up on a dandi. For the night we halted at a place called Chisapani, I think. An interesting sight was to see motor cars being carried up. Their wheels had been removed and the cars tied to pairs of long pine trunks. Then a hundred people would lift up the car and carry it up and down the hill as required. We wondered where they were taking the cars until we got the answer the next day.

Next morning we crossed another range and came down to a place about seven miles from Kathmandu. Before reaching Kathmandu, we could see the large Kathmandu valley before us. As we got down we found asphalted roads and motor cars waiting to meet us and take us to Kathmandu. The drive to the city and the city itself was a veritable Shangri-La. Black-topped wide roads and huge palaces, the biggest being the Singh Durbar, which housed the offices of the Nepalese Government. This was a big building with six or eight storeys and some fifty or sixty doors in the front and some on the side—a rectangular structure. It housed large gardens with fountains.

Kathmandu was cold in December. There would be fog till about ten or eleven in the morning and then the sun would shine forth. The days were pleasant and one had a glorious view of the Himalayas. Nights were again cold.

Power and administration was in the hands of the Rana, who ruled as a family hierarchy. The eldest in the family became the prime minister and the others, following precedence, went on to become the commander-in-chief, ministers, and so on. The legitimate children were born generals of the Nepal Army, while the illegitimate ones were mere majors, colonels, etc. Almost every Rana had one or more legitimate wives and several mistresses. The prime minister was addressed as 'Teen Sarkar'—i.e. 'Shree shree shree' written usually as 'shree 3'. At the time of our visit the prime minister was General Padma Shamsher Jung Bahadur Rana, the distinguishing name being 'Padma', since all others were common to every high dignitary. While all power rested with the Ranas, a fiction of Kingship was kept alive. The king was addressed as Maharajadhiraj and 'Panch Sarkar' (shree 5). He was more or less kept confined in his palace but every moning he was, so to say, worshipped with an aarti performed for him. The sovereign lord of Nepal was however Lord Pashupatinath addressed as 'Shri 1008'. Here resides a famous idol of Lord Shiva and this is a very big pilgrim centre, especially on Mahashivratri day. Babu was really most anxious to worship before the great deity Lord Pashupatinath.

When we went to pay our first formal call on the Prime Minister, we found him and other ministers dressed in their most flamboyant and colouful military uniforms with plumed helmets, sword and khukri—some covered in gold and some even diamond studded, helmets with pearls and scarlet tunics. They looked most magnificent. We could converse with them directly in Hindi or English. All the Ranas were highly educated having read in schools and colleges of India and several in England. The audience with the King was however different. He was dressed very simply like any ordinary Nepali, and he spoke to us only in Nepali. It was not that he did not understand or speak Hindi or English, but according to royal etiquette everything addressed to him was translated by an interpreter, as also what he said. However, a Rana minister was always present to note what conversation took place.

One day, we had a very unique experience. The Prime Minister Padma Shamsher, while talking with Anugrah Babu, burst into tears. We were all very embarrassed. Later one of the younger Ranas told us that Padma Shamsher, though a great soldier of his time, had become too old and senile and that he often burst into tears as he could not control himself. We also learnt that the Rana hierarchy had decided to remove him from the office of the prime minister. Soon Padma Shamsher himself spoke about it and requested Anugrah Babu to help him get a piece of land in Ranchi where he would like to settle down after retirement. He said he had been contemplating purchasing some land, but the buyers and negotiators on his behalf were demanding very high prices. He then added that, after all, he had been prime minister for only two years and so did not have all that much money. We learnt that as prime minister he had control of the exchequer, and whatever was surplus from the revenues collected after meeting the expenses of the state, was his. As a gesture of goodwill to Nepal, and as this was the first direct request made by the Prime Minister, the Bihar Government later decided to give away a large area in Doranda to Padma Shamsher free of cost for his private use.

Babu bought two special items in Nepal. A rudraksh mala which he had with him till his death and that is now with me. He also bought a cat's eye ring for me to wear. We were also presented with a gold plated khukri, and some brass and copper statuettes of the Buddha and Shiva at the end of our stay in Kathmandu. I think, in all, we spent three or four days at Kathmandu and had returned to Patna in a week's time. Both Vimla and I have wanted to go to Kathmandu but thereafter no opportunity arose, although now it is only a forty-five-minute journey by air.

*

The year 1948 opened with the death of the Father of the Nation, Mahatma Gandhi. He was shot by a fanatic Hindu Brahmin on the evening of January 30 which cast a gloom over the nation. That evening, no cooking fires were lit in any house. Not only India, but the world, mourned.

The year was memorable in our personal lives for another event. Our second son, Lalit, was born on November 15 that year at the Patna General Hospital. People said Lalit had been born literally with a silver spoon in his mouth. I was then secretary, Supply Department and we were living at 3 Strand Road in Patna.

Next year, L.P. Singh and I took three or four months' leave and came to Almora. Almora in those days had no water supply or electricity. But despite this, and mainly because of my father, Vimla used to come to Almora for varying periods, either alone or with the children and my sister. This continued until 1950 or '51 by which time Raja could not miss school and we were going to Ranchi every summer. Moreover, Babu was over seventy, I did not want him to stay alone in Almora while I was so far away in Bihar. But things were also slowly changing in Almora. We got piped water supply in our house in 1950 and that meant a considerable increase in comfort. We got electricity about five years later, sanitary-fitted bathrooms in 1971, and geyser and overhead tanks and gas for cooking around 1984. In 1943, Babu had a severe accident when a wall collapsed on him and he fractured his right arm. Again in 1950, he suffered severe bronchial trouble and a mild heart attack. I asked him to stay with us from that time onwards in Patna and Ranchi.

In 1949, L.P. Singh and I went on a trekking pilgrimage to Kedarnath-Badrinath. On my return from this trek, I was appointed Finance Secretary of Bihar. I remained finance secretary of Bihar for four years till 1953 and all this time we lived at 6 Circular Road in Patna.

This house was a lucky one for us in many ways. The two boys continued to grow well. On 2 January 1953, our third and last child, a daughter, was born—we named her Ratna. Later while coming across the name of a Javanese queen, I added Mangala to her name—Ratna Mangala. She completed our family.

Work went on pleasantly enough; it was heavy but I liked it. There was again a severe food crisis and great scarcity in 1951. At that time, the government was talking in terms of 'monopoly procurement' and 'total rationing'. These terms however were never more abused. Already the tendency to double talk had begun to creep into our public life. So were these terms bandied about. Some states, especially Bombay, were taking great advantage of this situation. K.M. Munshi was then food minister and P.C. Bhattacharya, of the Indian Audit and Accounts Service (IA & AS), the food secretary. He was later governor of the Reserve Bank of India. Bihar was a highly food deficit state, it had no really big urban centres, but it had important industrial centres like the coal belt of Dhanbad and the steel city of Jamshedpur. Talk of 'monopoly procurement' with very high market prices was a misnomer. The government would not allot us foodgrains according to our requirements. We needed at least 20,000 to 30,000 tons of foodgrains a month. Against this we were allotted a bare 10,000 tons. Later with the onset of summer and rains, the scarcity began to increase, but not the allotment of foodgrains. The central government began to throw the entire blame for the deteriorating food situation in Bihar on the Government of Bihar. I think it was in May 1951, when K.M. Munshi, and later Prime Minister Jawaharlal Nehru, wrote to Chief Minister Shri Babu that if things did not improve immediately, the government would be compelled to intervene and take over the administration of the state. This was a very serious matter and amounted to a serious political crisis.

A Cabinet meeting was held in Ranchi to discuss this letter and the next steps. The Food and Civil Supplies Department were then under a new secretary and he had really no solution to suggest except that Bihar may have to submit to the centre. While discussions were going on and the Chief Minister was thinking of tendering his resignation to the Party High Command for lack of confidence in him and his government, L.P. Singh, who was then chief secretary, suggested that I might be asked to come to the Cabinet meeting and give my assessment of the situation. He suggested this because I had been in the Supply and Food Department for six long years and was familiar with the subject. So I was called in and shown the letter from K. M. Munshi. Certain statistics had been provided on the basis of which conclusions had been drawn. What the letter said was that on the basis of twelve ounces of foodgrains per adult per day—this was considered to be the appropriate requirement—Bihar's food production was sufficient to meet the needs of the people, and therefore what was needed was better internal procurement and distribution and not assistance from outside. I told the Cabinet that all these figures were fallacious as also the conclusions drawn from them. They had been examined on a number of occasions and found erroneous. It was a pity that the government was still quoting them.

The Union Food Minister had called an All India Conference a few days later to discuss this matter and take a final decision on the letter from the Prime Minister. The Chief Minister asked me to attend the conference as the Bihar Government's representative, instead of the Food Secretary. So in a hurry and at very short notice I went to Delhi. This conference has remained in my memory as one of the most important ones that I have attended. After some speakers from other states had spoken, I was asked what Bihar had to say on the subject, and also why Bihar was not falling in line with the rest of the country in regard to its food policy and food administration. I said Bihar would adopt and follow any policy for the country which imposed the same burdens and privations on all its people. Bihar should not be singled out for a step-motherly treatment. I then gave them facts and figures. I argued that if the centre wanted the Bihar Government to meet its requirements from its own production on that scale, then the same standard could be applied to the whole of India; this way the country could produce a surplus to the extent of five million tons of food instead of importing three million tons. The centre should immediately stop imports, acquire the surplus from the food producing areas and give it to the food deficit states. I gave figures to show how disproportionate the availability of food was in different states. Bombay, with its so-called 'monopoly procurement' and 'total rationing', was given extra food imports, so that the actual availability was roughly twenty ounces a day per person against Bihar's bare twelve ounces. This statement of mine had an electric effect. I had attacked K.M. Munshi's home state, I had attacked the state whose food administration was being held as an ideal. I asked that my figures be contradicted if they were wrong. This could not be done as I had based my arguments on the figures supplied by the government itself. I was supported by several other food deficit states. There was consternation in the meeting—hurried consultations on the dias between the minister and the food and agriculture secretaries (the latter was Vishnu Sahay). They could find no fault in my argument. I also said that the Chief Minister would be writing to the Prime Minister on these lines in reply to his letter. The Food Secretary stepped down from the dias to come and ask me why I had not brought these facts to their notice earlier, instead of raising them here in the open meeting. I replied that they had given us no option as they were threatening the Bihar Government which had to fight back. He went back and there was further consultation. I was asked how much food Bihar wanted. I said it had to be one lakh ton a month for the next four months, and thereafter it could be reduced as the first harvest of maize would have come in the market. Then arose the question of what food was needed, because rice and wheat were scarce. I said that a starving man is not choosy about his food. He wants anything edible. Bihar would accept anything: maize, barley, milo (a minor millet like jowar and which was used as chicken feed abroad). They asked whether we could handle such a large quantity to which my answer was that the government should ensure that the railways move the stock—we would do the rest thereafter. We would move the stock by trucks, bullock carts and boats. We would utilize family ration cards and village shops to ensure equitable distribution throughout the state. The government accepted our demands. We fulfilled our part and as a result there was no famine. Prices came down. For this task, in addition to being the finance secretary, I was also appointed the food commissioner of Bihar for two years from 1951 to 1953. This was a challenging task but the whole administration rose to it. Later, we received kudos and appreciation from the Government of India. Sometime later, K.M. Munshi wanted me as a deputy secretary in his department. Shri Babu, then chief minister, refused again. I was happy enough to continue in Bihar.

*

In the aftermath of Partition and Independence, an offer was made to ICS officers wherein they could ask for a change of their state. Some people did so. I was also asked to think of coming to Uttar Pradesh. But I declined. I was happy in Bihar. The government had treated me well. I was able to act independently. There were no pressures on me. Babu and Vimla also agreed. So I never asked for a change and I did not regret it.

This period of my life, from 1951 to about 1960, was at a personal level, perhaps the happiest. In retrospect, the most fruitful and satisfying job which I consider I have had, is that of Development Commissioner, Bihar from 1956–60. This was at the time of the Second Five-Year Plan. But more about this a little later.

In the summer of 1953 I again took two or three months' leave. I had had a severe attack of vertigo at Patna. Some said it was due to low blood pressure, some a disturbance of the fluid in the inner ear, and others very long hours of work. We decided to spend the holidays in Nainital and rented a small cottage. I had another attack of vertigo in Nainital, this time at 5 a.m., while in bed. I was advised several things, a glass of port at night before going to bed, more hot food with chillies, a cup of hot milk with honey at bedtime and five almonds, five raisins, five black peppercorns at breakfast. I adopted the last two and by God's grace there has been no recurrence of the vertigo attacks all these years.

I was also hoping that upon my return I would be posted out as a collector, as my turn for promotion as commissioner was drawing near. However, on returning, I had to again join as finance secretary. But a short-term vacancy for a commissioner did open up in September of that year. The government decided that my experience as food controller would count towards a district experience and I was thus posted as commissioner, Tirhut with headquarters at Muzaffarpur. At thirty-six, I was perhaps one of the youngest officers to be a commissioner.

The house of the commissioner was huge. It was one of the biggest houses that I have ever lived in. I think it was bigger than the Punjab or Haryana Raj Bhavans at Chandigarh. It had a huge drawing room and an equally big dining room separated by a sliding door. It had a fine wooden floor suitable for ballroom dancing. There were two long corridors inside, a bedroom with a dressing room and bathroom, an office room with a bathroom, and a stenographers' room on the ground floor. On the first floor were six big bedrooms with equally large dressing rooms and twelve bathrooms. On all sides were large, wide and long verandahs. It had a fifteen-acre compound with mango and lichi orchards, a kitchen garden and a well. Servants' quarters were galore. For the first and only time, I kept a cow here. There was plenty of grass and a number of people to look after it. The large house was explained by the fact that in early British days, North Bihar was a planters country with indigo as the main crop. Also the Lt Governor of Bengal used to come and stay there.

I had kept books in several book cases in the drawing room. I realized this a little too late when white ants began coming up through the floor and eating up several of my books. This was the second time this had happened, the first was in Gaya. I had brought a number of books from England, although six of my books had been confiscated by the Indian Customs on the grounds that they were either seditious or pornographic. Among the 'seditious' ones were publications of the Left Book Club of England—books like *The Road To Wigan Pier* and the *Theory and Practice of Socialism* by Strachey. Among the 'pornographic', a title I remember was the *Autobiography of a Prostitute*. At Muzaffarpur, I gave away a number of books to libraries as by that time their number had increased greatly. Much later, in July 1977, the godown where my furniture was kept was flooded and several boxes of books were reduced to pulp. Whatever books could be salvaged, along with my further acquisitions while in Calcutta and Chandigarh, now form a fairly good collection at my old house in Almora. I like to sit surrounded by them and there are several I could find the time to read only now.

My stay in Muzaffarpur was altogether short, only about nine months. I was then sent to Bhagalpur as commissioner again on a leave vacancy of three months. The Bhagalpur house was an old Dutch factory near the banks of the Ganga—a single-storey building almost flush with the ground without any plinth. I was there during the rainy season. One evening after dinner, while I was working in the office room, there was a sudden commotion among the chaprasis and the police guard. I came out and enquired what the matter was. They said a big snake had just gone inside through the drawing room into the sitting room. Fortunately, Vimla and the children had gone into the bedroom just minutes ago. The place was searched and the snake could not be found. After some time it was seen to be at the top of a wooden 'jhil mil' door. It was felled and killed—a cobra!

*

North Bhagalpur was in the grip of a severe flood in the Kosi, described as the 'river of sorrow'. The Kosi used to sweep straight down from the Nepal hills to meet the Ganga. But North Bihar being a flat inland delta, the river would swing in its course—a hundred miles east and west and back again every hundred years. Wherever it went, it left thick coarse sand as its silt, thus ruining all the crops and making the land infertile. I decided to go and see how the relief operations were going on. So I headed to North Supane in Saharsa and took a boat to travel down the Kosi therefrom. The boat we boarded was a big flat bottomed one and could carry more than fifty passengers although we were fewer. The boatman said *'Jai Maharani Kosi'*. I was curious, as rivers in India are usually addressed as mothers—'mai' like Ganga-mai—so why 'Maharani' for Kosi? I was told this was because Kosi was temperamental, wayward, imperious like a Maharani—there was no knowing when she would get angry or in what direction she would turn—so they dare not displease her. The journey down the river took time as we stopped at several marooned villages on the way. People were complaining that no one had come for innoculation against cholera. I recalled that ten years earlier at Bihar Sharif I had to fine people for not taking or giving smallpox vaccination to their children. We also saw a number of water snakes following our boat. Then we passed through special paddy fields. There is a peculiar variety of tall paddy, gowing up to heights of eight feet or even more, on the bed of the Kosi. The paddy rises with rise in the river water and has to be harvested on boats. The seed that gets scattered and embedded enables a new crop to be raised the following year. Before we could reach our destination at Madhopura it had gone dark. The sky was overcast, we were surrounded by paddy fields and had lost our way. We could not figure out the right direction. So we spent the whole night in an open boat. The boatmen—mallahs—kept us entertained by singing boatmen's songs concerning the Kosi. As dawn arrived, we found that we were hardly a couple of furlongs from the shore and a jeep and other vehicles had been waiting for us the whole night.

I spent just about three months in Bhagalpur and was then posted back to Patna. As there was no clear vacancy in the Super Time Commissioner's scale, the government appointed me against leave vacancies and in short-duration special posts so that I did not revert to the senior scale.* Thus from about October '54 for the next two years, I was successively land reforms commissioner, officer on special duty to rewrite the Famine Code of 1885, then to recommend the reorganization of the DM's and SDO's offices—the previous report being dated 1901, and finally to recommend redrawing of the district and sub-divisional boundaries in Bihar. I flitted from room to room in the Secretariat and changed at least two houses in the new capital area of Patna. Although some officers would perhaps have protested against such changes, I did not mind. In fact it gave me an exposure to various aspects of administration and gave me a knowledge of several departments, which I would not have otherwise acquired. These postings were therefore of considerable benefit to me personally.

As land reforms commissioner, I became familiar with the detailed revenue administration of the state. This post had

---

*Salary bands for ICS/IAS officers progress from 'Junior Scale', 'Senior Scale', 'Super Time Scale' to 'Above Super Time Scale'. The reference to 'Super Time Commissioner's Scale' is to a salary band. Appointment to a leave vacancy is at the same level as one's entitlement. For special posts, salary would be set according to the entitlement of the person posted there.

been created consequent to the abolition of zamindari after Independence. Bihar was the first state to do so. Lord Cornwallis' Permanent Settlement of 1793 was abolished. This was one of the most profound and far-reaching measures that was taken in Independent India. A 150-year-old legislation—which over the years had given rise to a parasitic class of absentee landlords, led to the impoverishment of the tenantry and reduced them practically to serfhood and great poverty, caused a decline in agricultural production and made one of the richest states into the lowest per capita state—was abolished. I personally attribute the extreme poverty of Eastern India principally to this legislation. Cornwallis had, no doubt, enacted the legislation with good motives—he had wanted to create a class of landlords loyal to the British on the lines of the English gentry. But within ten years it was found to have been ill-conceived and ineffectual.

Therefore, this law was not extended to the rest of Northern India, Bombay or Madras presidencies where the Ryotwari system prevailed, that is, direct assessment and collection of rent by government through its own official hierarchy of tehsildars, patwari and kanungos. This Permanent Settlement law had led to such an exploitation of tenants by the landlords and so much oppression that there were numerous peasant revolts in various parts of Eastern India, which all came under the old Bengal Presidency. In 1885, the government had to therefore enact the Bengal Tenancy Act protecting the tenant from unjustified eviction. Special terms for the protection of tribals were enacted in the Chhotanagpur and Santhal Parganas Tenancy Acts. Zamindars were divided and sub-divided over the years into a host of subordinate zamindars.

The collection of government revenues was very interesting. I witnessed it once in Gaya. The landlord was required to pay the revenue before sunset on March 31. This was called the 'sunset law'. To beat the deadline, the landlords would come to the Treasury to make the payment. It was physically impossible to handle such large collections in one day. So a big enclosure would be erected outside the Treasury, magistrates and armed guards posted. The landlords would fling the money in special bags which contained details of their zamindari into this enclosure. The penalty for non-payment by this hour meant that the estate could be sold free of all encumbrances, and if necessary, purchased by government in satisfaction of its dues for the amount of rupee one. It was basically confiscation and the government acquired large properties when it so desired by this method. The landlords were most anxious to avoid this sale and they would somehow pay the revenue. The government had very little expenditure to incur in this collection. The greatest negative aspect of this Permanent Settlement was the distance it created between the government and the mass of the peasantry—in fact the mass of people—and over the years it led to greater and greater estrangement. Upon the abolition of zamindari, the government had to create a new administrative set up, somewhat on the lines of the system in Ryotwari states and also to work out the modalities for payment of compensation to the ex-zamindars. This measure, in the course of years has been, I think, the most potent not only from an economic perspective but a most powerful instrument of social and economic change in the rural areas of Eastern India. The reverberations are still being felt and adjustments, some painful, are still being made.

The revision of the Famine Code was a somewhat different matter. The economic history of India of the eighteenth and nineteenth centuries is full of stories of famines throughout the country. Eastern India also had its full share. Around 1880, a Famine Code was promulgated to lay down measures for amelioration of famine, symptoms to be watched, etc. Although this did help, we witnessed one of the greatest famines of the century in 1943, the year of the Bengal famine. The failure to tackle this was one of the reasons of the transfer of then Viceroy Sir Wavell. After Independence, it was not only food scarcities and famines that had to be tackled, but floods and calamities caused by fires, earthquakes and other natural disasters too. The Famine Code of 1880, with the scale of relief indicated therein, had become out of date. So I was asked to undertake the work of its revision and bring it up to date. I think I took about six months to do so. When in 1967 I had to go to Bihar again in the midst of yet another severe food shortage—we imported nearly twelve million tonnes of food—it was gratifying to note that relief operations throughout the state were being carried out in accordance with the revised code of 1955.

The pattern of staffing of the district and sub-divisional office was based on the report of the Board of Revenue in 1901. A great many changes had taken place since, especially in the Revenue and Development departments. Some old offices in the Revenue Department had become redundant due to the abolition of zamindari while new ones had had to be created. Development was a new field of activity. The report on staff reorganisation was quickly accepted and implemented.

Bihar, at that time, had very big districts and sub-divisions. There were only sixteen districts and about fifty sub-divisions. Although it was only two-thirds the size of UP, this number did not compare favourably with the fifty-five districts of UP and its 150 odd sub-divisions. Only Madras had such large districts and sub-divisions. I recommended the formation of eight new districts and seventeen new sub-divisions. This recommendation was however not implemented for another twenty years. In 1976, when the first new district was created, I was invited by then Chief Minister, Kedar Pandey, to attend the ceremony. I was cabinet secretary at the time. Although I could not go, I was happy that at least the recommendations were being accepted. Today in fact there are many new districts, subdivisions and commissioner's divisions that have been created.

During this period, I was permitted by the state government to visit Madras and Bombay to study their district and revenue administrations. I borrowed many ideas from the set up in these states which had the Ryotwari system of land administration. However, I also found that the administration in Bihar compared favourably with other states, although unfortunately due to the statements of its ministers, parliamentarians and legislators, the public impression throughout, then and even now, is of an administration totally run down, caste-ridden and corrupt. In fact, it is not so.

In 1956, I was appointed development commissioner, Bihar. I held the post for the next four years and we moved into 4 Strand Road. This was the most satisfying job I have held in my thirty-nine years of government service. This was the period when the Second Five-Year Plan was being implemented and Community Development blocks were created. There was optimism throughout the country. People were cooperating enthusiastically in implementing the various development plans. The politicians, still of the old breed, had not felt the necessity of using the administration for their selfish interests. I always look back to this period with considerable nostalgia. For a short period of about six weeks I also acted as chief secretary in Bihar in addition to my duties as development commissioner.

In this job, I travelled throughout India and saw the great variety and diversity of its culture, archaeology, and people. I found the most beautiful, scenic parts of India to be three extremities, Kashmir in the north, Assam and its environs in the east and Kerala in the south. During a trip to Assam, I learnt of the matriarchal system in the Khasi and Jaintia Hills and the proud cultures of the Adivasis. The Chief Minister of Assam B. P. Chalika said that 'a Naga does not know how to bend his head'. He is so proud. I also saw the developed state of the women of Manipur, with a big, flourishing bazaar in Imphal entirely manned and run by them. These travels involved meeting so many people from different parts of India and revealed the true 'unity in diversity' of our country. I relish all the memories. And as they are mostly happy and uneventful ones, one also tends to forget them!

*

As I write, I recall that I went on a short holiday with Raja to Kashmir in 1956. Vimla, Lalit and Ratna stayed with Babu at Ranchi. Among other places of usual interest in Kashmir, we also went to Amarnath caves. The Sheshnag Lake was one of the most beautiful sights I have seen in my life. We brought back many souvenirs some of which are still with us, the wooden 'man in the moon' in the front verandah of the old house, a fish shaped walnut bowl and a nut cracker. In 1959, Babu celebrated Lalit's yagyopavit ceremony in Patna. It was a big affair, from a traditional point of view and as a social event because a number of our relatives came to stay with us as did our friends and acquaintances from Patna and Bihar.

At the end of 1959 and early 1960, I went as the leader of an Indian co-operative delegation of six people to Yugoslavia and Israel, spending six weeks in each country. The visit was very educative. The communist system of Yugoslavia under Marshal Tito and the definition of words like 'socialism' and 'democracy' acquired new meanings. The privileges of the members of the Communist Party had to be seen to be believed. In one of the farm cooperatives, north of Belgrade, we found great difficulty in answering the call of nature. There were no indoor toilets and one had to go out in the field to an enclosed one, open at the bottom and the top, with a deep hole in the ground and temperatures all around at -5ºC. When we said we were not used to such facilities we were allowed access to a special portion of the hostel, reserved for party members with the most modern facilities. We were advised to only drink mineral water in Yugoslavia for fear of hepatitis. Yet the country was prosperous; communism certainly had some advantages. There were numerous museums and memorials devoted to the two years of German Nazi occupation to remind one of its horrors. They were erected in order to unify the people of Yugoslavia, belonging to different language groups, religions, etc., into one body, as being united under a common object of hatred. Also the question came repeatedly to one's mind—does one need to lop off the tallest poppies in order to have all round development? Otherwise it appears that one creates islands of prosperity in a sea of desert.

In Israel, one saw the tenacity of an oppressed people united by love of religion and a fanatical regard for their language—Hebrew—dead for nearly 2000 years. Yet they were reviving it. And what hardships had the people endured to create a homeland for themselves, after the most inhuman and brutal attempts to exterminate a whole race under Hitler's Nazi rule in Germany and the conquered territories. There is no recorded instance of such genocide in world history. And here in Israel were Jews from all over the world, building up a new and powerful country even though surrounded by a hostile Arab population!

I often like to repeat a conversation I had in a Jewish Israeli kibbutz with an ex-minister, an educated and widely travelled person. He had visited India several times and was acquainted with its development programme. He was enthusiastic about Jay Prakash Narain's Bhoodan-Gramdan movement under the direction of Vinoba Bhave. We began to talk of the Community Development programme in India. I said that as long as we were dealing with a few hundred blocks we were doing very well, but when we attempted to cover the whole country, we had to multiply our efforts a hundred-fold. Staff requirements, training and supervision also increased in the same proportion with the result that the programme had got considerably weakened. Jawaharlal Nehru had talked of a lamp lighting hundreds of other lamps and thus shedding a bright light all around. But this seemed to not be happening somehow. Then we talked of the availability of educated manpower in India and other requirements. At this stage this gentleman told us a tale that I never quite forgot. He spoke of a newly married couple, the husband went out to work and the wife started to cook with the help of a cookery book. She put in all the ingredients as directed and waited. The husband came back and asked if the food was ready. She said she had been waiting but it was not ready. He looked down and found she had not lit the fire. The cookery book did not say 'light the fire'. So what was happening in India was that, although we had all the necessary wherewithal for a tremendous advance, the 'fire' was somehow missing. Who will light it and when?

On my return from Yugoslavia and Israel in early 1960, I was transferred to Delhi as joint secretary in the Ministry of Community Development and Cooperation headed by S. K. Dey. I had completed about twenty-one years in Bihar, fifteen of which were in Patna.

*

Raja was now at the Allahabad University. This marked the third generation of our family to attend this university: my father had attended the then Muir Central College towards the end of the last century, I was there in the mid-thirties, and Raja between 1959 and 1961. Lalit had gone to Doon School, Dehradun. An important chapter of my life came to a close. We had been very happy in Bihar, especially during the fifties, in Patna. All of us had good friends and good company. Vimla had her ladies' groups, the children their playmates. I had my own circle and heavy but satisfying work. Even Babu had the company of some senior retired officers with whom he shared some common interests. Since coming to Patna I had given up playing bridge as I got little time for it. I used to play tennis now and then, but even that stopped after coming to Delhi. When we were due to leave we had a round of parties, and moreover, when we boarded the Delhi Express in the morning, a very large number of our friends came to see us off at the station. The farewell was touching and Vimla wept. Babu said that this was due to her— she had so endeared herself to everyone.

Babu and Vimla got down at Allahabad to spend a few days there, and I went on ahead to Delhi. They were to wait until I found us a place and our luggage arrived from Patna. Government accommodation was not so difficult especially for senior officers. I had come as a fairly senior joint secretary—so I was soon allotted a ground floor flat—83 Wellesley Road, now known as Bapa Nagar on Zakir Hussain Marg. I got the ground floor flat because of Babu's old age. The flat was two stages below my entitlement, but then better than nothing. And what a contrast from Patna! From a house with seven big bedrooms, bathrooms, drawing room, dining room, office room and a large compound, this flat had three smallish bedrooms, with two bathrooms, drawing-cum-dining room, a tiny verandah and a patch of lawn. We could not put all our luggage inside the house. And from an army of servants, peons, etc., at Patna, there was nobody to lift our luggage here. Vimla and I had to carry our boxes inside ourselves. Some that we put on shelves stayed there for a year until we changed house. So that marked the end of an important chapter in my life and a major part of my official life as well.

*

Some other memories before I close this chapter. By and large happy ones. Life seemed to be going on well. I was moving up the bureaucratic escalator smoothly enough. I liked working in Bihar, the people were genuine and friendly. Government had also been considerate to me and treated me well. The people of Bihar also, I think, liked me. Even now I meet people at Almora who tell me that their parents or grandparents knew us well in Bihar. Despite all talk of casteism and divisions in the ranks of politicians and differences among Shri Babu (Shri Krishna Sinha)—a Bhumihar Brahmin, and Anugrah Babu (Anugrah Narayan Sinha)—a Rajput, I found in my long years in Bihar that these two leaders were always united and spoke with one voice on any matter concerning Bihar as a whole. They put the interests of their State much above the interests of their constituency, district or caste. I came to the conclusion that it was their followers, or supporters, who were constantly trying to create a rift so that they themselves could benefit. This was also a period of political stability, mature and sincere leadership with towering personalities like those of Jawaharlal Nehru and so many others at the helm of affairs, of an optimism bordering perhaps on a euphoria among the people, of a bright future ahead (perhaps even without working very hard). So many gains had been consolidated, so many crises averted, that confidence in the future was justified.

CHAPTER FIVE

Delhi and Bombay: 1960-66

So I moved on to Delhi and thus began the second half of my official career. I was in the Ministry of Community Development and Cooperation (Department of Community Development) for about two and a half years from April 1960 till about October 1962. The first six months in Delhi were a period of adjustment. We had to form a new circle of friends and acquaintances. This is always difficult. Babu was happy about my move to Delhi as he had always been of the view that for further advancement in service, one had to go to Delhi. But he would also add that Delhi was a most impersonal city, everyone was busy in the rat race and no holds were barred for progressing through it. Pushing one's way up was the thing to do, even if it meant elbowing your way through or tripping another man. But then such was life. I did not see myself fitting in such a circle, yet I stayed on in Delhi for over fifteen years.

Babu was happy reliving his memories from thirty years earlier. Some of his old friends and acquaintances were still alive and he met them after several years. However, his own stay in Delhi was short. Towards the end of the year, in late December, he was suddenly taken ill after returning from his evening walk. He had caught a chill and a chronic bronchial patch flared up into a pneumonia, and with an illness lasting just over twenty-four hours he passed away on 23 December 1960 at the age of eighty-two. Raja and Lalit were both at home for winter vacations. Dada and his family were at Kailash Colony and came immediately. My sister, who was in Allahabad, could come only a day later. He was cremated at the Nigambodh ghat in Delhi and I performed the last rites in Delhi itself. A number of our relatives came and this kept Vimla and the rest of us very busy. Sometimes I feel that the custom of relatives and friends coming on such occasions lessens the bereavement, as the mind has to deal with other duties and cannot think so much of what is missed. Babu however left us with his blessings. He was performing his meditations right up to the last day and died with his rosary in his hands. He did not say anything to me, Vimla or the children towards the end.

*

Official work continued its usual pattern. In Delhi, each of the central ministries were almost as large as some of the state secretariats. The people one met in meetings and at conferences were only those more or less directly connected with a particular issue. Thus, in the community development ministry, I mainly met people from agriculture, health, education and planning. There was a different circle in other ministries and quite often one circle did not touch or intersect with another circle. As in Patna, so also in Delhi I moved from one ministry to another in a fairly frequent manner and in the course of these movements worked in several buildings. To start with, Community Development was located in the Krishi Bhavan. Then I was in the Ministry of Economic and Defence Coordination (Department of Supply) for a year which was located in the eastern end of the North Block. Then for another year and a half, I served as additional secretary, Ministry of Finance, Department of Revenue—as a gold control administrator, and for a while, chairman of the combined old Central Board of Revenue (being the last Chairman before it was bifurcated into the present two Boards of Direct and Indirect Taxes) at the Western end of North Block. After a gap of a little over two and a half years that I spent in Bombay, I was back in Delhi in August 1967 as Secretary, Planning Commission in Yojana Bhavan. Two years or so later, I headed to the Udyog Bhavan, first as secretary, Department of Heavy Industries and later as secretary, Industrial Development of the combined department. In May 1971, I was back in the North Block as secretary, Department of Revenue and Finance, and from there finally to the Cabinet Secretariat in the Rashtrapati Bhavan as cabinet secretary for almost four and a half years—the longest tenure in any post in my official career.

Among the initial adjustment difficulties I recall, one was getting Ratna enrolled in a good school in Delhi. We went from school to school and drew a blank. At last she was given admission to Mater Dei Convent School on Purana Qila Road just behind Tilak Marg. When I went to the Life Insurance Corporation (LIC) for about two years and came back, there were again difficulties with Ratna's school, although at the end of her school tenure she came first in her class.

While in Delhi, some years later during a conversation, Cabinet Secretary Vishnu Sahay gave me his assessment. He said that I was not classified in the category of 'high flyers' like L.K. Jha or K.B. Lall, but was considered a high, above-average officer, solid, unruffled, but with little brilliance. Most people have attributed my move from one job to the other mainly to the escalator I have already described. This is a digression, however.

*

Let me come back to the community development (CD) ministry. The Community Development programme continued to expand rapidly. Prime Minister Jawaharlal Nehru gave it full encouragement. It was also popular with the people. Development administration through the National Extension Service was—for the first time in several hundred years of India's history—going down to the villages. For every group of ten villages there was a village-level worker. For every 100,000 people there was a block with roughly a hundred villages therein. Every block had a block development officer (BDO) who would coordinate all development activities. He had with him an agricultural graduate extension officer, a veterinary doctor, a cooperative inspector, a social education worker, two women village level workers (VLWs) and so on. This team was required to work as a unit with full horizontal coordination among them. They were supported by a non-official Panchayat Samiti as an advisory committee. It had the heads of all elected gram panchayats as members, together with special representatives of women, Scheduled Caste and Scheduled Tribe members. The programme mainly consisted of providing drinking water and irrigation wells, minor irrigation schemes, desilting and repairs of tanks, building of panchayat bhavans, village roads, drains, evening schools for adults and children, women's handicraft centres, balwadis for the very young, health programmes and more. The programme was determined on the priorities suggested by the villagers themselves. Funds and authority to sanction were vested with the Block Panchayat Samiti. There was full delegation of powers to them, with the result that work was completed quickly, generating an enthusiasm among the villagers in turn. They were required to meet half the cost of any scheme, in the form of labour, materials, or cash. And this came in generously. India's success in this programme attracted world-wide attention. The Ford Foundation, under Dr Douglas Ensminger, played a key part in formulating and starting off this programe. Later, the United Nations too adopted this framework. Many visitors came from other developing countries to observe our model and our officers went on deputation to several countries to help start off similar programmes.

At this stage two things, in my view, proved to be major handicaps. The first was a desire to cover the entire country with CD blocks before the end of the Third Five-Year Plan in 1966. This meant funds had to be found for some six thousand blocks, including the arrangement of attendant staff and ensuring their training. This strained our resources, the programme got thinned out, funds decreased, the staff was ill-trained and ill-equipped, and proper supervision could not be ensured. All this, in turn, affected the quality of the programme. The second decision, taken at about this time, was to give a statutory base to it, by creating legal gram panchayats, block and district level bodies, and by having elections and giving them a formal status. While this was a desirable thing, it was perhaps somewhat premature in timing. Our politics was not yet mature enough and as a result wrong people began to be attracted to these bodies because of the funds and patronage they commanded.

But some other developments took place which effectively killed the programme by the mid-60s. First and foremost was the death of Jawaharlal Nehru, the staunch supporter of this programme. His successors, Lal Bahadur Shastri and Indira Gandhi, gave it lukewarm support. Indira Gandhi, while not openly condemning it, nevertheless, did not hide her lack of support for it. Soon after Indira Gandhi became prime minister, S.K. Dey—India's first union cabinet minister for cooperation and panchayati raj—left the government and the CD and cooperation ministry lost its identity. It was later merged as a wing or cell in the agriculture ministry. Perhaps there was an element of personal dislike. I remember an occasion when S.K. Dey asked me to seek Indira Gandhi's support for some programme which the CD ministry was sponsoring. He asked me to go in his place. I made an appointment for my first ever meeting with Indira Gandhi. She seemed to be visibly annoyed and brusque at the meeting. The first question she asked was why S.K. Dey had not come. I said I did not know. Then she gave some non-committal reply to the proposal I was carrying. It appeared to me that whenever S.K. Dey went to see Mrs Gandhi, which was very frequently, perhaps he did not show her the deference that she expected. Any minister in Nehru's Cabinet or among officers who had even remotely treated her only as Nehru's daughter and not as a future prime minister were soon shunted away when she came to power. This happened, for example, with my colleague Kesho Ram who was Jawaharlal Nehru's secretary. He was removed from the Prime Minister's Office to the periphery of government until his retirement.

Then the CD programme, especially the horizontal coordination under the BDO, was disliked by the departmental chiefs and secretaries to government of India and in consequence by the departmental ministers. They began to complain that their programmes of development were suffering because they did not exercise direct authority over the village and block level staff, although this was wholly unjustified. They wanted a line chain of command—an undiluted one. So they succeeded in breaking an essential element of this programme, namely close horizontal coordination at village, block and district level. They had their way, but the basic concept of Community Development was broken and destroyed.

And lastly, but equally importantly, the elected representatives, MLAs in the state legislatures, and MPs in Parliament, did not like the emergence of powerful elected representatives at block and district levels. Their self-importance in being able to dispense patronage, in pleasing one set of their supporters and denying their opponents the benefits of developmental programmes, felt receding from their hands. While MLAs and MPs could influence state ministers, threats of withdrawing their political support as a quid pro quo was important, they could also influence the district level authorities in various ways. But if these locally elected panchayat bodies and chiefs came into position and power, they would have to be wooed. Therefore, the national political parties, influenced by their MLAs, MPs, and party chiefs, saw to it that the panchayat bodies did not function. The easiest thing to do was to accuse them of favouritism, casteism, or corruption and then supersede these bodies. Thus, no elections were held for decades, at some instances even as long as fifteen years, to any local body, whether rural or urban. This is the position even today.

In this way a programme which started with great promise and fanfare in 1952, and had achieved country-wide coverage in just fifteen years, was allowed to die a premature death. Yet it left some achievements of a permanent nature. For example, an extensive development administration extending right down to the village still exists. It was this, and the ground work that had been done earlier, which was responsible for the breakthrough in agricultural production from the second half of the '60s. But what has been lost and not been recovered in the last twenty years is horizontal coordination between the various development departments and agencies. They are each going their own way to the great detriment of the people and the nation. I do not know when, if ever, we will again be able to secure and achieve this coordination.

*

In August or September 1962, I was appointed director of the National Academy of Administration at Mussoorie. The Academy trains IAS and other central government officers for a year or so after they pass the UPSC exam. It has been renamed the Lal Bahadur Shastri Academy of Administration. My friend, A.N. Jha of Uttar Pradesh, was then director and he was stepping into the Planning Commision as additional secretary—there was no secretary in the Planning Commission then. He and the other officers at Mussoorie kept asking me everyday about when I was reaching Mussoorie. I could only reply that I had no orders. One day I was asked to meet Lal Bahadur Shastri, then home minister. I first went to see Home Secretary V. Vishwanathan who told me about the appointment and asked me to go in and see the Home Minister. Shastriji asked me if I was willing to go to Mussoorie. I said I had no personal choice or preference in the matter and was willing to go wherever government sent me. He then said I had been selected for the post and I should prepare to go soon. On my way out I saw Vishwanathan again and asked him when I was required to go. He said very soon. The formal orders were now only a matter of time, the Home Minister had agreed and the Prime Minister would just sign on the proposal. He also said that the idea was that I would spend one year in Mussoorie and go to Harvard the following year on a senior fellowship for one academic term. In fact, I had been selected when the awards were first instituted in 1958 or 1959, but I had then declined saying that I could not be away from India for a year due to my father's old age. So this suggestion was again presented.

I came home and told my wife about this. She wanted to know if she should start packing. Just then I met a senior colleague of our service, S. Ranganathan, and he asked me about the posting. I told him the details, and that we were getting ready to leave. He suggested from experience that I wait until the actual order was received. So we took his advice and waited. A few days passed and nothing happened. I then made some enquiries, and learnt that S.K. Dey was witholding my release for he wanted my successor instated before my departure. Character rolls of officers were called from the Establishment Officer, scrutinized and returned as they were not met with S.K. Dey's approval. I was getting somewhat impatient. I even went to the extent of asking a very senior colleague of mine, S.N. Mozoomdar, who had been my Chief Secretary in Bihar and was a good friend of S.K. Dey, to speak to him—something which I had never done before in my life. Part of the reason was that it would mean a promotion to the post of additional secretary. I felt I would lose out in seniority if the promotion was delayed.

Just about this time, S.K. Dey went on a month's tour to the USA. He had been invited to give a series of lectures on the Community Development programme in India at various American universities. Just as he was boarding the plane, he told M.R. Bhide, secretary in the CD ministry, that I was not to be relieved until his return and that he would bargain and get an officer of his choice in my place, especially as the home ministry wanted me. So matters stood as is.

Then suddenly in early October 1962, major international developments took place. China attacked India. There was a virtual turmoil and the country was in the throes of an unprecedented crisis. Defence Minister Krishna Menon had to resign. T.T. Krishnamachari (better known as TTK) was reinducted into the central Cabinet as a minister incharge of a newly-formed Ministry of Economic and Defence Coordination. He was given vast powers of coordinating various matters and had direct access to the Prime Minister. S. Bhoothalingam was appointed secretary and P.V.R. Rao from the CD ministry was appointed additional secretary. TTK had also been given full authority to make a selection of the officers he wanted and other ministries were told to relieve those selected. He selected me—I do not know why or how—I had never met him or worked under him. Perhaps P.V.R. Rao recommended my name. TTK wanted me to step in as additional secretary but the home ministry was creating some difficulty. S.K. Dey had returned from the USA by then. One day in office I got a sudden order to immediately report to the new ministry. I changed my office within three hours. Initially I was very unhappy. I had lost the chance of a promotion; S.K. Dey had objected to releasing me without a substitute and yet here I was, relieved without a substitute. P.V.R. Rao told me that TTK was trying to get my post upgraded to that of an additional secretary's but this was not agreed to and I had to wait another year to secure a promotion. This was yet another instance when my career took a sudden and most unexpected turn—on the whole, perhaps for the better.

In the economic and defence coordination ministry, I was placed incharge of the Department of Supply. The importance of this department then was the urgent need to re-equip the defence services following the Chinese attack, our withdrawal, their capture of vast Indian territories and their subsequent withdrawal. Until then the Supply Department had been a part of the Ministry of Works and Housing. Military missions came from the USA and UK and they asked for a list of equipment that India would like to import. They were shocked to find that we were still on the First World War specifications! Moreover, among the items needed by the Army on an emergency basis were tinned peaches from California! So a drastic review of all defence intends was made and this task fell to TTK's ministry. I remember, we were still importing large quantities of wool from Australia to make heavy overcoats for the winter. These had been used by the British Army in the First World War and were still in use in the Indian Army. They were so heavy that they made it difficult to trudge through the higher Himalayas. If they got wet they became even heavier. The Chinese, on the other hand, were using waterproof coats filled with cotton or feathers which were not only warm but very light. Such coats could be manufactured locally in India without any difficulty, save precious foreign exchange and would be most suitable as warm overcoats for the hills. So a changeover was made and what came to be known as parka coats came into use.

Another example where I had a row with the defence ministry was over the supply of medicines. The Army Chief complained to the Prime Minister that the Supply Department was not meeting the Army's demands for medicines and the hospitals were running short. The Prime Minister spoke to TTK and I was called in to provide an explanation. I consulted the concerned officers of the Supply Directorate, the Directorate General of Supplies and Disposals, to find out the facts. They said that millions of tablets of various medicines were ready, packed with the manufacturers, but the Army Inspectorate was not accepting delivery. It was found that the Army specifications provided that all such bottles should have cork stoppers. Now cork used to come from Portugal and we had severed all diplomatic and commercial ties with Portugal over the question of Goa. Moreover, better plastic stoppers were now being manufactured and all civil hospitals were buying medicines in bottles with plastic stoppers. So I informed Jaisukhlal Hathi, who was the minister of state incharge of supply and TTK about this, and said that I was ringing up the Army Chief and Defence Secretary to let them know that if the specifications were not changed by the evening and instructions issued immediately to the Inspectorate, we would inform the Prime Minister. The changes were of course made at once. Then we found that waterproof tarpaulins were being imported by the Air Force from the UK. These were a few examples that I came across. The result of all such revelations was a thorough revamping of the Defence Services rules and regulations and modernization together with indigenization of the Indian Army, Navy, and Air Force.

Sometime in the summer of 1963, in June or July, TTK suggested that Jaisukhlal Hathi and I go to England and USA to inspect and visit our old supply missions and thereafter recommend improvements in their working. The idea was to cut down staff as much as possible, save foreign exchange and make purchases in India itself wherever possible and necessary. Our first stop was London. The India Store Department (ISD), as it was then called, was a very old establishment from the days of the East India Company. There was another similar department called the Crown Representatives established for British colonies other than India. Before Independence, practically every manufactured article came from England and this office was thus important. The Defence Services and the Railways had their own representatives and purchase procedures, albeit under the overall control of the Director ISD. This office was more or less independent of the High Commission though technically a part of it. The High Commissioner was in favour of a big reduction in the staff and its amalgamation with the High Commission office. The Defence Services, especially, as also the Railways, were in favour of retaining their identity. This gave officers of these departments an opportunity of a three-year posting to London. But we made some major reductions in the staff and changes in purchase procedures which were accepted by the government. This translated into savings of hundreds of thousands of pounds a year in expenses.

During this visit, I went to Cambridge for a day to see Raja who was there at the time.

From London, we flew into Washington via New York. Some of the indents pending in our London office were for vacuum seals costing a paltry two shillings and sixpence! In some cases the manufacturers and suppliers informed us that these items were now out of production. They all advised that we change to more modern products or try and fabricate these small items ourselves. These examples go to show just how ancient the equipment with us was.

The Washington office, called the India Supply Mission, was a more recent creation having been set up during the Second World War. It had been set up for the procurement of military supplies from USA for the use of the Indian Army in the Eastern sector. After the war, the mission was seen mainly purchasing food grains and fertilizers for India out of funds made available by the US backed India Aid Funds. P.P. Agarwal was the director at the time of our visit and I stayed with him. We found that fertilizer purchases could be better made in India as worldwide quotations from Europe and Japan could also be taken into account. But food purchases were best made in Washington. Also shipping was best arranged in New York. We made our recommendations accordingly.

We made a day's halt in New York mainly to meet the shippers. Our effort was to explore the utilization of Indian shipping as much as possible. A memorable visit was made to the New York Radio City—or am I forgetting the name—it had the biggest show in town—the biggest revue programme, widest stage and a big hall. This was closed down a few years later.

From New York we headed to San Francisco, and therafter from Honolulu to Tokyo. San Francisco and Honolulu were just sightseeing trips. Jaisukhlal Hathi knew some wealthy Gujarati merchants there who played host and showed us around the famous sites.

Tokyo also had a small purchase setup, created fairly recently. I think we suggested that it need not exist as a separate entity. Our purchases from Japan were very few except for fertilizers, which in any case could also be purchased from Delhi. We saw the sights of Tokyo, including a dinner party at a Geisha's place in the traditional, old-fashioned Japanese style. We returned via

Hong Kong. The whole trip around the world took a fortnight, or maybe even less.

In September 1963, Bhoothalingam called me one day and said that the home ministry was asking about my plans to go to Harvard for the promised fellowship. He also added that TTK was not very keen to let me go, but would not disregard my personal wishes in this matter. I told him that he could say no to the home ministry. I was not very keen myself. So the Harvard fellowship never materialized.

Towards the end of 1963, there was a major reshuffle in the Cabinet portfolios. TTK again became the finance minister after having resigned in 1956, following the Mundhra deals by LIC and subsequent enquiry by Justice Chagla. Justice Chagla had held on that occasion that the correct prescribed procedures had not been followed by LIC in purchasing Mundhra's shares. He had also held TTK and H.M. Patel, one of the most outstanding officers and then economic affairs secretary and part-time chairman of LIC, responsible. Both of them had resigned. So this was a big comeback for TTK.

One of the most drastic, highly unpopular, yet considered a most patriotic and essential, measures taken by Morarji Desai following the Chinese aggression, was the Gold Control order. It was intended to curb the demand for gold and gold ornaments in the country and also to collect funds for the war. At many places, people donated considerable quantities of gold and jewellery to the government. But as I said, this measure was very unpopular. When TTK became finance minister he persuaded the Prime Minister to modify the order and make it a little more palatable as also enforceable. This was agreed to. A change in the departmental set-up followed. TTK decided to appoint me as gold control administrator and additional secretary in the Department of Revenue, Ministry of Finance. This appointment of mine was the most publicized one in my entire career. The news was carried by all newspapers, not only in English, but all vernacular papers across all states of India. Gold Control was a burning topic, and not only jewellers, but even ordinary housewives all over the country were interested. The revised order modified the 14-carat rule for ornaments and made some concessions in regard to the possession of ornaments and liberalized rules for remaking of ornaments and for export purposes. Special programmes and funds were also instituted for the rehabilitation of displaced goldsmiths and jewellers.

As gold control administrator, I had another opportunity of visiting different parts of the country. One special memory is a visit to Saurashtra, Rajkot, famous for its fine silver work and Porbunder, the birthplace of Mahatma Gandhi and home to a temple of Sudama. I could not visit Dwarka, one of the four dhams, nor the newly built Somnath Temple nor the Gir Lion Sanctuary. I also had occasion to see the enamel jewellery work of Jaipur, and the diamond-cutting and polishing work in Bombay. This job brought me in contact with the gems and jewellery traders in India. Besides keeping alive the especially high artistic knowledge, skill and craftsmanship of our workmen, it is a flourishing industry and one of the most valuable foreign exchange earners today. Under the new Gold Control Order, possession of gold coins was illegal, so we changed the light gold sovereigns and a Nepali gold coin I had for gold bangles. In 1940, a gold sovereign was worth Rs 15. Today I think it is worth more than Rs 1500 (almost a hundred times more), which gives an indication of the inflation over the last forty years or so. Rehabilitation of goldsmiths and jewellers was one of the tasks assigned to me. I remember giving several of them loans to go into scooter-cycle and taxi trade, cloth shops, and other small industries. But it was a hard job and several people faced difficulties. Over the years, however, jewellery trade continues to thrive and the Gold Control order has been made more and more liberal. I do not know why the government does not abolish it altogether. It has ceased to serve its purpose.*

For a short while, around six weeks or so, I was appointed Chairman of the then undivided Central Board of Revenue (CBR). This dealt with both direct and indirect taxes. During this period, TTK piloted a bill in Parliament, bifurcating the CBR into two separate boards—the Board of Direct Taxes and the Board of Central Excise and Customs. This brief tenure enabled me to get acquainted with the procedures and the senior officers of the Revenue Department. I was also placed incharge of revenue intelligence that dealt with smuggling and international currency rackets and Custom evasions. Opium and other narcotics were also under my charge. So I got a peep into another big branch of central government administration.

A totally different assignment also came my way as additional part-time work. Vishnu Sahay was then governor of Assam, and his work at that time also comprised overseeing the administration in NEFA—the North East Frontier Agency, now called Arunachal Pradesh. This was the area overrun by the Chinese in 1962. Vishnu Sahay proposed that a committee be formed to review the administrative set up of NEFA. D. Ering, the MP of that area hailing from Pasighat, was appointed chairman. There were four or five others; I was the most senior. We travelled all over NEFA, and the visits were memorable. We travelled from Bomdila via the famous Sela pass (though 'pass' is redundant—'la' means 'pass') to Tawang, the famous monastery near the Tibetan border. I still have two of the woollen asanas made in Tawang. We also traversed through all the other district towns and several remote settlements. What dense jungles there are in NEFA! Flying over that area was an

---

*The Gold Control Act was repealed in 1990.

unparalleled experience and I took my hat off to the pilots who negotiated these difficult hills and passes and landed at airfields in remote areas without any modern aids of communication.

The various tribes were most interesting. Each had their distinctive cultures, dresses, and modes of living. Some were friendly and some intensely hostile to intruders, whom they eliminated as soon as they could get a chance. And yet, even in these areas, mythological stories uniting this vast subcontinent existed. For example, at the source of the river Lohit, which merges with the Brahmaputra is a 'kund' known as Parshuramkund. It is said that it was only after bathing here that Parshuram could be absolved of the sin of matricide committed by him, and the axe which had got stuck on his shoulders then came off. Then there was a tribe where men and women wore similar dresses and cropped their hair in identical styles, so that one could not distinguish a man from a woman easily on first sight. They said this custom came from the days when Arjun, of Mahabharat fame, kidnapped Rukmini from this tribe. The custom described above was to minimize chances of future similar abductions.

There was a group of Buddhists in southern NEFA, who said they had come some 700 years ago from Thailand to escape local persecution and take shelter under the Ahom Kings of Upper Assam who then ruled this territory. We saw some of the manuscripts they had brought with them in their flight across the forests of Thailand, Upper Burma, into this part of NEFA.

We were once discussing the language policy to be adopted for this area. We alighted from our plane at a place called Along (Aalo) or Pasighat, I forget. There was a high school nearby where we were meeting and a number of school boys had gathered there out of curiosity. We decided to ask for their views on the language to be adopted for school education. I have always remembered the reply that one of the boys gave us. He said that they wanted to be taught in the language which will enable them to fly the airplane in which we had come there. This was a most revealing reply. They said that learning in their local dialects had no meaning, the teachers did not know the dialects and even if they learnt they could never be as fluent as they were in their own mother tongue. Assamese was, of course, the easiest language for them. But there was also some traditional rivalry between the hill men and the plains men—the plains people have always exploited the hill people and called them backward. The hill people are simpler, more trusting and therefore easily cheated. I have found this antagonism wherever I cast my eye—in Chhotanagpur, the hill tribes surounding Assam, in Himachal Pradesh, in our own hills of Kumaon-Garhwal, in Yugoslavia, in Scotland, in South America, in Thailand, in Burma.

So the people in NEFA did not want to learn Assamese, but suggested Hindi and more importantly—English—to enable them to fly the plane. Nowadays I think of the education policy in my hometown. Almora used to be a centre of advanced education and at that time English was also a subject, an important one, of study. Now all teaching is in Hindi and even the best students who secure several distinctions in their high school and Intermediate exams are unable to get into medical or engineering colleges and find themselves handicapped even in the state government's competitive examinations, leave alone the all-India ones. There are two primary government schools close to our home in Champanaula. Each of them has perhaps five teachers each, highly qualified, BA BEd, MA BEd, MA MEd, etc., with a salary of not less than Rs 1000 per month. The total strength of children in these two schools is not more than a hundred. The education is free and the medium of instruction is Hindi. There is also a primary school close by with English as the medium of instruction. It is a private school and charges Rs 25 or more per month per child. It pays the teachers less than Rs 200 per month. Yet it has more than 250 boys and girls on its rolls. It has no proper school building or even well-ventilated rooms, no playing grounds, etc. And the son of our municipal safai-karamchari (sweeper) attends this school and not the free primary school. Why? Because English is taught at this private school. But our educationists and government do not see what the parents and pupils want. Furthermore, the children of all senior politicians, bureaucrats and other well-to-do people read in English-medium schools, so they are not worried about this state of affairs elsewhere. How correct was the demand of the young student of Arunachal Pradesh way back in 1963!

Our Committee's recommendations were accepted by the government. Thus the administration was transferred from the Ministry of External Affairs to the home ministry, the name 'political agent' was changed to 'district officer', as elsewhere, 'agencies' were called 'districts'. When in 1980 I revisited Arunachal Pradesh, especially their new capital Itanagar, I had an opportunity to go through our earlier report once again. It was satisfying to note that our recommendations had been found to be satisfactory over nearly two decades of time.

In April 1965, that is after about a year and a half, my assignment as gold control administrator and additional secretary in the Finance Department came to an end. I was posted as chairman, LIC of India at Bombay.

*

B.K. Kaul had been appointed chairman of LIC some three years ago. He had been joint secretary in the finance ministry, economic affairs department. Morarji Desai liked him and although he was quite junior to me in service he was appointed chairman. He had retained his house in New Delhi and functioned as chairman from there, visiting Bombay only from time to time. With the change of ministers there was a change in the policy regarding LIC. TTK had his own ideas and wanted them to be implemented. Soon there was trouble with the LIC staff. B.K. Kaul had some suggestions for meeting the demands of the officers but TTK would not approve of them. In fact things deteriorated to such an extent that he would not even see Kaul. No proposals or suggestions for LIC were accepted. On the other hand, LIC's business had stopped growing and that in turn was causing further trouble. By the beginning of 1965, TTK had decided to make a change. I was sounded out to see if I would be willing to go, and in accordance with a policy I had followed since entering the service until my retirement, I said that I had no special views on the subject and I would agree. But there was some delay. TTK this time insisted that I go with a secretary's scale of pay, viz., Rs 4000. There were some objections. Nagendra Singh, who was a year senior to me, was still an additional secretary as was H.C. Sarin, who was one position below me. They had become additional secretary before me and insisted that they too rise to the rank of secretary before me. Because of this uncertainty I agreed to remain in my existing rank. But this time TTK was insistent that I must get a secretary's rank as I deserved it. So after some hesitation and huffing and hawing, my appointment as secretary was approved, along with those of Nagendra Singh and H.C. Sarin. This was at the beginning of March 1965.

By then the two-thousand-strong Class I Officers' Union headed by K.K. Shah (Congress), who was later governor of Tamil Nadu, and the eight-thousand-strong Class II Officers' (Development Officers) Association led by a socialist Hind Majdoor Sangha and General Secretary Kelkat of Gwalior/Indore, had served notices of strike. And by a coincidence the strike was to begin the very day I was to join LIC. So I sent instructions to Bombay for the Managing Director and also the representatives of the two unions to meet me at Delhi a day earlier to see if we could sort out the matter and prevent the strike. They responded to my invitation and I remember starting a meeting with them at 8 a.m. in the Zonal Manager's office. We sat through the whole day and night—having all our meals there—an eighteen-hour session. Then at 2 a.m. an agreement was signed, calling off the strike and agreeing to resume discussions. This has been one of the longest days in my memory—most tiresome but in the end, it made for a successful outcome.

When I came to Bombay a few days later, I was alone as Vimla and the family were to join me later. At the airport, I was greeted by senior officers of the LIC. However at the office I was greeted by 'hai hai' and thumping and banging of fists on my car. This was my experience for the first few months whenever I visited the offices of LIC—demonstrations, shouting, etc. All this was because negotiations were going on with the staff unions, who felt that they could get the best terms only if they negotiated from a position of strength. The negotiations took quite some time, mainly because I found that tripartite negotiations had to be carried out with two parties always absent. This is one of the greatest drawbacks in our public sector management practices. In the case of LIC, whenever I had discussions with the Board, which was a government-appointed body, the government representatives and staff were absent. And moreover, the Board did not have a final say in staff pay matters (as also in others) and did not know if their recommendations would be accepted by the government. When I talked with the staff, the government representatives and the Board were absent, and the staff did not know how far they could make the government yield. Although in the matter of the LIC, I always felt that if the demands were impractical and the staff did go on strike, the government could afford the business of the LIC being suspended for some time without any material damage being done. When I talked with the government officials, the other two were absent, and the officials would not indicate how far they were prepared to go. Fortunately in this case I had the full backing of TTK, who was prepared to accept my recommendations and gave me a free hand in the negotiations. I have always felt that it would be best if all these public sector enterprises were run like government's commercial enterprises, like say the railways, posts and telegraph or the defence ordnance factories. There would be better discipline and better management. Maybe government procedures would need to be changed in regard to several matters.

LIC at that time was a big organization. As I have mentioned earlier, it had 2000 Class I and 8000 Class II officers. In addition, the Class III and Class IV employees came to be nearly 50,000. And there were independent, part-time or full-time agents ranging over 300,000. So the government was also keen to satisfy this large number of people. Fortunately the negotiations, though taxing and laborious, ended satisfactorily for all parties. And LIC's business which had been stagnant at the level of Rs 700 crores for nearly three years began to climb up again and reached nearly Rs 1000 crores. In its growth, LIC has not looked back since.

*

Towards the end of 1965, work at LIC became more or less normal, agreements with the staff unions had been signed and life was more peaceful with less tension. There was also a change of government at that time. Lal Bahadur Shastri died and was succeeded by Indira Gandhi. TTK had to again resign as finance minister. He never came back to the government after this. He was succeeded by Sachin Choudhury, a leading barrister of Calcutta. He did not stay too long in the government but we got on reasonably well. However I do remember one particular incident when the two of us were alone and discussing LIC matters. He was saying something, and as is the habit with most of us Indians, I interrupted him. He reprimanded me for this and said that this was not done. His training, especially as an advocate, had instilled this principle in him. I was subsequently very glad for this reprimand, and ever since have tried hard not to yield to the itch to interrupt. I met Sachin Choudhury later, in Calcutta in 1981, and we got to know him and the family well and met socially fairly often.

In April 1966, Vimla and I went on a pilgrimage to Gaya. We went to Allahabad, then Benares, before arriving at Gaya. From Gaya, we travelled to Patna for a day or so and then returned again via Allahabad. Subsequently in 1977, we went to Badrinath where Vimla and I performed my father and mother's shradh again at Brahma Kapal. After these shradhs, which have a high position in our tradition as expressions of our deep reverential homage to our ancestors, I have felt much better mentally.

I had hardly settled down at LIC and was looking forward to a year or so of a pleasanter period with an extensive tour of the South, when suddenly, around the end of November in 1966, I got telephone calls from Delhi to inform me that I was being considered for the position of secretary in the Department of Steel. They asked if I would like to come to Delhi. To the latter I said yes, because despite the comforts at LIC, Vimla and I liked Delhi better. Then I began to get telephone calls from the steel ministry to enquire when I was joining, as some important talks and negotiations were to be held with a British consortium of steel manufacturers. Since I had received no orders I could not say anything. Then once again the wholly unexpected happened. In Bihar, the food and famine situation as well as the political situation were becoming very serious. The earlier stalwarts, Shri

Krishna Sinha and Anugrah Narayan Sinha, were no longer on the scene. Krishna Ballabh Sahay was then chief minister of the Congress party-led government. One day, then Cabinet Secretary D.S. Joshi rang up to say that the Prime Minister wanted me to go to Bihar immediately as chief secretary instead. I asked why me of all people, but he answered that that was the Prime Ministers's decision. I said if I was ordered I would go, but this transfer would mean a loss of Rs 1000 per month in pay plus a reduction in my rank. Till then a chief secretary in most of the states, except the three old presidency states, ranked with a joint secretary in the centre. Then he said that the Government would protect my pay by giving me a personal pay of this amount. I said this was not acceptable. They should give me full 4000/- and as the assignment was meant to be only for six months or so (I was being deprived of a secretaryship in the Government of India), I should be given a house in Delhi so my family could be there and my children's education would not suffer. The government accepted these conditions. I was allotted 13 AB Tilak Marg for the family, given the designation of commissioner general-cum-chief secretary (while the cadre post of chief secretary was kept in abeyance), given a salary of Rs 4000, and asked to proceed to Patna. In early January 1967, Vimla, Ratna and I came to Delhi and stayed for a few days with Vinod, my brother-in-law, in Nauroji Nagar. I went on to Patna to take over my new post. The night before, I was rung up by the Additional Chief Secretary T.C. Puri, who incidentally happened to be my senior, to be told that there had been violence and arson in Patna, police had had to open fire, some people had been killed and a curfew had been imposed. The Government of Bihar required more central police personnel and I was supposed to speak to the home ministry about this before leaving for Patna the next morning by air.

 I arrived at Patna airport, I think at about 9 a.m. or so, with a couple of suitcases, while a curfew was imposed in the city. I drove straight to the Chief Minister's residence which was then at Chhajju Bagh in Patna, to attend an emergency Cabinet meeting. After that I came to the Secretariat to take formal charge of my new office. And thus began a new chapter.

CHAPTER SIX

Patna, 1967 and Delhi, 1967–72

In Patna, I found the circuit house and the government guest house too crowded and so decided to live in a ground floor room of the Irrigation Department's Kosi bungalow on Bayley Road. It was quiet and I could walk to and back from the Secretariat.

Before I left Delhi, I was advised by several officers, in particular by the Cabinet Secretary and the Food Secretary A.L. Dias who was then dealing with famine relief in Bihar, that the government had given me a blank cheque to take as many officers as I pleased from Delhi to Patna. They suggested that I recruit a special confidential assistant, a senior officer whom I could trust, as the Bihar cadre was caste-ridden and politicized. It was suggested that I transfer certain DMs, SDOs, and BDOs that were messing up the relief work. I told them that I would decide on this only after getting to Patna and making my own assessment. Several Bihar cadre officers who were then in Delhi came to me, wanting to get out of the list of people to be recalled to Bihar. I gave them all the same reply. In fact, I had been given similar advice by TTK while I was at LIC that pertained to selecting an officer as second-in-command. I refused both times. In my long career, I have always found that the best thing to do is to trust the local officers completely. And it has never let me down. Local officers have always given me their free and frank advice, knowing full well that I would protect them whenever necessary.

So in Bihar I did not transfer the charge of any single officer, and whenever the Chief Minister wanted to do so I told him it would interfere with the relief work. Moreover elections were around the corner and doing anything to disturb them would have been unwise. I also did not go on tour to see the relief work. I called a few district collectors of certain important districts to come to Patna and explain to me what they were doing. The result was that the famine works were implemented without any mishaps. I did not allow the ministers to give orders locally. I had told the officers that if they received such orders they must refer the matter to me. Additionally, I told the ministers that if they found anything remiss in the field, they should tell me, and I would get it set right. I also found the certain departments of the Government of India, like Food and Information, were directly writing to the district officers for information. I ordered the district officers not to write back to Delhi, but to send the information to me and I would see how to relay it to Delhi. Similarly, I told officers at Delhi not to write directly to the district officers because if they did so, they would get no reply. These simple steps prevented back-seat driving by the powers residing in Delhi and local political interference. I found the Famine Code, which had been issued by me in the fifties, coming in very useful as all work was now being done in accordance with the instructions laid therein. In June 1967, when the rains set in and the spectre of famine receded, I looked back with comfort that nothing seriously detrimental—no loss of lives, no setback in the food distribution system or relief work programmes—had taken place.

And now I come to some political developments. The general elections were scheduled, I think, for late February 1967. Chief Minister K.B. Sahay was blatantly partisan. He wanted the processions of all opposition parties to be banned, but those of the Congress to be allowed. Inspector General (IG) of Police, R.A.P. Sinha, a friend from my Bihar Sharif days, and I had a closed-door meeting with K.B. Sahay. Both of us objected to the Chief Ministers's proposal and said that preferably, all processions should be disallowed in view of the tension prevailing; or if the Congress procession was to be allowed I could grant permission to the other political parties as well. K.B. Sahay exploded at this and said that President's rule had not been imposed and that I could not talk to him in this manner. I responded that President's rule or not, I would not agree to this very partisan order, further, I would refuse to pass it on to the district authorities and if that also did not work, I would quit. This quietened him. He realized that I meant to have my way in the fair and impartial conduct of the elections. After that there was no further interference. R.A.P. Sinha said I had been very strong in my views, but he acknowledged that this was the only way to deal with K.B. Sahay.

But the Congress was entering the elections as a very divided party. Indira Gandhi was openly supporting Mahamaya Prasad Sinha, a rebel Congressman. She would constantly telephone him from Delhi and send emissaries to meet him. On the other hand, the official Congress leader was K.B. Sahay, who did not enjoy a rapport with the Prime Minsiter. Thus, there was constant bickering about the candidates. Before the actual election, Mahamaya Prasad Sinha's group went out of the official Congress. The elections were held in a very tense atmosphere with several incidents of booth capture, rioting, etc., in Bihar but on the whole the elections passed off more peacefully than was anticipated. In Bihar, as in all the North Indian states, the Congress suffered a huge loss and the opposition parties, though lacking agreement on any positive policy, were united in their anti-Congress stand and formed the Sanyukta Vidhayak

Dal—or SVD, as it came to be known. Mahamaya Prasad Sinha was elected leader of this group and the first non-Congress government in Bihar since Independence came to office. There was some jubilation at this change because the Congress had become very corrupt and people were generally disgusted. But the SVD experiment proved to be very short-lived. Ministries began to change in Bihar with extreme rapidity. One chief minister lasted one day, another eighteen days, some others a few months.

*

There are some interesting episodes connected with this new SVD ministry. The first one was about the Cabinet papers and proceedings being in Hindi only. Up until then an English copy was also attached. Soon some ministers began ringing me up to say that they could either not read or understand the Hindi version properly and asked that the English version also be supplied. So much for having only Hindi! I remember in the first Janata Cabinet meeting in Delhi in March 1977 under Morarji Desai, some members said that all discusions must be in Hindi. Morarji Desai pointed out that the lone Tamil representative did not understand Hindi and would not be able to participate in the proceedings. Another minister, Atal Bihari Vajpayee, who sat next to him kept on translating. Later, English began to be used by several cabinet ministers.

There was a proposal mooted in the Bihar Cabinet that the salaries of the ministers be reduced from the then Rs 1500 per month. One of the ministers, Ramanand Tiwari, an ex-constable, sent for me. He told me about his family background, about how he had lost his father when he was only three or four years old. His mother had brought him up by cooking food and sewing clothes in other people's houses and had thus enabled him to read upto the fifth grade. They had no land or property. After a few years, he began selling water on railway platforms—in those days we had 'Hindu pani' and 'Musalman pani' that was distributed from separate 'gharas' to the travellers. Then he became a household servant of an assistant station master. He then grew up and qualified to become a constable, being well-built. However in 1942, while in Jamshedpur, he and some others revolted. He was dismissed from service and then joined politics as a rebel. Now he had become a minister. It was impossible for him to even serve tea to people who came to his house as he had no tea cups. He mentioned that another minister, who was the Raja of Ramgarh, was supporting this proposal but the latter had money enough to employ several people at Rs 4000 a month. I told him he was right in opposing any proposal to reduce the salary of ministers. In fact, they were low enough, and one of the main causes of corruption. People took gifts in kind if not in cash, and this was very vicious and undesirable. Fortunately, this impractical proposal got quashed.

Internal dissensions in the SVD ministry soon surfaced. Every political group began to press their own point of view, some ministers espousing the cause of their district, or caste and so on. The Chief Minister began to find it very difficult to control the discussions. I soon found that the meetings were so loud that voices carried to the corridors, and clerks and peons would crowd outside to overhear. I had to order the police to keep the corridor in front of the Cabinet room clear of people. I also had to lock the main door and allow entry only from a side door. Some meetings became very difficult and ministers exchanged blows. On several occasions I found it to be so embarrassing to be present that I quietly withdrew until things settled and I was called in. I should mention here that the chief secretary of a state acts as secretary to the Cabinet as well.

Things came to a head over the re-employment of retired

officers. The Cabinet wanted to pass a resolution that re-employment or extension of service to officers would not be allowed under any circumstances. I pleaded with them not to adopt such a resolution but instead refuse requests on a case-by-case basis when they came to the Cabinet, and to let it be known generally that the Cabinet does not favour re-employment. I tried to argue that this was a special privilege of the government and they should not shackle themselves if some deserving case came up in the future. They however did not agree. Soon a case concerning a Tribal peon from Chhotanagpur employed in the Bihar Public Service Commission surfaced. The Chairman had recommended the case strongly on the ground that this person had been employed in the first instance on very compassionate grounds which still held. He belonged to a Scheduled Tribe and a year's extension would enable him to complete his minimum service period and earn a pension in his old age. This was a very deserving case and quite a number of ministers were prepared to agree, but because of their own self-imposed ban the Cabinet rejected this request. I told the Cabinet that if they later agreed in any other case, I would cite this example and either disagree or request them to reopen the case. Soon enough, the case of a professor of medicine at the Patna Medical College came along. He was a very well-known physician, family doctor to many ministers and senior officers, and very competent with a good private practice. He belonged to what are called 'backward classes' in Bihar. One of the ministers, probably the Health Minister who himself belonged to this caste, championed his case very strongly. I brought up the case of the Tribal peon. The Cabinet found themselves in a very difficult position. They kept on postponing the decision from one meeting to the next. Sometime after I left Bihar, the Mahamaya Prasad Sinha Government fell on this issue and therafter, for almost two years, no ministry in Bihar survived any significant length of time.

The six-month period of my assignment to Bihar was over. Famine conditions had been averted and elections had been successfully held. I was pressing for a posting in Delhi and was told that two secretaryships were likely to fall vacant—secretary, personnel department in the home ministry and secretary, Planning Commission. I opted for the latter. So in August 1967, just before Independence Day, I returned to Delhi and joined as secretary, Planning Commission. Before I left Patna, the Chief Minister Mahamaya Prasad Sinha invited me to tea. I thought it would be a small party with a few ministers and some senior officers present. It turned out to be a very big gathering. The entire Cabinet—all secretaries to government and heads of departments—were present, as also some prominent people of Patna. Later the Chief Minister read out a valedictory address for me and presented it to me on a salver. I refused to accept it saying that as a government servant I was prohibited from accepting such a costly gift. He then gave me the necessary permission to accept his gift, as only a chief minister could do. This was when I took my second and final leave from Bihar and perhaps the only example where a serving chief secretary was honoured in this fashion. I have never forgotton the love and affection that Bihar, its many governments, my colleagues in the government, and Bihar's people have so generously given to me over the years I spent there.

*

Now I come to the last decade of my service and life in Delhi. In October 1967, I was allotted 3 Tughlak Road, classified as a 'Type VIII' bungalow. I moved into it on Vijaya Dashmi day and lived here until my retirement in March 1977.

I was in the Planning Commission from August 1967 to February 1970. There was a thorough reorganization of the

Planning Commission conducted by Indira Gandhi at that time. Tarlok Singh—who had started the Planning Commission in 1951 and had been with it uninterruptedly since, all while rising to become a member of the Planning Commission—was dropped. In fact he had become so synonymous with the Planning Commission that in common parlance the Planning Commission was referred to as 'Tarlok Sabha' to rhyme with the 'Lok Sabha'. An eminent administrator, he was a year or so senior to me and had been a favourite of Jawaharlal Nehru. And as happened to so many others, like S.K. Dey, he also went into the wilderness after Indira Gandhi came to power. He went abroad on a UN posting for some time—and has been writing books since then.

The new Planning Commission had Prof D.R. Gadgil as deputy chairman. He was a very well-known economist, albeit somewhat old school, but an erudite person nonetheless. He had been head of the Gokhale Institute of Economics at Poona (Pune). R. Venkatraman was another member. He had been industries minister in Tamil Nadu when Kamraj was the chief minister there. He had a very good reputation, especially in the field of industries. Then came Venkattappaiah—a member of the ICS, followed by Pitambar Pant who had also been associated with the Planning Commission since the beginning, as member-in-charge of Perspective Planning. He was basically a statistician and a great favourite of Mahalanobis, who established the Indian Statistical Institute at Calcutta. And lastly there was Dr B.D. Nagchaudhuri, who was then director of the Saha Institute of Nuclear Physics at Calcutta. It so happened that Dr Nagchaudhuri and I had been class-fellows at Allahabad and had studied together under Dr Meghnad Saha. The team in the Planning Commission was a very cohesive one and work went on smoothly and without any difficulty.

Before this Planning Commission, planning in India had

gone for a spin. The Third Five-Year Plan (1961-66) based on the 'Mahalanobis model' had gone wholly awry. It had laid stress on the development of heavy industry, but a crisis in agriculture and shortfall in resources meant that most of the set targets were nowhere near being achieved. Inflation was also increasing at an uncomfortable rate. As a consequence, the Fourth Plan could not be formulated and the three years, from 1966 to 1969, came to be known either as 'annual plan' years or 'no-plan' years or years when there was a 'plan holiday'. Both economic and political conditions became critical in the country. The Congress lost power in all eight or nine of the most important Northern states from Punjab to West Bengal for the first time. The food situation became dire. We were forced to import ten to twelve million tonnes of food a year, which was an unprecedentedly high level of imports. As the country did not have the resources to pay for this, we had to depend on aid from the USA and that meant accepting their conditions. The aid came under what was called PL 480 (i.e. Public Law 480). Once, in 1967, I think, President Johnson held up the authorization of more aid for a couple of months and our whole distribution system began to totter. We were living on what was called as a ship-to-shop system. The rupee was also under strong pressure in the international money market and was said to be artificially over-valued. All kinds of solutions were being thought of, such as having a dual exchange rate as in some countries, like Israel. Smuggling, especially of gold and currency, was on the rise. Many popular and unpopular measures were taken. Among the most important was the devaluation of the rupee. Many said that India should not have done this, it certainly raised internal prices somewhat, but I personally have been of the view even then and thereafter, that this was the one single measure that enabled us to correct the imbalance of our import-export trade and adjusted prices which had been artificially plugged too low or too high.

An important consequence was the adjustment and change in our agricultural policy. This had been badly neglected in the post-war years despite the lip service paid to it in the plans and policy statements. It was not backed by resources and specific measures. Moreover, the huge food surplus in USA and Canada, the falling international food prices, and the euphoria of PL 480—which enabled us to import cheap food and make payment to the US Government in rupees in a special account kept with the Reserve Bank of India—also lulled the country to extreme vulnerability on the food front. The critical years, 1966–69, woke us up and ushered in what has come to be known as the Green Revolution. Its main components were an assured economic price to the producer, with guarantee of government purchase if prices fell below the minimum; import of new variety of 'high yielding wheat' which had been developed in the International Wheat Centre in Mexico by Dr Borlaug, the Nobel prize winner; import of artificial chemical fertilizers; more money for irrigation projects; manufacture of fertilizers and so on. There was thus a shift in focus from heavy industry to agriculture which was a very major change in the Mahalanobis model which was greatly influenced by the Soviet model on economic planning. But the Soviets had to pay a heavy price for it—a price they could pay because of their political system after the Revolution of 1917. India could not follow the same path given its different political and social system.

The main task before this new Planning Commission was to prepare the Fourth Five-Year Plan for the years 1969–74, and to put the country back on the rails of planned development, so to speak, from the 'ad hoc-ism' of the annual plans. This task was successfully completed by March 1969, when the draft plan was published. These two years were full of moderate work for me but devoid of the tensions of the previous years at LIC and in Bihar, and therefore a welcome change. I liked the work because it was not directly concerned with administration. Moreover, it gave me an insight into practically every aspect of working of the central government and also that of all the states and union territories. I found that the Planning Commission had more information on many subjects than individual ministries. For example, it had a better perspective of industrial development in the country than the nodal ministry of industries.

In 1969, yet another major political change took place which had its outfall in the Planning Commission as well. This was the first major split in the Congress at the insistence of Indira Gandhi. She accused then Congress President and the High Command of pursuing anti-Congress policies. As I have already mentioned, the Congress had lost in several Northern states and had been able to achieve a bare majority in Parliament. The party had to think of its future line of action. The old guard of the Congress led by the Congress President, Nijalingappa, and by what was called the 'syndicate', comprising of Atulya Ghosh of West Bengal, S.K. Patil of Maharashtra (Bombay), and Morarji Desai, wanted to veer right and get the support of the Conservative elements in the country. On the other hand, Indira Gandhi, with her supporters and advisors, wanted to turn left and get the support of the youth and the more radical elements. The first faction thought of joining with the Jan Sangh and the second with the Communist Party of India—at least tacitly.

There was thus a clear ideological split. Indira Gandhi, who had supported the candidature of Sanjiva Reddy put up by the syndicate for the Presidentship of India, withdrew her support and put up V.V. Giri—then Vice President—as her candidate. Morarji Desai was unceremoniously removed from the post of deputy prime minister and finance minister. Indira Gandhi put before the Working Committee a radical programme of bank nationalization, abolition of the privileges of the ICS, and abolition of the privy purse of the princes. The last two items were against the solemn commitments made by the Congress that were enshrined in the Constitution at the time of Independence in 1947. They were pronounced by Sardar Vallabh Bhai Patel with the full support of Jawaharlal Nehru even though the latter may not have liked them in view of his socialist line of thinking. But they had greatly helped in the consolidation of the country. The guarantee of privileges to the ICS had brought the unstinted support of the entire civil service in the country towards the policies of the government and had greatly helped in tiding over the extremely difficult post-Partition days. The abolition of ICS privileges was more an exercise in public relations than an actual practice. For example, the pay and pension were not touched. The only 'privilege' that was abolished was the date of retirement. The ICS men retired after thirty-five years of service (excluding the year of probation) or sixty years of age, whichever was earlier. This was changed to the uniform fifty-eight years of age as for all other central services. This measure affected a few officers who had to retire earlier than their due time, some had to retire as much as two years before their due dates. At the same time some officers benefited by periods ranging from one to seven months or so. I was one such beneficiary.

In contrast, the effect on the privy purse of the princes was more widely felt. The guarantee of the privy purse and the scheme of payment had enabled the consolidation of the political map of India without bloodshed. The princes had voluntarily agreed to enter into an agreement with the Government of India and had handed over the administration of their states to the latter. There were only three cases where these states did not accede at that time—Junagadh, Hyderabad and Jammu and Kashmir (J&K). The last continues to be a major hindrance in our settlement with Pakistan, who refused to recognize J&K's

accession to India and invaded it with Tribals of the North West in late 1947.

In regards to bank nationalization and the privy purse issue there was prolonged litigation in the Supreme Court, but the decisions were in favour of the government. And a number of former communists, like S. Kumarmangalam and Rajni Patel joined the Congress of Indira Gandhi. So also did several socialists. The Congress was split into two—the old Congress calling itself Congress (O) or 'organization' and Congress(I) or 'Indira'. But this split paid Indira Gandhi its dividends. The first favourable result was the election of V.V. Giri and the defeat of N. Sanjiva Reddy. Then Congress(I) won the Parliamentary elections, and later, following the birth of Bangladesh in 1971 and victory over Pakistan, a massive victory in all the states where the elections had been lost in 1967.

Now for the fall out of this split in the Planning Commission. Sometime after this break, it became evident that the Prime Minister was not happy with the Planning Commission. But the reason was difficult to figure out. The draft Plan had already been published with her approval. She had not indicated any special change to be made. Prof Gadgil told me on more than one occasion that he had tried to meet with Mrs Gandhi. Often he got a chance to speak to her after considerable delay but could never get a reaction from her. She would just listen to him and not say anything. He was unable to understand what she had in mind. R. Venkataraman, however, told me that the Prime Minister's dissatisfaction was only with Prof Gadgil, as it was well-known that his sympathies were with Congress (O), although as a member of the Planning Commission, he had not been taking part in active politics. He told me that he had offered to resign if so desired, but the Prime Minister had not indicated anything. However, a few months after I had left the Planning Commission, the then Cabinet Secretary was sent to meet Prof Gadgil and suggest to him that he, along with the other members of the Planning Commisson, should submit their resignations to Mrs Gandhi. Prof Gadgil was most affected of all. He did resign along with the other members. Far be it from receiving any appreciation for the tremendously difficult work that he and the other members had done in putting together an implementable Fourth Five-Year Plan before the country, the Commission was being disbanded in such a cavalier fashion. He was an old man, in his seventies, given to certain cultured values. He could not stand this ignominious treatment and unfortunately, died in the train on his way to Bombay after he relinquished office. Venkataraman went into the political wilderness for some years, until he rejoined Indira Gandhi. He was one of the few eminent people from Tamil Nadu to do so and therefore he was again inducted into the Cabinet and is now the vice president of India. Venkatappaiah and Pitamber Pant were given other jobs, as also Nagchaudhuri, who became scientific advisor to the Defence Minister and later vice-chancellor of Jawaharlal Nehru University, Delhi. So the only losers immediately were R. Venkataraman and Prof D.R. Gadgil.

As far as I was concerned, I was transferred as secretary to the Department of Heavy Industry in February 1970. This was, in a sense, a lighter and less important charge, but the work in connection with the Fourth Plan had been completed, and moreover the Prime Minister wanted Asoka Mitra, who was in the information and broadcasting ministry, to be transferred immediately for some reason. So, he joined the Planning Commission as officer on special duty for a few days before I joined the Heavy Industry Department.

The workload in the Department of Heavy Industry was very light—one of the lightest I had had for years. I used to go to office at about 10.30 a.m. and be back by 5 p.m. after having had a lunch break of an hour or more at 1 p.m. The heavy engineering public sector units, the motor car industry and the machine tools industry were under this department. While working here, I had the opportunity to visit Bangalore, especially the Hindustan Machine Tools. This was one of the units which had been doing consistently well and had been able to set up several new units out of its own profits. The watch unit has been one of the most profitable. Bharat Heavy Electricals (BHEL) units at Bhopal and Haridwar were other centres. At that time there was constant criticism of the fact that the BHEL was not making a profit and it was described as a white elephant. The original project report for this unit had stated that it would not make any profits in the first ten years. And this was so. It was after eleven or twelve years that it turned a corner and wiped out all accumulated losses. Since then BHEL has consistently made profits and declared dividends. In fact, today it is not only one of the most profitable units but is also a player in the international market having set up many units abroad. Two very important units, the Heavy Engineering Corporation and the Heavy Machine Tools at Ranchi have, however, not yet turned the corner. Both are, what may be called, real 'mother' units, in the engineering world. The first can fabricate machinery for building a million-tonne steel plant a year. It can manufacture the biggest turbines and has the heaviest forge in India. The Heavy Engineering Corporation is manufacturing some of the most sophisticated units for our atomic power plants. The Heavy Machine Tools Unit is capable of making 'machines' that make other 'machines'. But in respect of both these units, the plant utilization factor is below the minimum economic level required. We had invited some foreign experts to advise us on these plants. One of them gave an interesting analogy. He asked for how much time in a 24-hour day is a lavatory or a bathroom engaged, and yet no house can do without them. Similarly, he said, for self-sufficiency in the field of engineering, including armaments manufacture, both these units are essential.

I made a visit to the Hindustan Motors factory at Uttarpara, near Calcutta, during this period. West Bengal was then under President's Rule and a drive had been launched against the Naxalites. While going to Uttarpara, I found several areas completely cordoned off by Army units where a house-to-house search for arms and extremists was being conducted by police contingents. The areas looked under full siege. As a result of these operations, several people were arrested, some killed and a great deal of arms and ammunitions seized. This brought about peace in West Bengal and enabled the Congress(I) to win the elections in 1972. At the same time it enabled the CPI(M) to consolidate its hold in West Bengal and has been in power since 1977. There is also no immediate prospect of the Congress(I) being able to dislodge them even in the general elections due next year in 1987.

One of the first things that the Industries Minister Fakhruddin Ali Ahmed asked me to do was to prepare a memorandum on the small car project for the Cabinet. I told him that the Planning Commission had turned it down and not included it in the Fourth Plan. That notwithstanding, he said we should prepare the note for a car project which would not mean any strain on public resources. After several informal discussions, a note was prepared. It had, I would say, three important points. The first was that any private entrepreneur who was prepared to set up a plant and manufacture cars entirely indigenously would be permitted to do so. They could not import any foreign technology or foreign machinery or equipment or employ any foreign technicians. The vehicles must have passed the strictest tests of safety before being put on the road. The note added that, in the department's view, India did not have the technical capacity to manufacture a passenger car without foreign collaboration. The second point was that the Department of Heavy Industries would be allowed to start negotiations with foreign car manufacturers on the condition that the foreign manufacturers would provide the technology and equipment from their own resources, buy back some components, and assist in export of vehicles so that India could service the loan of the foreign company out of these foreign earnings; and finally, that the public sector outlay would be kept at the minimum and funds would be found out of allocations made for the Heavy Industry Department. The Planning Commission and the finance ministry appended their objections to the proposal. However, when the memorandum went up to the Cabinet, the first part was approved and as for the last part it was said that specific proposals should be brought before the Cabinet after discussions with the car manufacturers.

On the basis of this, two licenses were issued for manufacture of an indigenously designed car—one to Sanjay Gandhi for his 'Maruti' car and the other to a Bangalore firm. This was what Indira Gandhi had been wanting to do all along. In retrospect, I think, that one of the major reasons of the Prime Minister's dissatisfaction with the Planning Commission was that it did not support the small car project. Mrs Gandhi had indicated her preference in this matter to Fakhruddin Ali Ahmed, and was keen that Sanjay Gandhi's proposal regarding the small car go through. As soon as the letter of intent was issued to Sanjay Gandhi, Bansi Lal—who was then chief minister of Haryana—allocated to him a very big area of land near Gurgaon. The company collected some money from local industrialists and businessmen and a building with a compound wall was also constructed. But despite a number of notices in the newspapers, no car came out of the assembly line. After the Emergency was imposed, some German experts were invited who ostensibly came as tourists. Some engines were found in their luggage and the Customs inspectors impounded them as unauthorized. The inspectors were punished, suspended and later transferred. Attempts were made to get licenses issued for machines, but they were rejected. At this, the Customs and Excise's office was blamed. Later, Mantosh Sondhi, who was secretary in the Heavy Industries Department, was summarily removed because he would not help in getting the conditions of the license modified regarding import of technology and machinery. It was only after the elections of 1980, and after Sanjay Gandhi's death, that the indigenous car idea was given up and the Maruti car manufacture was taken up in the public sector in full technical and financial collaboration with Suzuki, the Japanese car manufacturers. This was to perpetuate Sanjay Gandhi's memory.

Soon after the Cabinet memorandum referring to the license above was approved, Fakhruddin Ali Ahmed was transferred and Dinesh Singh stepped in as industry minister. He asked me to start work on the third part of the memorandum, viz., negotiations with foreign manufacturers for a public sector plant. I told him that the government had had two earlier infructuous discussions on this and the foreign parties were reluctant to revisit. On both occasions the proposal was turned down by the Planning Commission. In any case the cars being manufactured in India, mainly the Fiat and Ambassador, could only be described as 'small' or 'small-medium' cars. If their prices were high it was not due to the cost of manufacture. In fact, the ex-factory price compared favourably with the ex-factory price of a Fiat manufactured in France or an Austin-Morris in England. The price of the Indian car on the road was however double, only because of the extremely high excise duty on the manufactured car, or double taxation both on the input and the final car, and very high rates of sales tax. So unless these were removed the cars could not become cheaper. And the finance ministry would not agree to reduce the duties. So I told

Dinesh Singh, that I could reopen the negotiations only if there was an assurance for government's approval of the programme. He was confident of this but wanted the proposals to be put up for approval soon while he was still the minister and before the general elections approached. With his assurance, I reopened the negotiations. There was good response, but naturally such a project needed detailed examination. Several small expert committees were set up, but even then the matter took two or three months. The best proposal was from Renault, France. But before the proposal could get to the Cabinet, Dinesh Singh was transferred to the commerce ministry and Moinul Huq Chaudhary of Assam stepped in as industry minister. When the proposal was sent again, it was shot down by the Planning Commission and the finance ministry. The Prime Minister also supported them as she was against any public sector project which could jeopardize Sanjay Gandhi's scheme.

There was further fall out on this when the Janata Government came to power in 1977. They set up a Commission of Inquiry on Maruti's affairs under Justice Gupta of the Supreme Court to go over all circumstances under which Sanjay Gandhi was given a license to manufacture a passenger car.* I had retired by then and was living in Ranikhet. I was summoned twice by the Commission to give evidence and was cross-examined at length to find out if any concessions had been given to Sanjay Gandhi. I told them no, and also that anyone could come forward to indigenously manufacture a car if they thought they had the ability to do so, but I maintained that the department was clear and explicit in the Cabinet memo that it did not think it possible. My contention, as far as I was concerned, was upheld, and there was no reference to me in the final report. But

---

*Report available at https://www.scribd.com/document/221722724/Commission-of-Inquiry-on-Maruti-Affairs-1977

many other irregularities were unearthed—large withdrawals by Sanjay Gandhi and Indira Gandhi in various forms, irregular land allotments, etc., were brought to light. This chapter thus ended with Sanjay Gandhi's death and a car plant in the public sector, which of course has been getting all the patronage from the government unlike the other older and established car manufacturers.

Another important and interesting issue that came up during my tenure in the Department of Heavy Industry was the question of price control on passenger cars. The car manufacturers were demanding an upward revision of the prices because of an increase in the price of steel, tyres, batteries and central excise duties, but the government was refusing to grant this increase. Later, a very modest increase was proposed. The car manufacturers went to the Supreme Court calling the government's proposals inadequate, and saying that the whole price control system was defective. They won, and the system was more or less abandoned thereafter. One of the points put forth by the manufacturers was that the price control and distribution order was not in the interest of the general public, but only that of government servants and politicians. This was indeed true. The order was being used to favour them, but more than that it was being misused. Some government servants were changing their cars every two years and making a big profit thereon. Legislators were buying the cars 'benami' or on behalf of some businessman, who would pay for the car, its upkeep and use by the legislator whenever required by him, but mainly use it for his business purposes. Even if this person was in great need of a car, he could not buy it directly and had to adopt this subterfuge. Over the years our whole system of price controls has got completely askew. Certain powerful vested interests have been preventing a change and in some cases dismantling the system where it is not required. Price controls at artificially fixed levels have prevented increase in the production of some essential commodities like cement. It has prevented steel plants from working profitably and affected the proper growth of the chemical and pharmaceutical industries. On the one hand, essential public sector companies have been working at a loss and have not been able to expand their production resulting in black marketing, creation of a parallel economy of black money, tax evasion, and loss of public revenues. On the other hand, it has enabled many private sector companies—including multinationals like Hindustan Unilever and Colgate-Palmolive—to make huge profits, declaring dividends of 100–500% in the manufacture of luxury and non-essential consumer goods. Of late, some changes have been made in the price control policies, but we still have a long way to go, before the economy can be considered to be free of such serious price aberrations.

*

I used to say, as a young man, that I had three ambitions. One was to smoke a pipe, but then I never liked smoking. The second was to possess a copy of the Encylopaedia Britannica, but I could never get together the amount of money required. The third was to grow a 'goatee'. This, I now decided to do. When people came to see me and found me unshaved they used to ask if all was well. This was because it was during a mourning period that one did not shave. So I used to tell everyone as soon as they came in, that everything was alright. Since then I have kept this beard. Some of my friends used to call me 'Maulana' Pande, some said I was becoming like a Marx or Lenin. Once at an official banquet for some Arab visiting dignitary, the visiting team thought that I was an Arab. So also did a taxi driver once in Bombay. He even asked me how I could speak Hindi like an

Indian! So at least one of my three ambitions has been fulfilled. But the beard is straggly—somewhat like that of Ho Chi Minh!

*

In November 1970, T. Swaminathan, then secretary in the Ministry of Industrial Development, was appointed cabinet secretary. Two years later I succeeded him. At my suggestion the post of secretary, Heavy Industry was not filled up as I felt that a separate secretary for the post wasn't necessary.

The general elections were drawing near and preparations were in full swing. These included collection of funds for the political party. I had a very interesting experience. One day I was suddenly called to meet Prime Minister Indira Gandhi immediately at her residence-office, 1 Akbar Road. I was ushered into a room where she was alone. She asked me why Dinesh Singh had not deposited the full amount, given to him by a certain industrialist, in the party account. I said I did not know anything about this matter. The sum in question was a few lakhs. Dinesh Singh was now the commerce minister so I asked her if she would like the Commerce Secretary to see her. But she said that she would look into it herself. This was a very clear confirmation of money being collected by ministers, for the party and other purposes. And what was also clear was that even some officers were helping the ministers do so, otherwise I would not have been called. That personal assistants, special assistants and selected officers were involved in these transactions was common talk. The outfall of this incident was that Dinesh Singh was out of the ministry after the election, had never been able to rehabilitate himself again in the party, and even now is in the political wilderness. And at one time, not so many years earlier, he was said to be a member of Indira Gandhi's Kitchen Cabinet—one of her closest confidantes and advisors.

Later in 1976, when I was cabinet secretary, I saw the unfortunate case of another minister—P.C. Sethi. He had been a successful chief minister in Madhya Pradesh for almost five years and had come to the centre with a good reputation. At the time, he was union minister for petroleum and chemicals. In preparation for the election, he had been appointed the party treasurer. In this capacity, he had to deal with large amounts of cash, apart from making collections himself. He used to come to Cabinet meetings with a briefcase full of currency notes. He began to behave in a very peculiar fashion in the office and at the headquarters of public sector companies under his department. He would openly ask for money from the industrialists in the office itself. It became a scandal. Also he began to drink intemperately. He was a diabetic and heavy drinking affected his mental health. He began to ring up embassies of foreign governments and ask for cratefuls of whisky bottles to be sent to his house. The secretary of the department, Praxy Fernandes, came to see me and brought some files where absolutely biased orders had been passed. I took them to the Prime Minister and told her what was happening. An order was passed that henceforth for some time no files were to be sent up to P.C. Sethi, but would instead be marked to the Prime Minister for orders. During this period, Sethi once went to Bombay and created a huge ruckus. In a matter of days he had run up a bill of over Rs 30,000 at a five-star hotel. Once he even drove on the wrong side of the road in Bombay, an accident was averted providentially. His wife went to see Mrs Gandhi about his condition and asked her to intervene. I was asked to make arrangements for sending him to some clinic. I telephoned the Chief Secretary, Bangalore and the Director of the mental home to make provisions. The Chief Secretary, Bombay rang up to suggest that we should immediately arrange to have him brought back to Delhi. At that time, Dhirendra Brahmachari—who ran a yoga school in Delhi, had a yogic ashram in Jammu, gave lessons on the television and was close to Mrs Gandhi and her household—offered to help. He probably went to Bombay and was able to take P.C. Sethi to his ashram in Jammu, and after some months Sethi was more or less back to his normal self. Indira Gandhi again put him incharge of important portfolios, although he was totally ineffective by then. But she always retained him. Did he know too much? Rajiv Gandhi, however, had him dropped later.

In May 1971, there was yet another sudden change in my job profile. P. Govindan Nair, a year or so my senior, was the finance secretary. He was taken seriously ill and found to be suffering from intestinal cancer. He died soon after. The vacancy had to be filled. Y.B. Chavan was then the finance minister. M.R. Yardi, a year or so junior to me, was the expenditure secretary and Dr I.G. Patel the economic affairs secretary. One evening it became known that Yardi had been appointed finance secretary. I heard about this at a party I was attending. They said that the Establishment Officer was issuing the orders. Next morning, at about 8 a.m., Cabinet Secretary T. Swaminathan rang me up and asked me to meet him in an hour. At the meeting he told me that I was to take over as finance secretary immediately. I said that we had all heard that Yardi was to take over. He said that was so, but last evening there was a Cabinet meeting and in that the Prime Minister had ordered for my appointment as finance secretary. Yardi was held up and Swaminathan had spoken to the Industry Minister intimating him of the same. I was to report as finance secretary as soon as possible.

I joined the finance ministry that very day and remained in office till November 2, 1972, for just a year and a half. The general elections had just been held and a new budget was to be presented. So I was immediately immersed in work on the budget which was due for presentation in another month or so. This was the budget for 1971–72. Then the country was engulfed in the Bangladesh turmoil—and with it the huge influx of refugees. So a supplementary budget was presented in Nov 1971, I think. The following February we had the annual budget for 1972–73. So in my short stint as finance secretary, I had been involved in three budgets. As finance secretary my maincharge was the Department of Revenue—and therein dealing with the two Boards of Direct Taxes and Customs and Excise, and as overall coordinator in the Ministry of Finance, by virtue of being the most senior secretary as well as finance secretary. The work load was heavier than that in my previous two asignments. As finance secretary I almost always sat in the Cabinet meetings to represent the views of the finance ministry as there was hardly a subject or matter in which finance was not involved in one way or another.

Major changes took place politically in 1971. It started with the elections in Pakistan, where the Awami League of Eastern Pakistan got a majority. But Western Pakistan parties did not want this. Martial law was in force. Mujibur Rahman of East Pakistan was jailed. Refugees from East Bengal began to flow into West Bengal, Assam, Meghalaya, Tripura in very large numbers—at one time we had nearly a crore of them. India appealed to world powers to persuade Pakistan to stop the atrocities in East Bengal and stop the influx of refugees into India, otherwise we would have to take measures to protect ourselves. Nothing was done. In July 1971, India signed a treaty of peace and friendship with Moscow. Help began to be given to East Bengal refugees. A Mukti Bahini was formed by the East Bengalis. Border skirmishes and guerilla raids began to take place. In December 1971, Pakistan attacked India and we were ready for it. The Indian Army marched into East Bengal and within fifteen days Pakistan's Army was overrun and they surrendered at Dacca (Dhaka). There was an apprehension that India may march into West Pakistan also but then we called a halt on the Western front. Bangladesh had emerged as an independent state. In March 1972, elections were held to the state assemblies and Congress(I) emerged victorious with an overwhelming majority. The opposition had been routed.

This was Indira Gandhi's hour of crowning glory. The opposition parties in the Lok Sabha, including the Jan Sangh, hailed her. Atal Bihari Vajpeyee called her 'Durga' and likened her to the goddess. M.F. Husain, the famous painter, portrayed her riding a lion, like Goddess Durga. The President conferred on her the Bharat Ratna. The London Economist in one of its articles addressed her as the 'Empress of India'. Both nationally and internationally she was acclaimed as one of the greatest leaders, world statesman and in India a power to be reckoned with. She had proved her supremacy over all other political leaders in the country. Her programmes and policies stood fully vindicated, even including the split in the Congress Party. She stood supremely unchallenged. But then when you reach the summit, you have to come down. As the old proverb goes, absolute power corrupts absolutely. She could not stand any opposition and was seen surrounding herself more and more by an inner coterie of advisors. But she continued to be at the top for some time thereafter.

CHAPTER SEVEN

Delhi: Cabinet Secretary (1972-77)

I now come to the last phase of my official career. It was, I think, sometime in the last week of October 1972, that P.N. Haksar called me. We had been friends for long and used to meet often. This was the time when he was secretary to the prime minister and the most powerful civil servant—the man behind the throne. A lawyer from Allahabad, he joined the IFS on Independence and was appointed by Indira Gandhi. He informed me of the decision to appoint me as cabinet secretary in succession to T. Swaminathan who was retiring on November 2, 1972. I pointed out that K.B. Lall, who was then defence secretary and had seen the country through the Bangladesh war, was senior to me. But Haksar said that K.B. Lall had only six months left before his retirement. As I had about two and a half more years of service, I was the preferred choice. So, once again my career escalated and I took over as cabinet secretary to the Government of India, the highest post that a serving civilian can hold. The cabinet secretary not only acts as the secretary to the union cabinet, but also heads the Civil Service, advises on all postings of officers above the rank of a joint secretary, and initiates the postings of additional secretaries to the government. This post was created after Independence, somewhat on the lines of a similar post in Great Britain. Although I was due to retire on attaining the age of fifty-eight in March '75, I was given extensions from time to time, totalling a period of two years. So I finally retired at the age of sixty, relinquishing charge on 31 March, 1977, after nearly four and a half years in this post—the longest held by anyone thus far.

However, K.B. Lall protested about this posting. So both he and P.N. Haksar had their posts upgraded to the level of a principal secretary to government and equated with the cabinet secretary in the Warrant of Precedence. K.B. Lall was also posted for the second time as our ambassador to Belgium and the European Economic Community at Brussels for a three-year term. A year later, when D.P. Dhar became deputy chairman of the Planning Commission, I was also appointed principal secretary to the Planning Commission in addition to my duties as cabinet secretary.

As cabinet secretary, the file work was not heavy, but the meetings that one had to attend and the people one had to see were galore. First, there were the meetings of the Cabinet and its sub-committees, and then the innumerable inter-departmental meetings presided over by the Prime Minister that one had to attend. The cabinet secretary also served as chairman of a number of committees of secretaries to government as also of several ad-hoc committees. This took up most of the time. I found my working days to be usually long, from about 9 or 9.30 a.m. till fairly late in the evenings, sometimes as late as 8 p.m. Then there were ceremonial functions and duties to perform. For example, whenever any foreign dignitary, head of state or government came to or went back from India, I had to go to Palam airport and line up for welcoming the dignitary. After a couple of years, I requested the Prime Minister to excuse me from this protocol duty as too much time was wasted in this. Then there were a number of official banquets and dinners and lunches that one had to attend. These official banquets were often followed by a cultural programme, some of which were quite good. Among the more magnificant functions that I now recall was the dinner for President Brezhnev of the USSR and the Shah of Iran. A horseriding show by the President's bodyguard in the forecourt of the Rashtrapati Bhavan in the evening, just at dusk, was one of the best shows of horsemanship that I have seen. This is a general description, but let me describe some important events that I can recall.

In 1973, the first major problem that I had to tackle was concerning the deteriorating food situation and rising prices. We had to again resort to importing food from abroad and this time there was no PL 480. We made commercial decisions while ensuring that the grain was purchased at the lowest price. I remember T.N. Kaul was our ambassador in the USA and I had to make several long-distance calls to him, at unearthly hours in the morning, to get to him in Washington. Then there was a write up in the *Statesman*. Its editor, Kuldip Nayar, had put out a story that Food Secretary G.C.L. Joneja had gone to Washington to make purchases of wheat. This news was also published in the *Washington Post* and other US papers which led to wheat prices firming up. I got a frantic call from Washington as the news was false. Joneja had not gone out of Delhi. When I contacted Kuldip Nayar to inform him of this, he responded that Joneja may have gone and come back. This opened my eyes to the travesty of truth put out by such an eminent paper. I stopped reading the *Statesman* thereafter. This experience also gave me an insight into the very unhealthy trends in journalism. Unfortunately, it has tended to grow. Nobody is anxious or wants to muzzle the press, but the press must also realize that it has a duty to the society and the nation. In fact, it is not above blackmailing the governments, politicians and officials. Some have been able to secure government quarters, special house building colonies, travel concessions, and so forth, for themselves at hugely subsidized rents. They keep politicians on their toes by promising to write in their favour or by threatening to expose their misdeeds. The small district newspapers are usually rags of yellow journalism with their main aim being to extract concessions from the local harassed officials. This is the general picture. But there are several good papers and good journalists and on the whole the Indian press commands respect abroad and the government here has not imposed curbs unlike in many developing countries. The picture would have been much brighter if only they had been more enterprising, more objective and more aware of their social responsibilities.

The food situation was tackled fairly satisfactorily, but the price situation proved more intractable. For this, the government gave a direction to the secretaries of economic departments to come up with a scheme for controlling inflation. I presided over a number of meetings and we evolved measures for controlling the supply of money and increasing production. The measures recommended bore fruit and, for the first time in over a decade and a half, the wholesale price index actually fell. Monetary restraint and curb on deficit financing were important elements in this. At this time we were also faced with the first oil crisis. As a result of the decisions of OPEC—the Oil Producing Exporting Countries—the price of crude oil went up from $3 per barrel to $10 per barrel. Various measures to meet this situation were suggested. I vehemently opposed rationing of petrol, based on my experience of the Second World War. Instead I suggested a hike in prices to mop up the surplus as much as possible and thereby compel people to use less because of the high price which proved successful. I consider the economy management of this period a plus point in my career.

In 1974, we faced one of the worst industrial crises in the form of the All India Railwaymen's strike. The strike was politically motivated and posed a great challenge to the government. In fact if successful, it was aimed to overthrow the government. The railways, the police and paramilitary forces, the home guards and the territorial Army were mobilized. It was decided to cut down passenger traffic to the minimum and confine freight traffic to the most essential items, viz., foodgrains, oil products, coal for electricity and industrial use, ores for essential industries like steel, fertilizers, etc. The list was very small. When the strike actually happened, the railways were able to keep the country going. There were arrests, and attempts at intimidation and sabotage were ruthlessly suppressed. But then the strike fizzled out and the country heaved a sigh of relief. Thereafter, the deterioration that had set in the working of the railways also stopped. It was a big turning point and showed the government's determination to deal firmly with such threats. I remember that V.V. Giri, President of India at the time, was worried about the measures the government was taking. He had been an active railway men's leader who had organized the first major strike within the Kharagpur railway yard in the South Eastern Railways back in the 1920s. His sympathies were with the workmen, but he also realized that calling a nation-wide strike was not the right thing. I remember he called me several times to discuss the situation and I always referred him to the Prime Minister or the Railway Minister.

However, the political and economic situation continued to deteriorate and public dissatisfaction increased. Despite a massive mandate in the central and state elections, resentment against the authoritarian and dictatorial rule of Indira Gandhi continued to increase. One very potent source of dissatisfaction was her attempt to build up her younger son, Sanjay, as a potential successor. The opposition was loud in its cries against the dynastic succession that was being built up. Chief Ministers who supported and openly expressed blind allegiance to Indira Gandhi and her son Sanjay were put in power, and those who did not do so by word and deed were removed. Dossiers of important political men were kept from the police and intelligence sources, democratic norms were being thrown overboard. Resistance was met with an array of criminal charges. Office bearers at all levels were nominated from the top. Corruption and unethical practices were increasing manifold. Jayaprakash Narayan and Morarji Desai started a very powerful campaign against it all. The former was held in high respect because he had never accepted any political office, was close to Vinoba Bhave and was generally considered to be incorruptible. Meetings and rallies began to be organized on a large scale. Strikes—including the railway strike referred to earlier—were part of this programme. At several places, attempts were made to paralyze train services as closures and bandhs became the order of the day. In Gujarat, Congress(I) had been forced to resign by a massive student movement against corruption. Individual MLAs were forced to submit their resignations. So President's rule had been enforced, but fresh elections were being put off. This was when Morarji Desai started a fast unto death to compel Indira Gandhi to order early elections. Thus, towards the middle of June 1975, the general climate in the country was one of great discontent and disorder.

Then a couple things happened almost simultaneously that had one of the most profound effects in post-Independence India. Soon after the Lok Sabha election of 1971, in which Indira Gandhi had been elected from the Raebareilly constituency in Uttar Pradesh, Raj Narain, one of the defeated candidates, filed an election petition challenging her victory. He cited several instances of corrupt practices during the elections. Yashpal Kapur, Indira Gandhi's election agent, was said to be distributing large amounts of cash from an ostensible sick bed in a hospital. Kapur had been her private secretary for years and had come to acquire enormous power behind the scenes. Formerly, he was only on her private staff but was later given an official position in her Secretariat. I remember that when I came to Delhi, I do not quite recollect when, someone advised me most seriously that I should cultivate relations with Yashpal Kapur. He even rang me up once. I gave him no encouragement but I could not help running into him after every Cabinet meeting. Later R.K. Dhawan came to occupy his position. Now just before this election, Kapur had submitted his resignation from the official post, but there was a delay of a few days in issuing the official gazette notification. This election petition had been pending before a judge of the Allahabad High Court. Several witnesses had been examined and the judge's decision was expected any day. It was rumoured that an advance copy of this judgement had been clandestinely obtained some days earlier and had been made available to Indira Gandhi. Elections had also been announced in Gujarat as a result of Morarji Desai's fast unto death.

On the same day, that is 11 June 1975, the judgement on the election case came in at about 10 a.m. The judge held Indira Gandhi guilty of corrupt practices in the election on two counts, and as stipulated in the law, disenfranchised her for six years. The first charge was that Yashpal Kapur was still a government servant when he started acting as her election agent and she was thus held guilty of misutilizing the services of a government servant in the election. I have already mentioned that there was some delay in processing Yashpal Kapur's resignation. Indira Gandhi did not know about this. Nor was Yashpal Kapur a regular government servant. He had been her political secretary and been appointed to a temporary government post. The second charge was that the government machinery had been utilized for constructing the election podium, making arrangements for electricity, etc. Even though Indira Gandhi was contesting the election as a party leader, she was still the prime minister, and the security regulations required that all arrangements be made by the government. The sentence was something in which the judge had no discretion. Now most people felt that Indira Gandhi had been held guilty on purely technical grounds, no charges of corruption, of bribing of voters, of exceeding the prescribed limit of election expenses, etc., had been proved. In fact the judge acquitted her of all these charges. Most people felt that the judgement would be set aside on appeal by the Supreme Court. People around the world were amazed that our election laws were such that they could hold a prime minister guilty of election malpractices on such charges. However there it was, and soon thereafter an appeal was filed in the Supreme Court. The High Court judgement's operation was held in abeyance till the disposal of the appeal, with the stipulation that while Indira Gandhi could participate in the debates she could not vote nor draw any salary as a Lok Sabha MP. The appeal was expected to be heard in two or three months' time.

That same day, the Gujarat election results were announced. Congress(I) had lost.

The opposition, led particularly by Jayaprakash Narayan, began to organize huge meetings throughout the country demanding Indira Gandhi's resignation immediately. On the other hand, Congress(I) people, especially the close associates of Indira Gandhi, began to organize support rallies in front of the Prime Ministers's residence. Everyday, people were brought in buses, trucks, taxis, and several groups demonstrated their support for her. Newspapers were full of it. But there were no fights, no clashes with police or between groups of people. While the political tension was very high, as also the number of meetings and rallies being held, there was no increase in crime, and law and order was generally undisturbed. Excitement, on the other hand, was very high.

During this time, intense internal confabulations were taking place. The Prime Minister rarely came to office and instead worked from her house. A new coterie of 'palace advisors' had sprung up which included Sanjay Gandhi. Rajiv Gandhi kept himself completely out of political activity. Others included Siddharth Shankar Ray, Rajni Patel, Om Mehta—then minister of state in the home ministry, and Kishen Chand—a former member of the ICS who had been appointed It governor of Delhi. Many people were visiting her—Congressmen, MPs, etc. Some were advising her to step down temporarily, others for sticking it out. The Defence of India Rules promulgated in 1971 were still in force, and the declaration of emergency was also on the statute book. However at this stage Siddharth Shankar Ray, a Bar-at-Law, by all accounts came forward with the view that an internal emergency should be declared and thereafter measures to curb the activities of agitationists, especially Jayaprakash Narayan and his group, be taken. A very closely guarded strategy was worked out. Important official functionaries like the Home Minister K. Brahmananda Reddy, or the Home Secretary S.L. Khurana, who had replaced N.K. Mukarji, (because it was felt that Mukarji would prove to be difficult), or I, the cabinet secretary, and even the Secretary to the Prime Minister, P.N. Dhar, were, I think, not consulted and not even in the picture. Another person who was in this coterie was then Chief Minister of Haryana Bansi Lal. He in fact wanted N.K. Mukarji to be returned to Haryana so that he could 'deal' with him. Bansi Lal was known to be very difficult with civil servants who did not toe his line. But with great effort, and with P.N. Dhar's support, I was able to get the Prime Minister's orders to transfer N.K. Mukarji to the Ministry of Tourism and Civil Aviation.

Things were moving very fast. On June 25, there was a very big public meeting attended by Jayaprakash Narayan at the Ramlila grounds in Delhi. At the meeting Narayan said that Indira Gandhi should be forced to resign, the police and Army should refuse to obey illegal orders, and the people should surround her house. It is a moot question whether this eventuality could or could not have been met by the laws and regulations already in force. However, as far as I was personally concerned, I had no knowledge back then of some of the facts that I have described above. That same day, at about 6 p.m. or so, I left office and walked back home unaware of any impending crisis. I think it was four in the morning when the RAX telephone (a special secret telephone connected to only a few selected people—ministers, some secretaries, etc.) began to ring. Lalit answered the phone and woke me up. The call was from the Prime Minister's house and I was informed about an emergency meeting of the Cabinet—at 5 or 6 a.m. I was also told that the ministers were being informed separately.

I arrived at 1 Akbar Road a few minutes before time. I thought to myself that perhaps Indira Gandhi had decided to resign. Jagjivan Ram and Swaran Singh reached at the same time as I did. We were all equally clueless about the reason behind this sudden meeting. Y.B. Chavan arrived and shared with us the news about the arrest of Jayaprakash Narayan, Morarji Desai and some others. This news set everyone thinking. Soon thereafter, Mrs Gandhi was seen walking from 1 Safdarjung Road with Om Mehta and some others. Their faces showed that they had not slept the whole night. The Cabinet finally assembled and in a terse few words Mrs Gandhi announced that a proclamation of internal emergency had been promulgated by the President last night, several people had been arrested, and that she had decided that the disorders be put down by a firm hand. No minister said anything. She then asked me to call Home Secretary S.L. Khurana and ask him to come immediately. On arrival, he was handed over a copy of the proclamation and asked to take further action. The Cabinet had duly ratified the decision and the meeting soon dispersed.

It was later discovered that the said notification was taken to President Fakhruddin Ahmed the previous night and signed by him then. It was actually published in the morning, but was dated the previous day. At about ten or eleven in the morning there was a meeting in the Home Secretary's room to discuss the further course of action. At that meeting, Khurana read out the names of the dozens of people who had been arrested the previous night. It appeared that some BSF and Air Force planes were sent to various state capitals to carry some chief ministers and other designated people from Delhi. They had all been given lists of people to be arrested immediately. The ministers had called their chief secretaries and IGs of Police and given them the lists along with orders to make the arrests immediately. The places where they were to be confined were also indicated therein. The ministers were also given intructions to add more names to these lists. Most of the names belonged to the opposition, but included some dissident Congressmen like Chandra Shekhar Singh, once a great supporter of Indira Gandhi and leader of what were called the Young Turks in the Congress(I).

Under the Emergency proclamation, fundamental rights, especially the right of habeas corpus had been suspended. We had a debate whether the full list of names of those arrested was to be given out. Most of the secretaries were in favour of doing this. P.N. Dhar said he would check up with the Prime Minister, but she declined. Further, a press censorship would also be imposed to curb the reporting of the news concerning arrests. Someone remarked we were living in Idi Amin's Uganda!

The declaration of Emergency was not only ratified by the Cabinet, it was also voted by both Houses of Parliament. The legality was upheld by the Supreme Court in a writ petition. Thus, both constitutionally and otherwise, the Emergency was valid in law. Although the initial reaction of the people was one of shock or disbelief, yet for the first six months there was general approval. Government offices functioned better, corruption was less, many long-standing difficulties of the people were removed and railways, following the collapse of the rail strike, functioned much more efficiently. Some people, with older memories, began to compare the situation with Mussolini's Italy. Some programmes of development were presented in new bottles, the Prime Minister's twenty-point programme and Sanjay Gandhi's five-point programme.

But things did not rest there. After the Emergency proclamation, Parliament amended the election law, the Representation of People's Act, retrospectively nullifying the High Court decision on the election petition. It also amended the rule regarding appeals, so that the Supreme Court had to set aside the order of the high court judge. The Constitution was amended to increase the term of the Parliament and state assemblies from five to six years, as elections to the state assemblies were due shortly and the Congress(I) was not willing to face them. All these measures were resented by the people. Then two programmes of Sanjay Gandhi were enforced with vigour—the first related to demolition of unauthorized structures in various cities including Delhi, and the other was the family planning programme. Both these caused widespread resentment. More so with the family planning programme as it was spread far and wide into the villages. In some states, the officers told me that they could not enter a village because of the fear of being beaten up or chased away. And this was the case not only for those connected with family planning, but other departments too. People who expressed even the slightest protestations were arrested! Thus Bhim Sen Sachar, a veteran Congressman in his eighties, was arrested because he along with five or six others wrote a letter to Mrs Gandhi about the excesses taking place. His son was a high court judge. Then Pt Haksar, from the well-known New Delhi shop—Pandit Brothers, also in his eighties and a Kashmiri Brahmin (most likely to be distantly related to the Nehru family also and an uncle of P.N. Haksar), was arrested for voicing his criticism—that too in private. To add to these arrests was the strict censorship on the press that prevented any news from being published, so that all kinds of rumours began to float about and gain currency. Yet again, most of these actions were not taken through the official machinery or official channels. Thus the Cabinet Secretariat was left out completely. Even the Prime Minsiter's Secretariat was often not in the know of what was happening. Other departments of government were also unaware. Instructions were issued by Sanjay Gandhi to chief ministers or other ministers directly for carrying out certain programmes. And the inner coterie became powerful. No one could meet the Prime Minister directly. They had to go first to Sanjay Gandhi and could meet with Indira Gandhi only if he approved. Otherwise he gave them instructions on what to do. The chief ministers that had the temerity to ask for, or insist for, a meeting with Mrs Gandhi, or refused to act on Sanjay's orders only, got removed. This was the fate of H.N. Bahuguna of Uttar Pradesh and Nandini Satpathy of Orissa—both once close associates and admirers of Indira Gandhi. On one occasion, a Cabinet memorandum on family planning was supposed to be sent out. Gian Prakash, who later became the comptroller and auditor general of India, was then health secretary. He brought the draft memorandum to show me, because it made a reference to some deaths that had taken place in the family planning vasectomy camps. When this went to the Prime Minister, a great objection was raised. But at the meeting, except for a homily that more care should be taken in the camps, directions were given to carry on with the family planning programme with greater vigour. Some ministers, like K.C. Pant, advocated legislation for compulsory enforcement of the programme. Later when protests against this programme became vehement, the Prime Minister put the entire blame on Health Minister Karan Singh.

At this time Mrs Gandhi also began making statements asking for commitment on the part of officers. The question that followed was, commitment to what—the Constitution of India or the person of the Prime Minister? While publicly it was said to be the former, in the case of several important and sensitive appointments it was meant to be the latter. A few cases that came my way gave me an inkling into it. Proposals were made for the appointment of some officers to certain posts, but the Prime Minister's final orders were not received, even though reminders and telephonic messages were sent her way. Then one day the officers were rung up and called to see her. They went and were told that Sanjay Gandhi would meet them. The one or two who gave an undertaking of loyalty and were found fit had their appointment proposals approved. For the rest, it was reversed. The officers whose proposals were not approved came and told me about their interviews. In some cases the ministers were asked by the Prime Minister's Secretariat to withdraw the file and recommend others. This also caused great resentment among the civil servants. Some of them went out of their way to what may be called 'out-Herod Herod'. Among them, then Lt Governor of Delhi Krishan Chand, and Jagmohan, then in the Delhi Development Authority, come to mind. Krishan Chand could not survive the collapse of Indira Gandhi's Government and committed suicide soon thereafter. His was one of the most tragic cases of being too loyal.

Come 1977, and the six-year tenure of the Lok Sabha was coming to an end. Some Indira-loyalists wanted elections to be further postponed, bringing the six-year tenure to seven years. Others however advised against this. They anticipated an explosive situation if there were to be further delay. I think that even some foreign governments, both the Conservative and Labour parties of England, the US Government and some others that had supported Indira Gandhi and were friendly to India, were in favour of elections being held. However, despite possible loss of power and its consequences, and to her great credit Indira Gandhi decided on elections. In this respect she showed her democratic bent of mind. Personally, I think, this was the greatest decision she took which greatly helped in the strengthening of the Indian Constitution and India's nascent democracy. The elections were announced to be held in the third week of March 1977.

Meanwhile, the political prisoners so far under detention, like Jayaprakash Narayan, Morarji Desai and others were all released, the ban on public meetings was cancelled and press censorship was lifted. All measures to enable the exercise of a free vote were taken. The opposition party leaders had been in jail for about eighteen months and several of them had been together. For once they saw that their only chance of winning was by coming together. Jayaprakash Narayan especially helped in this process, so that several centrist parties joined together to form one single party—the Janata Party. The old Congress (O), the Jan Sangh, the Socialists, etc., merged together to form this new party. Only the parties of the left, like CPI(M), CPI, Forward Block, RSP, remained outside, though they said they would also fight on the anti-Congress(I) programme. The extreme right wing and communal parties like the Akali Dal, the Muslim League, etc., remained outside the Janata Party.

As the election campaign was just gathering momentum, in the beginning of March, Jagjivan Ram shocked everyone by resigning from the Cabinet and Congress(I). He went to meet the President and gave him a copy of his letter of resignation addressed to the Prime Minister, and announced his decision in a press conference, even before Indira Gandhi had any time to react to his letter. This sent shock waves in the Congress(I) and I remember ministers ringing me up to find out if this were true. Till then I had no news, officially, of this development and told them so. There is, however, no doubt that Jagjivan Ram's departure from the Congress(I) meant a big blow to the party.

The opposition organized very enthusiastic and well-attended election meetings. The people's mood was also anti-Congress(I) mainly because of the large-scale arrests, the rumours concerning the family planning programme, and the general mood against the imposition of the Emergency. As a result, the Janata Party won big, although Congress(I) emerged as the second largest party and formed a sizeable opposition in Parliament for the first time. Its victories in the South—in Andhra Pradesh, Karnataka, and Tamil Nadu were impressive. For example, the Janata could get only one seat from Tamil Nadu and also only one or two from Andhra Pradesh, but swept the polls in northern India.

As soon as the election results began to come in, with clear indications of a defeat for Congress(I), news of Indira Gandhi's defeat also came in. An emergency Cabinet meeting was called at about 11 p.m. This time the meeting was at the residence of the Prime Minister—1 Safdarjung Road. It was held in one of the small rooms where Indira Gandhi used to meet visitors. She announced that she would be sending in her resignation, and that of the Cabinet, immediately to the President. The other important issue that came up for discussion was whether the proclamation regarding the Emergency should be formally revoked or not. There was some discussion, but the majority felt that this should be done, otherwise the Janata Government may use the provision of the Emergency against Congress(I) members. So I was asked immediately to record the Cabinet decision and prepare the notification to be signed by the President. The Home Secretary and I sat in an adjoining room and got the papers typed out, ready for the Prime Minister's signature. I went back to the room where the ministers were sitting. I read out the papers and they asked me to take them to Mrs Gandhi who had gone inside.

When I went in, there was a sight which I had not expected. Mrs Gandhi was standing in the main corridor and Sanjay and Maneka Gandhi appeared from the other side looking visibly upset. They went up to her and Maneka asked what would now become of them. Rajiv Gandhi was not there. I gave the papers to the Prime Minister for her signature and was asked to take them immediately to the President and get his signature. By then it was past 1 a.m. The Home Secretary and I went to the President. Vice President B.D. Jatti was then acting as President following the death of Fakhruddin Ahmed who had suffered a heart attack in early February. He was staying at 6 Maulana Azad Marg. I told him about the Cabinet meeting, showed him the proceedings and also requested him to sign the proclamation revoking the Emergency. I gave the papers to the Home Secretary for further action and returned home at about 2 a.m. Thus this chapter came to an end.

A couple of days later, Morarji Desai was sworn in as Prime Minister. The Cabinet formation took some time—discussions and personal ambitions within the Janata Party had begun to crop up and it was only Jayaprakash Narayan and Acharya Kripalani who were able to virtually force a decision on the other leaders, principally Charan Singh and Jagjivan Ram. They were both later inducted as deputy prime ministers. One of the first things I had to do was to ask Morarji Desai to select my successor. I told him I was due to leave on March 31 and this decision was urgent. I told him that my recommendation was that Nirmal Kumar Mukarji—the last serving ICS officer and the seniormost officer—should be appointed as Cabinet Secretary. He approved of this. A few days later, there was an urgent notification to be issued for which I suggested an emergency Cabinet meeting. Morarji Desai said he had no time, but would approve the notification which could later be ratified by the Cabinet. I am mentioning this to highlight how the procedure to which these very Janata Party leaders had greatly objected to back in June 1975, when Indira Gandhi had proclaimed the Emergency, was now being adopted by them as one of the first acts after taking office.

Before demitting office, Indira Gandhi agreed to meet the secretaries to government whom she thanked. She had been in office for about eleven years. She met them at a tea at 1 Akbar Road and said goodbye. It looked then as if she would be out of office and Parliament for some time. But how rapidly and unexpectedly things change!

I attended two or three of the Morarji Cabinet meetings and recall the discussions about using only Hindi in the meeting (protests arose from the only minister from Tamil Nadu); and about abolishing the Padma awards when the proposal to confer Bharat Ratna on Jayaprakash Narayan arose. I bade farewell to the ministers at a Cabinet meeting on my last day. After I left the room, the Cabinet, in accordance with previous traditions, passed a resolution appreciating my services and keeping them on record. So ended this chapter. Technically, I was on refused leave for 120 days from April 1, 1977, and began to draw my pension from the end of July 1977, having signed my covenant with the Secretary of State for India in September 1938. I was thus in the ICS for one month short of thirty-nine years. I ended up in a position which I had never dreamt of when I joined. So many things happened in nearly four decades.

*

In a few more paragraphs I will relate some official matters and also some personal matters during the time I was cabinet secretary.

First, the official matters. There was the incident of a bomb explosion at Samastipur where Railway Minister L.N. Mishra became a victim. He had been a very important part of the Indira Gandhi Government. This was also the first political murder in independent India, if one excludes the murder of Mahatma Gandhi. This mystery was never solved. Several enquiry commissions were appointed, but the person responsible and the motive behind it were never found out. Another important minister, Mohan Kumaramangalam, who had joined the Indira Congress Government died in a tragic plane crash near Palam airport. Mohan Kumarmangalam had been an important member of the CPI (when it was undivided) for years. In the obituary notice that was officially published, there was no reference to this most important and long period of his public life. He was in Cambridge in my time—late thirties—and had been known to be a communist sympathizer even then.

Then there was the case of Sikkim. It is true that at the time of Independence, Nepal, Sikkim and Bhutan all sat in the Indian Chamber of Princes. None of them had any external dealings except through the Government of India and in many respects they were no different than the other states in India, like Hyderabad, Mysore, etc. When it came to internal matters, however, they were fairly independent and guarded access into their land rather zealously, making it difficult for people to go there. The mountainous nature of their countries and lack of communications enabled them to keep to themselves. In Nepal, there was a movement towards democratic reform. This was mainly started by some Nepalese, especially those living in Benares, and among them the Koirala brothers. With the initial success of democracy and parliamentary rule in India, officially and unofficially, India encouraged the movement started by the Koirala brothers. In the mid-50s, this movement gained momentum. With C.P.N. Singh as our ambassador at

Kathmandu, every possible encouragement was given. From the Indian side, namely the Tirhut division and neighbouring Gorakhpur districts, thousands of people began to move into Nepal terai. Many of them held land and had relatives there. The border was open. But this groundswell went against the Rana regime and gave power to the people. The King of Nepal, who was virtually a prisoner in his palace, escaped and took shelter in the Indian embassy. India began exerting pressure. The 200-year-old Rana regime and its rule collapsed. They abdicated their traditional, hereditary offices and the King was recognized by all, including the Nepalese in India. The mountain kingdom had a great respect for the office of the King, so it was retained while some political reforms were affected. But when the old King Tribhuvan died and his son Mahendra succeeded, things began to change. The young King asserted himself and in order to keep Nepal independent, he began to woo China, who had by then occupied Tibet in the north. Gradually, he began to keep an equal distance from both China and India, politically, with the purpose of ensuring and safeguarding Nepal's independence. He succeeded in this and got the support of all classes of Nepalese people plus some foreign countries. So India had to change its role. In fact, today, our influence in Nepal is much less than it was in the first few years after Independence. Not only that, there are visible anti-Indian signs and demonstrations at times, although culturally, linguistically, ethinically, and geographically, Nepal and India are very close and are also connected by ties of religion, marriage and more. But politically we are now much weaker in Nepal.

Coming back to Sikkim. The Chogyal of Sikkim, as he is called, after the death of his first wife, who was Tibetan, married an American woman—Hope Cooke. The ruling tribes of Sikkim—the Lepchas and Bhotiyas—are Buddhist, the majority, now Nepali, is mainly Hindu. However, Sikkim was considered to be predominantly and basically a Buddhist country. Seeing the developments in Nepal, this young Chogyal wanted greater independence for his state, including representation in the UN and an Ambassador in India. For quite some years, Sikkim was really governed by Indians. At first, the dewan, or prime minister, was an Indian official selected by the Government of India and additionally there was a political officer from the Indian Foreign Office. This desire for greater political freedom by Sikkim was not to India's liking, and there were strategic considerations as well, as Tibet and China were putting their own pressures on the Sikkim-Tibet boundary. There was another ambitious Sikkimese—Kazi Lhendup Dorji—living in Kalimpong in the Darjeeling district. His wife, known as the Kazini, was a European of uncertain origins, but probably a Belgian, was equally ambitious. She responded positively to feelers for Sikkim's merger with India and the Kazi becoming the chief minister of the state. India's Research and Analysis Wing (RAW) had been working towards this end to cut down the Chogyal and his American wife's dream. So one day, Foreign Secretary Kewal Singh called a meeting in his room. Several people were present and among them I recall were R.N. Kao, the head of RAW, the Home Secretary, Director Intelligence Bureau and several other officers. Kewal Singh said that the Prime Minister had asked for some action to be taken regarding Sikkim. There was some discussion and RAW was told to take necessary action. Very soon, a number of people from Kalimpong and Darjeeling began to move into Sikkim. The Sikkim police hierarchy and the Chogyal's palace guards had been infiltrated. As the people began to move into Gangtok, the Chogyal was presented with a demand to agree to have a referendum about Sikkim's merger with India. The record of this meeting was kept by Kewal Singh. He circulated it to all senior officials present. I remember having returned it to him saying that no such record should be kept. The Chogyal was pressured and compelled to announce the referendum, which was overwhelmingly in favour of India. And so, Sikkim became a state of India. Some safeguards were provided, but its independent or semi-independent identity was obliterated. Later, Morarji Desai, on becoming the prime minister, talked of the annexation of Sikkim by Indira Gandhi, but by then this had become a fait-accompli and no one supported him, not even his own party. But this move made Bhutan and Nepal more zealous in guarding their independence. Since then there have been no further moves by India. But other neighbours, like Sri Lanka and Pakistan, have continued to be wary in their dealings with India.

Then there was the first, and so far the only, atomic explosion in the Rajasthan desert by India. This event was kept a most closely guarded secret, and even though the planning and execution must have taken over a year or so, no word of it escaped. So when it happened in 1974, the world was astounded. India had entered the atomic age and joined the world's select club of nations possessing the secret, the technology, and expertise to manufacture an atom bomb. India however always held that it wanted to use atomic energy for peaceful purposes and not to make the atom bomb. But our military potential has been substantially enhanced in this region.

During my tenure as cabinet secretary, I also acted as governor on behalf of India in the Board of Governors of the International Crop Research Institute for Semi-Arid Tropics (ICRISAT) which had been set up near Hyderabad. The meetings of this body gave me an opportunity to get out of the work of the Cabinet Secretary and meet agricultural scientists from all over the world. In one of the meetings during my tenure they said that wives could also accompany their husbands. So Vimla accompanied me and we were both able to go to Madras and Tirupati as well.

On the evening of 31 March 1977, I held a farewell party and invited all secretaries to government and the three chiefs of staff along with their wives. There were then nearly fifty secretaries so it was a big party. But the interesting thing was that many secretaries did not even know each other—they had never met. The central government is now so big and so divided into compartments that only a few circles overlap. At this party people asked me what I intended to do. I said I had no firm plans yet but was thinking of going to the Kumaon hills if I could find a place to stay. General Raina was then the chief of army staff and also a colonel of the Kumaon Regiment. He said he would try and see if we could get a house in Ranikhet. A few days later he said that he had been able to locate a house called Jagati Bank that was rented out to a retired major and which would be available. We then decided to go to Ranikhet for some time. Satish and Kamla, my sister-in-law, were in Ranikhet so we would have their company too. And so, in early May 1977, we landed up at Ranikhet.

So ended forty years of my official life. By external standards, whether it be because of the bureaucratic escalator or whatever, I had risen to the highest position to which a civil servant could aspire. My record of service had been reasonably good and clean. The government and the people seemed to have confidence in my judgement. I felt I had nothing more to ask for.

CHAPTER EIGHT

Post-Retirement Years: 1977–81

Soon after I came to Ranikhet, people began to ask me if I was writing my reminiscences. They would not believe me when I told them that I did not, in fact, know many things which people assumed I would. Most of all, people asked me about the happenings of the Emergency. They would not believe me when I told them I did not know how it had really worked. But as I have now written, these were the actual facts. A coterie in Indira Gandhi's house ran the show directly through chosen chief ministers, union ministers and selected bureaucrats and officials. Anyone they assumed to be difficult or prone to raise objections was excluded.

We spent a happy time in Ranikhet. It was a quiet, peaceful life. We entertained frequently and kept ourselves busy. In June, Minu (my eldest daughter-in-law) and the children came over for a month and we travelled about in the hills. I faced a lot of trouble in securing my pension, provident fund repayment and commutation. This was most harassing and made me wonder how difficult it must be for others. Everyone contributes to this, the departmental people are callous, the accountant general's office and the Treasury Office downright corrupt.

In October 1977, I travelled to Almora with Ghanda, my cousin. I stayed for a week or ten days and got our house here white-washed and generally habitable. I did this as it was not clear if we would be able to stay on in Ranikhet. We were certainly not getting a house there on a permanent basis.

*

The most important event of this period was the setting up of the 'Shah Commission of Enquiry'. Justice Shah, who headed this panel, was a retired chief justice of the Supreme Court. He was asked to investigate all events leading up to the declaration of the Emergency, its legality, and the reported or rumoured excesses that took place during the Emergency. It was set up amidst tremendous fanfare, with a high-powered team of police and other officials to help, leading lawyers and advocates to examine and cross-examine witnesses. Loudspeakers were set up and placed round the lawns. All India Radio, television and newspapers gave it great publicity. The idea was to pin-point the entire responsibility on Indira Gandhi and, if possible, set about prosecuting her later.

I was also summoned to give evidence. I was asked about the circumstances and what I knew about the declaration of the Emergency. I told them that I had no notion of it and learnt about it only at the Cabinet meeting, where the decision was ratified by the Cabinet. I was then asked if I thought it was necessary. At one stage, I wanted to say that this was a matter of opinion, but before I could say this, Justice Shah said he wanted to have my opinion on the subject. I maintained that perhaps it was not necessary, because the government already had all the powers under the Emergency Proclamation of 1971 which was still in force; the Defence of India rules and the Maintenance of Internal Security Act were in force; and this notification did not confer any additional powers which the government did not already have. I also said that the previous year's railway strike had been effectively handled by the government and they could meet any threat to law and order even now. I was also asked about the law and order situation. I said that it was tense, a number of public meetings were being held, but there had been no reports of violence or of the breakdown of the law and order machinery.

Many others were also examined, including several ministers. At this stage, a rift began to appear among the Congress leaders. I think, Indira Gandhi wanted there to be a common strategy which would enable them all to give more or less the same reply, in particular, pleading protection under the oath of secrecy and not expressing their personal opinion. Some ministers did not follow this and so, effectively, went out of Indira Gandhi's coterie. The most important was her own statement. She was asked to take an oath before giving evidence. However, she read out a prepared statement, challenged the authority of the Commission to summon her to give evidence, and refused to take the oath. Thereafter she walked out. This created a very piquant situation for the Commission. After some days, Justice Shah filed a complaint before the competent court that Indira Gandhi be prosecuted for her refusal to take the oath. She said she had not taken the oath as she was not required to do so, and her statement would have been used against her. An adjudication of the simple issue—was she, or was she not, required to take the oath—the facts not being under dispute—could not be made by the trial court for two years, at the end of which it was held that she was not required to take the oath. By that time many things had happened.

I would like to digress a little here—and that concerns the role and function of our judiciary. I have quoted above where one simple issue could not be decided for two years. I would have thought that after hearing arguments from both sides, a judgement could have been delivered within a month at the most. But no, the case dragged on for two years, on what grounds I do not know: partly procedural and partly with the desire of not adjudicating. There are instances where the Supreme Court has delivered judgements two years after the hearing of arguments. The judgements themselves run into hundreds of pages, as if they were a thesis for a doctorate degree, quoting from judgements of the Supreme Courts of the world over—where there is no similarity of history, tradition, social customs and mores. Other countries do not quote judgements of our Supreme Court. Then the judgements are discursive, or rambling and in many important cases, one does not know what the real ruling is. There are any number of *obiter dicta*. I always get the feeling that instead of delivering justice, we lay more stress on the procedure and not on the substance. Delays are such that cases, even the simplest ones—like traffic offences and violations of prohibitory orders u/s 144 CrPC—do not come up for hearing for years, and then naturally justice fails them. We are currently witnessing the astounding drama of the culprits in the Indira Gandhi murder case still being under trial though nearly two years have elapsed. Writs of stay are issued without any regard to their effect on administration. In fact, I would say that the high courts have succeeded in ruining all universities, breaking down all discipline in government services, and made the maintenance of law and order a more or less impossible exercise. Our judiciary does not seem to understand that speedy administration of justice is a pre-requisite of a good government and essential for the maintenance of law and order. It is one of three arms of the government and not independent of it. I have a conviction that if one day, God forbid, democracy were to collapse in our country, the one single institution responsible for it would be the judiciary—despite all the public praise that is presently bestowed on it.

Coming back to the Shah Commission, despite an army of investigators and evidence from numerous people (barring a few cases of transfers which may be said to have been unjustified) no criminal violations of the law could be pinned on anyone. Teams of experts were sent abroad that found no illegal funds in foreign countries, no illegal transfers and certainly no illegal money with Indira Gandhi. They could not prosecute her on any charge. In one case, Home Minister Charan Singh ordered her arrest. It recoiled very badly on him and the Janata Government. Several states were asked to set up their own commissions of enquiry and institute cases against government servants. To my knowledge, not one offence was established, no officer was dismissed or found guilty, despite all kinds of rumours. In one case of Muzaffarnagar in Uttar Pradesh, where Charan Singh and his henchmen had made charges of police firing at people refusing to undergo compulsory vasectomy, he even wrote a letter to the Chief Minister saying that everything must be done to see that the enquiry commission establishes the guilt of the officers and the commission of high-handedness by the police. Despite this blatant interference, nothing could be established. This whole show had ended almost as a farce.

But there was considerable alarm among the officers. They were subject to a witch-hunt, were summarily suspended, and two secretaries to the government were even arrested and kept in police custody. The morale and cohesiveness of the services was broken. Later, when Indira Gandhi came back to power, she continued to discriminate against the officers even if she did not continue the same tirade against politicians.

The crowning folly of the Janata regime, and the hunger for power among its leaders, was witnessed when Charan Singh with his henchman, Raj Narain, played into the hands of Sanjay Gandhi. Expecting support from Congress(I), Charan Singh parted with Morarji Desai and brought about a downfall of his government. He then became prime minister and soon found that the Congress(I) would not support him. He remained in office for six months and had the most disastrous effect on Indian politics. He never faced Parliament. Elections were ordered, and in January 1980, Indira Gandhi was back in power.

*

In March 1978, we came to Almora. The Planning Commission set up a National Transport Policy Committee in April that year. V.G. Rajadhyaksha, who was then member-in-charge, Planning Commission, and H.M. Patel, then finance minister, proposed that I head the Committee. I agreed on the condition that it would be a part-time job. So, from May 1978 for the next two years, I was on this Committee. We travelled all over the country and I had an opportunity to meet my old friends and do a final 'Bharat Darshan'. We submitted our report to the Prime Minister as Chairman of the Planning Commission in March 1980 by when Indira Gandhi was back in power. This was a satisfying job and the report was well-received. I functioned from Almora and used to go to Delhi or other parts of India for about ten days every month.

Then, I think in 1979, at the suggestion of S. Bhoothalingam, my former secretary and retiring chairman of the American Express (AmEx) International Banking Corporation, I became chairman of their Indian Banking Division. This gave me an opportunity to travel to Bombay, Calcutta, Madras and Delhi once a quarter and meet several people. Also due to this assignment, Vimla and I could go to the USA and Europe in November 1980. This was Vimla's first and only trip abroad. We travelled first class and under diplomatic passports. We first went to Geneva, where Vinod was on a short assignment, then London, and Cambridge to visit Ratna and Sudarshan. From there we went to New York and spent a week, first meeting the AmEx head office people and then sightseeing. After the first few days, we stayed with SK (Krishnamurthy) and Bina (my niece). We then went on to Boston, Cambridge, where we stayed with Dr Preetinder Singh Virk, a class fellow of Raja at the Doon School and who had also known Lalit. From there we proceeded to Lafayette and Purdue to spend a couple of days with Lalit. After a day's halt at Chicago, on to Washington for the weekend, then back to London and Cambridge via New York. This time in Cambridge I dined at the High Table of Christ's College with the Master and their Fellows. We returned home via Paris and Rome. In all, we were away for about three weeks.

During Charan Singh's tenure, an Expenditure Commission was set up with S.N. Mishra of Bihar as its chairman. I, too, was appointed a member of this Commission. It functioned for about six months, submitted a few interim reports and was wound up soon after Indira Gandhi became prime minister—I think in March 1980.

During this period, I attended a conference on public administration at Manila. It was my first visit to the city. I had a brief stopover at Hong Kong. People told me how so many buildings had been built at such short notice due to the drive of Ferdinand Marcos' wife, Imelda. The city was clean. I also met many people at the Asian Development Bank. Life was tense and people did not venture out of their compounds after dusk. Nobody at that time could forecast such an early end of the Marcos regime.

About the middle of 1980, I was asked if I would agree to be the first director of a newly proposed Rajaji International Institute of Public Affairs and Administration, a very high-sounding name, to be established by the Bhartiya Vidya Bhavan of Bombay. I was not at all enthusiastic as this was far removed from my line. Then I received a personal letter from I.G. Patel, then governor of Reserve Bank of India, to consider this and at least agree to meet the people incharge. At a meeting in Punjab Bhavan in Delhi, I met with Jaisukhlal Hathi, then governor of Punjab, P.N. Bhagwati, Judge Supreme Court, C. Subramanium, former union minister and some others. They said I should give it a try. Vimla and others persuaded me to accept this assignment. But weeks and months passed and I heard nothing from them, though they had been pressing me to join at once. This baffled me. Then in November I told them that I was going abroad and I could join only in December, however if they wanted me to, I could utilize this visit by meeting people at places like Princeton, Harvard, Paris, where similar institutes were functioning. They agreed to meet my daily expenses for five days on this account. So during my trip abroad I had some discussions with various people and collected considerable literature. I returned at the end of November and then told them I could join them in Delhi in early December 1980. When I reached Delhi there was nobody to meet me, the room where I was to stay had not even been swept. I felt somewhat put-off. The first few days indicated some kind of non-cooperation. At a function organized by the Bhartiya Vidya Bhavan in honour of the President Sanjiva Reddy in Bombay, I met Jaisukhlal Hathi, C. Subramanium and others, and told them of my misgivings and that if they did not want me, they should say so. I left in mid-February 1981. This had been one of the worst judgements of my life. We returned to Almora after this none too happy interlude.

Then suddenly a month later, I was informed of my appointment as chairman of the Railway Reforms Committee for a period of two years with the rank of a union minister of state. I said I would not be able to do the job on a part-time basis from Almora, as the long travel now tired me. I came to Delhi and was allotted a good house, 4 Lodi Estate. I learnt that the Prime Minister had suggested my name. I had hardly settled down, set up the office and was about to start work on the Railway Reforms Committee, when in September 1981, I was asked to go to Calcutta.

CHAPTER NINE

Governor, West Bengal: 1981–83

In August 1981, rumours began to float of a change in the governorship of West Bengal, and my name began to be mentioned in this connection.

On coming to power in March 1977, one of the very first acts of the Janata Government—one which set a very wrong precedent subsequently—was to dismiss the state governments. The state governments to which this decision was applied were—Punjab, Haryana, Himachal Pradesh, Rajasthan, Gujarat, Maharashtra, Uttar Pradesh, Bihar, West Bengal, Assam and Orissa. The Congress(I) was in a comfortable majority in all these states and general elections were not due. However, the Janata Government ordered the imposition of President's rule in these states on the ground that people's confidence had been lost, as evidenced by the Lok Sabha election results. Then acting President, B.D. Jatti, initially refused to sign the order dismissing the state governments. He said there were no grounds to do so, as there were no reports of a breakdown in the law and order situation or collapse of any Constitutional authority. But the Janata Government threatened to resign and create a Constitutional crisis at the centre. The main moving spirit behind this move was then Home Minister Charan Singh. B.D. Jatti had to agree, the state governments were dismissed, a short period of President's rule was imposed, and general elections to the state assemblies ordered. The elections were held in May 1977. The Congress(I) was wiped out in all these states, Janata Government came into power, except in West Bengal where a left-oriented combination of parties with CPI(M) as the leader and supported by the RSP—Revolutionary Socialist Party and the Forward Block, called the Left Front, secured a thumping majority and formed the government. The CPI(M) leader Jyoti Basu became the chief minister. There was wild jubilation in West Bengal. Congress(I) was very disheartened.

It is worthwhile going back a few years. The Congress had held complete sway in West Bengal all through the days of Dr B.C. Ray who was a towering personality in many ways, and for a few years thereafter. However in 1967, when the first anti-Congress wave swept North India, the Congress lost in West Bengal too. While the Left Front, with CPI(M) as the principal party, emerged as the largest party, they could not form a government of their own. A section of the Congress, led by Ajoy Mukherjee, was supported by the Left Front and a United Front Government came into power. While Ajoy Mukherjee became the chief minister, Jyoti Basu became the deputy chief minister incharge of the home portfolio. But this Cabinet did not work harmoniously. The Left Front wanted an aggressive pro-labour and pro-tenant policy, but Ajoy Mukherjee and his group were not willing to go that far. The industrial sector was where the situation deteriorated the most. There were strikes and closures in establishments, accompanied by several cases of violence. A new agitational programme was adopted by the trade unions—called the 'gherao'. In this, senior executives and owners of firms were forcibly surrounded and kept in virtual imprisonment for hours on end, without water or access to a bathroom. Sometimes they were confined in such a manner in blazing sunshine. This was clearly illegal and a cognizable offence, but the police took no action as they were instructed not to interfere in labour disputes. Civic administration was also breaking down. The city of Calcutta was in chaos. We had the most extraordinary spectacle of the Chief Minister going on an indefinite fast in a public place against the decisions of his own government!

At about the same time a group of extremist leftist elements formed what was called the CPI (Marxist-Leninist) or CPI(ML). This group believed in violence as a means of rectifying social inequities. They started their campaign of terror from a village in North Bengal near Siliguri called Naxalbari. Hence this group became known as the Naxalites. They quoted Mao of China saying 'power comes from the barrel of the gun' and even declared him as the leader of their party.

The original Communist Party of India had split in 1963 after the Chinese aggression of India. The CPI was more inclined to support the Congress. It was led by Dange who considered the Congress foreign policy and some tenets of the internal policy worth supporting, especially as it was thought to be pro-Moscow and also acceptable to the Soviets. However, a small part broke away. This small group was led by E.M.S. Namboodiripad and supported by the communists in Eastern India, especially those in West Bengal and Tripura. They named themselves CPI (Marxist) or CPI(M). However, the extremist element considered the CPI(M) as revisionary because they believed in parliamentary elections even while strengthening the Communist Party. There was no love lost between the CPI(M) and CPI (ML). The original CPI commanded the allegiance of a minority section only in West Bengal.

Naxalite activity began to grow. There were killings daily, and the terrorist activities spread from North Bengal to South Bengal and Calcutta. Policemen on traffic duty were shot dead in the presence of thousands of people. The Vice-Chancellor of the Jadavpur University was shot dead on campus. It was a strange spectacle to see some of the brightest students join the Naxalites. This was a reflection of the deep social malaise that had affected Bengal.

This situation had grown over the years and was the culmination of years of exploitation and neglect of Bengal. One has to go back to the early days of the East India Company and British rule in India to understand it better. Bengal was then the richest state of India. The land was, and is, highly fertile. Trade, commerce and industry were highly developed. At the time of his impeachment, Warren Hastings said in his statement at the British Parliament that Dacca and Murshidabad were more prosperous and flourishing than London and Paris at the time. He also said that he had financed all the wars in India out of the 'revenues' of Bengal, along with remitting the largest revenues as income to the board of directors of the East India Company. This was followed by the Permanent Settlement of 1793 and exploitation by the landlords, the zamindars, with the help and connivance of the British rulers. The 'tribhaga' system in agriculture (where the peasants were compelled to grow indigo and opium and hand over two-thirds of the produce to the Company at a pre-determined rate), the continued increase in rents payable by tenants, the closure of handicrafts and handlooms to find a market for British manufactures, etc., resulted in the Bengal peasantry becoming utterly impoverished. Hence the anti-British agitation started originally from Bengal, and the statement 'What Bengal does today the rest of India does tomorrow' gained traction.

The next big blow to Bengal was the shifting of the capital from Calcutta to Delhi. Then came the two World Wars. Bombay began to develop as a rival port and business centre. The Bengal Famine of 1943, the Great Calcutta Killings, the Japanese bombing of Calcutta during the War years 1942–43, followed by the trauma of partition upon Independence in 1947 left West Bengal in a terrible plight. It had one-third of the area and population of undivided Bengal. It housed some industries, especially the jute mills, but all the raw material and the major hinterland was in East Bengal. West Bengal became like a tadpole with an enormous head at Calcutta. In fact, for a few years there was no direct contiguous terrain between South and Northwest Bengal. As if this was not enough, industries began to move out of West Bengal, so both agriculture and industry suffered further as unemployment increased. Young men were disenchanted and saw a bleak future for themselves which became a fertile enough ground for discontent and revolution. Many perceptive observers at that time sounded a warning, that unless Calcutta and West Bengal were rapidly rehabilitated, a communist takeover of that part of the country was a distinct possibility.

The Government of India had its hands full, however. There was not sufficient money or resources for this purpose. North West India, especially Punjab with the rehabilitation of millions who had moved across the borders in the West, the situation in J&K, the grim food situation throughout the country, consolidation of the newly won Independence, absorbed all energies of the government. The outbreak in West Bengal was thus bound to occur and 1967–69 saw it at its worst.

The Naxalite movement caused a great deal of killings, not only of police personnel and others by Naxalites, but inter-party killings between CPI(M) and CPI(ML) on one hand and CPI(M) and Congress on the other. The situation was dire. The Ajoy Mukherjee ministry was dismissed and Prafulla Ghosh, a veteran Congressman, was inducted as chief minister. But he could not last. President's rule followed. The Army had to be called out to maintain law and order and help the police. Flushing operations were carried out. At the same time in 1971, the situation deteriorated in East Bengal (then East Pakistan), following the elections in Pakistan and emergence of the Awami League, led by Sheikh Mujibur Rahman of East Bengal, as the major party. The history of the 1971 war with Pakistan need not be recapitulated here. However, the victory in the 1971 conflict, the return of refugees to East Bengal, the elimination of the Naxalite threat, meant that in the 1972 elections, the Congress(I) emerged victorious once again in West Bengal after a lapse of about five years.

A Congress(I) Government was formed with Siddhartha Shankar Ray as chief minister. His government had disparate elements, like Ghani Khan Choudhury who did not get on with S.S. Ray and kept up a continuous tirade against him, both openly and in party circles. Then there were some younger elements of the so-called 'Congress youth wing'—Subrata Mukherjee, Somen Mitra, etc. They were a militant group with the support of the lumpen proletariat and had at the same time played an important part in the Congress victory by their tactics of bullying and intimidation. They also got backing and support from the Congress High Command viz. Prime Minister Indira Gandhi. However, the ministry had a clear majority and continued without challenge.

Then came the Emergency of 1975. S.S. Ray fully supported Indira Gandhi in this. In fact, he was said to be the most important legal advisor who helped her to draft the notifications and advised on the steps that could be taken to get around the Constitution. He was one of her closest advisors. But when in March 1977, Indira Gandhi lost and Congress(I) was reduced to a minority in the Lok Sabha and the Janata Party set up commissions of enquiry against the Congress(I) for excesses during the Emergency, several of the older Congress people who had initially supported Indira Gandhi left her or ceased to give her active support. Among them was S.S. Ray. The Congress(I) was badly split in West Bengal.

So when the state assembly elections were announced for June 1977, the splintered Congress was no match for the Left Front. Several of the Left Front leaders, including Jyoti Basu, had been in detention during the Emergency. They emerged as champions of the peoples' cause. The Left Front secured an absolute and overwhelming majority. Jyoti Basu of CPI(M) was elected the party leader and formed the government. CPI(M) was the major partner in this government with RSP and the Forward Block playing a supporting role.

This time the CPI(M) acted very differently from its previous 1967 pattern. Jyoti Basu was also the home minister. One of the most important acts in public eye was to declare the 'gherao' as an illegal weapon of trade union activity. In the meanwhile some legal decisions had also been made by the high courts in this regard. The new ministry also began to suspend agitations in schools and colleges. Calcutta University began to function normally after almost a decade. Civic services were improved. Rural programmes were given high priority especially enforcement of land reform laws. Most of all, the ministry and the MLAs behaved with scrupulous honesty, set a new behavioral pattern of simple living with no display of official pomp. The result was that industries began to revive, law and order was better enforced, people's confidence was restored and on the whole things began to look up.

In 1977, the Janata Government appointed Tribhuvan Narain Singh as governor of West Bengal. He was an old Congress (O) worker, who had left Indira Gandhi in the 1969 split and gone along with Morarji Desai and others. Although politically not a Left Front ideologist, he was a keen supporter of the Left Front Government.

New elections to the state assembly were due in June 1982. From about the middle of 1981, Indira Gandhi began to think and prepare for the next election. Prospects in West

Bengal looked bleak. The ministry was well entrenched and the Congress(I) badly divided. It had no leaders of any stature and whoever remained, did not see eye to eye. The idea of removing the government, having a spell of President's Rule, rehabilitating the party and then holding the elections began to take shape. The first step in this direction had to be the removal of the Governor T.N. Singh. Emissaries were sent to him to get him to agree to a shift from West Bengal. He declined—perhaps he saw through the game. Then greater pressure was put on him. He finally agreed to resign and conveyed this to the President, Neelam Sanjiva Reddy. These moves went on for a couple of months or so. And it was around this time that my name began to be bandied about.

*

One evening in late August 1981, Dr P.C. Alexander and his wife came to see us at our house at 4 Lodi Estate. Dr P.C. Alexander was the principal secretary to the prime minister and a former IAS officer of Kerala, who had left behind a UN job in Geneva to take up this assignment. He asked me about my attitude to communism. I said that while communism obviously had some good features, its attitude of suppressing dissent, one-party rule, etc., were certainly not a welcome feature and could not be supported. In that sense I would be anti-communist and not pro-communist. The conversation ended there.

He came to see me again a few days later, and then said that my name was being mentioned for the governorship of West Bengal. He also hinted that the ministry was engaging in several unconstitutional acts that were against the interest of the country and the Prime Minister was not very happy about this. I think it was on 7 or 8 September that he rang me up in office and asked me to see him urgently. When I reached his office he said that T.N. Singh had decided to resign and leave Calcutta on September 11 (I am not sure of the exact date), and that the government did not want a stop-gap arrangement of asking the chief justice to act as governor, so they wanted me to immediately go to Calcutta. He also said that the proposal had been approved by the Prime Minister and President and that the Warrant of Appointment was being issued and would reach me in a few hours.

I began making preparations to leave. In the two days I had left in Delhi, I could not meet the Prime Minister despite attempts to find out if she had any brief for me. I met President Sanjiva Reddy who said he had asked T.N. Singh to go to some other state, Rajasthan or Gujarat, and not to resign, but he had not agreed. I did meet Pranab Mukherjee, who was then finance minister, and a very close and important confidante of Indira Gandhi. Although he had failed to get elected from West Bengal, and came to the Rajya Sabha from Gujarat, he was an important advisor on affairs regarding West Bengal. He vaguely remarked that nothing happened in West Bengal during the ten days of Puja activities as everyone was busy with the celebrations, so if changes were made during this period it would allow for some breathing time. This struck a chord with me and I said I would have to see after reaching Calcutta.

We arrived in Calcutta on September 11 or 12 in the morning at about 8.30 a.m. by an Indian Airlines flight. Jyoti Basu, together with the chief secretary and a few others, was there to meet us at the airport. From there we drove to the Raj Bhavan.

The Raj Bhavan at Calcutta is the biggest in India, second only to the Rashtrapati Bhavan. It was built nearly 200 years ago by Lord Wellesley, then governor general of India. He had wanted a fitting residence for the representative of Great Britain and did not want England to rule from the 'counting house'. It is a huge, three-storey structure with over a hundred rooms and a very broad and wide staircase leading up to the first floor. The main banquet hall on the first floor can seat a hundred people for dinner. The ballroom on the second floor at one time accommodated three thousand couples at a dance. Lord Curzon, who was the governor general and viceroy at the beginning of the twentieth century, has written a very interesting account of this building and some of its important occupants. This work was completed by Lord Curzon in 1925. This Raj Bhavan was the residence of the governor generals and later viceroys of India until 1911 when the capital shifted to Delhi. At that time many valuable portraits and paintings, furniture, and chandeliers were moved to Delhi. The building then became the residence of the governor of Bengal and later in 1947 that of West Bengal. There remain several interesting antiquities, such as the throne of Tipu Sultan captured after the battle of Seringapatam, trophies from the Burmese Wars—among them a canon, and some chandeliers going back to the time when the building was constructed. There are also the busts of twelve Caesars in marble which were shipped from England as part of the decorations. However, the building stands in the heart of Calcutta because of which the grounds are very inadequate, though it is surrounded by trees, flowering shrubs and a well-maintained garden.

Most of the building consists of public rooms, reception rooms, offices, and some godowns. The governor has just three rooms for his personal use on the second floor. One room is used as a sitting room, dining room and office room after working hours. There is a small pantry for cooking private meals. Then there are two bedrooms, with two bathrooms, but no dressing rooms. Admittedly the rooms are big, but guests have to be put up in rooms in another wing of the Raj Bhavan, quite a distance away. We had to communicate with our children in the other wing by telephone!

The lawn on the south side is the only private one. The main entrance which is also the entrance for staff and visitors is in the north. This southern lawn has unfortunately been somewhat marred and disfigured by the construction of an ugly dak-bungalow-esque single-storey structure consisting of four rooms by my predecessor, T.N. Singh. The Janata Government, in 1977, announced that the President and governors would move to smaller houses and not live in the present Raj Bhavans. However, it was found that the cost of constructing a so-called smaller house, with at least three or four bedrooms, two reception rooms, a dining room, with all the attendant security requirements would be quite expensive. The estimates varied from Rs 10–50 lakhs and upwards. Everywhere else, the idea was given up. Even in West Bengal, the state government refused to sanction a new building at the cost of Rs 10 lakhs. However, T.N. Singh got some old building material, marble slabs, teak timber, etc., from the Barrackpore property and then using bricks and a minimum of fittings got this ugly structure constructed at a nominal expense of about Rs 2 lakhs. But if the costs of all the materials, including that brought from Barrackpore, the fittings taken out from main Raj Bhavan etc., are all computed, then this building cost would work out to be about Rs 5 lakhs. It is an uncomfortable and ugly structure and has spoiled the lawns and the garden. Even before I left Delhi I had told everyone concerned that I would not live in this building, but would stay in the main Raj Bhavan, where the offices, visitor rooms, guest rooms, dining rooms continued to be located.

In Calcutta, there is an interesting custom that when a new governor arrives, he walks up the flight of steps at the front of the grand structure, lined with a red carpet, with the staff lined up on one side to welcome him. The next time this grand staircase is used is when the governor finally departs, dead or alive.

We went to call on T.N. Singh in his 'bungalow'. I was acquainted with him. We had lunch together. It was a hot and sweltering day. He was to move out of the Raj Bhavan at 3 p.m. and go to the Ramakrishna Mission's guest house at the Institute of Culture in Golpark for a few hours before entraining for Benares (Varanasi) at about 7 p.m. I told him he could have stayed in the Raj Bhavan itself as it was quite in accordance with precedent, but he had already made alternative arrangements. While conversing, he sounded somewhat bitter at the way he was being asked to leave West Bengal. He was critical of the centre's approach to Bengal and said all this was being done because, politically, he belonged to the opposition, the old Congress (O).

The first few days were busy with visitors. There was not much work. Chief Minister Jyoti Basu came to see me. He was very proper and affable. Earlier he had sent Finance Minister Dr Ashok Mitra to see me. Jyoti Basu offered me full cooperation, said I could send for him whenever I thought necessary. He even offered to ask his ministers, the chief secretary and senior government servants to call on me and explain whatever I wanted to know. In order to get to know the officers, I had requested that their confidential character records be sent to me for my perusal. As there were a number of callers, specially government servants whom I had known for a long number of years, I decided that I would best meet them in small groups for tea in the afternoons. As I held a number of such tea parties they were commented on in the press as 'tea parleys' held by me to assess the political situation in the state. Several interesting cartoons were published. We had a dog—Sheba—a fox terrier bitch. In one cartoon, I was shown with this dog and Jyoti Basu with another—an alsatian—both dogs on leash but snarling at each other. Then there was a widely quoted remark made by the General Secretary of the CPI(M) and Chairman of the

Left Front, Promode Dasgupta, who was a very influential and powerful political figure, saying that I had been sent to disrupt the Bengal administration. He called me 'Bangla Daman' Pande, i.e., Bengal Suppressor Pande. Promode Dasgupta had not met me then, nor did he for almost a year.

Large numbers of Congressmen came in groups to meet me and gave me memoranda listing atrocities on them by the CPI(M). Upon enquiry, most of these complaints turned out to be either family or land disputes, ten-year old disputes already settled by courts, or of clashes between groups of people who could only be called the lumpenproletariate. The Prime Minister would write to Jyoti Basu conveying the details of these complaints, and he would reply that on enquiry they had been found false or that action had already been taken wherever necessary. At the same time he sent her an equally large number of instances where the CPI(M) workers had been attacked or killed by Congress(I) workers. So charges and counter charges were being levelled against each other. Complaints regarding appointments were made, almost all on political grounds. One interesting thing I found in West Bengal was that there were no complaints relating to caste, communal, tribal or sexual discrimination—it was always political, whether from the Left Front or the Congress.

The local All India Radio and Doordarshan directors also came to see me and said that they had received instructions from Delhi to the effect that they should give maximum publicity to whatever I did or wanted to say. This was also part of the plan.

A few days later, a group of prominent Congressmen came to see me, headed by Ananda Gopal Mukherjee, president of the West Bengal Pradesh Congress Committee (WBPCC (I)). He was an MP from the Asansol area and a prominent trade union leader. After discussing the usual subjects of breakdown of law and order and attacks on party cadres by the Marxists, the deputation withdrew, but Mukherjee stayed behind to have a few words with me in confidence. He said that I should not recommend or impose President's rule. When asked why, he said that if President's rule were to be imposed the Marxists would become martyrs and whenever elections were held thereafter they would sweep the polls and the Congress would be completely wiped out. I asked him if he had made his views known to the central party leadership. He said he had hinted on it but it was not making any impact. He felt that my recommendation would have greater weight. Being a lifelong Congressman, he did not want the party to be eliminated from West Bengal where, over the years, it had played such an important part.

It was interesting to note that during the first few months of my stay in West Bengal, everyone who came to see me, especially from Delhi and also others, always advised me to get the rooms checked out in case they had been bugged. Some even went to the extent of advising that I should hold my talks with people, if they had any political concern, in the lawns of the Raj Bhavan to eliminate the possibility of bugging or eavesdropping.

Yet another point often raised was the existence of party 'cells' in all departments of the government, including even the Governor's Secretariate. It was common knowledge that any important decision taken in any department or office was immediately known to this 'cell' and promptly passed on to the party secretariat. The party then intervened if necessary; ministers were summoned to take corrective or appropriate action in the interests of the party. For this reason it was suggested to me that I should see that any letters I wrote to the Prime Minister, Home Minister, etc., which had any bearing on the situation in West Bengal, should not be allowed access by the Governor's Secretariat, but should be dealt with only in the private office or the office of the governor's secretary who again should be a reliable man, preferably a non-Bengali. As it happened, the secretary was one L.R.K. Prasad, a Bihari belonging to the Bengal cadre of the IAS, and he was to continue all through my tenure in Calcutta.

A fortnight or so later we again went to Delhi to bring our belongings and also to meet Mrs Gandhi. I told her about my preliminary assessment of the state of affairs, which included the difficult power supply situation, public dissatisfaction on civic and other services, the difficult financial situation in the state, and also mentioned the views of the president of the WBPCC (I). I also mentioned my plans of leaving for Darjeeling to spend a few weeks there during October which was the Puja season.

*

The Darjeeling Raj Bhavan is a very beautiful structure. It was built in 1936, after the great earthquake of 1934 when the old one fell down. The gardens are especially pretty and the flowers very lovely. The old compound was very large, but gradually portions had been given away for other purposes, such as the Mountaineering Institute which was established after the first conquest of Mt Everest by Edmund Hillary and Tenzing Norgay in 1953, and the establishment of a Himalayan zoo, later a public park, the offices of the Hill Development Secretariat and the headquarters of the Darjeeling Superintendent of Police. Despite this reduction in area, the Darjeeling Raj Bhavan remains a very attractive and pleasant place.

A few months later, I had again gone to Delhi. The President was hosting a banquet for some visiting dignitary and we were also invited. I met Mrs Gandhi there. She drew me aside and told me that I should be sure to meet Sankar Prasad Mitra (MP Rajya Sabha) and Ashoke Sen (former law minister). No mention was made of Siddhartha Shankar Ray.

Sankar Prasad Mitra had been the chief justice of the Calcutta High Court, earlier an active Congress worker, who upon retirement, was elected to the Rajya Sabha as a jointly sponsored candidate by the Janata and Congress parties of West Bengal. The Janata was, by now, not very happy with the Marxists in West Bengal as the latter gave them no encouragement. I asked Sankar Prasad Mitra to come and see me. He did so, and then gave me his private telephone number and asked for my unlisted telephone number so that he could talk to me in confidence. I asked him about President's rule. He asked whether the Prime Minister had suggested that I meet him. I confirmed that was why I was asking him for his opinion. He said he would let me know after sometime and would give me a note giving possible grounds. However, he never did so. Perhaps he had none.

I got a similar response from Ashoke Sen. He told me that there were very good grounds for such a course of action. I suggested he put them down in writing for my consideration. Again, nothing came out of it.

But propaganda from Delhi continued. Statements by people like Pranab Mukherjee or A.B.A. Ghani Khan Choudhury, about the desperate situation in West Bengal (financial mismanagement, bad law and order, etc.) continued to be aired in the press. Teams of officers would come and give somewhat similar reports. The war of nerves, shall I say, was maintained till well into the beginning of 1982, especially as the elections approached. The West Bengal Ministry proposed the elections for March which was a suitable time weather-wise, instead of the due date in late May or June when it would be very hot. But this was not agreed to by the Government of India or the Chief Election Commissioner. Complaints were made about the defective electoral rolls, about wholesale deletion of names, and more.

Some of the Left Front partners were also sought to be bought over to the Congress fold. One of these who appeared to be weakening was the Deputy Speaker of the Assembly—a Muslim gentleman from Gaya, but a trade union leader of the port workers in Calcutta. However, he ultimately did not go over to the Congress, though he gave me enough indications of his desire to do so.

The Congress(I) made desperate attempts to have the elections postponed or at least to see that they were not held by the due date. Writ petitions were filed by the Calcutta High Court about the defective rolls asking for a direction that elections be postponed until they were rectified. Calcutta High Court gave such a ruling. The West Bengal Government and others went on appeal to the Supreme Court against the order of the high court. The Supreme Court set the high court order aside and the stage was finally set for the elections. They were held on the last few days available in May 1982. The Left Front emerged victorious with a large and comfortable majority. The CPI(M) emerged as the single largest party with an absolute majority in the assembly. The Congress(I) also did well, doubling its membership from about twenty-five to a little less than fifty. Other parties, like the Janata, BJP, Lok Dal were wholly eliminated from the scene. In retrospect, the Congress was happy that they had improved their representation and the decision to not impose President's rule had helped.

An interesting episode ocurred during the 1982 elections. Just a few days before polling, after nominations had been filed and scrutinized and the last date for withdrawal had passed, one sitting MP and now a Congress(I) candidate in Nadia district, Krishnagar town—a Moitra—mysteriously disappeared after 10 p.m. The disappearance was reported to the police next morning at 8 a.m. and it was said that two other important local people had also disappeared. The story that then followed was that they had been kidnapped by a gang of Naxalite extremists. As no trace of them could be found by the police for a day or so, rumours began to float that they had been murdered and that therefore the elections should be postponed. The Chief Minister and the Marxists held that this was all a hoax, that Shri Moitra was always hobnobbing with the Naxalites and that the Congress was behind the drama. When the Election Commission refused to postpone the polling, these people resurfaced in Calcutta early one morning saying that they had been put on a train at Burdwan and had been kidnapped. The police refused to believe their story as it was not supported by any evidence. Later, Shri Moitra, who was himself a lawyer, refused to give any statement to the police or help in any investigation. There was no doubt that this was a drama enacted to win public sympathy for Congress and to discredit the government on grounds of failure to maintain law and order. Naturally, it had no effect.

The ministry was sworn-in in two stages: first the chief minister and four others, and after a lapse of about three weeks some thirty other ministers. In the interim I went to Darjeeling for the summer and came down for a couple of days for the second swearing-in ceremony. It lasted nearly an hour and a half and I had to remain standing all the while as minister followed minister. Later on, this practice of swearing in ministers individually was given up. A new precedent was set in Delhi by an en masse induction of cabinet ministers, ministers of state and deputy ministers. This saved a great deal of time. States also began to follow this practice later. But I have never liked it.

*

During my tenure, whenever Mrs Gandhi came on tour to West Bengal and had to stay overnight at Calcutta, she always liked to have a very quiet dinner alone. But often before dinner she had half an hour or so free. This is when she would send for me to discuss the prevailing situation in the state or to know my view on some suggestions made by her party members. At one such meeting I was able to suggest to her that the 200-year-old Asiatic Society be declared an institute of national importance.

My subsequent stay in Bengal continued to be pleasant enough. Relations with the party in power were good. We got on well with Mr and Mrs Jyoti Basu. They would often come over for dinner and stay on for a couple hours or so. Once when the swearing-in ceremony of the government was taking place, Promode Dasgupta also came and attended the function at Raj Bhavan. He told me that it was the first time he had come to Raj Bhavan and that they had all revised their earlier impression of me.

My wife and I were welcomed wherever we went—whether in Calcutta or the district—urban or rural areas. All political parties would attend the public functions. Several of my friends and relatives also visited.

We had a pleasant interlude when I visited Nainital and Almora in October 1982 as governor. I was the first person from the Kumaon-Garhwal hills to have become governor of a state. So some well-attended public functions were organized at the GIC in Almora where I had been a student.

Some of the more memorable visits include a very enjoyable visit to Gangasagar in February 1983, albeit a cold rainy day. Another was a visit to village Rangabelia in the Sunderbans area of 24 Parganas where one Tushar Kanjilal was doing very good work in rural development in a backward area. He received recognition and a Padma Shri award in 1986. Yet another was to Nawadwipa in Nadia district, the birthplace of Chaitanya Mahaprabhu and also the new temple and rooms built by ISKCON—the International Society for Krishna Consciousness. This society has published the original *Shrimad*

Bhagavad Gita and *Shrimad Bhagavad Puran*, in beautifully bound volumes in over fifty languages of the world. They propagate the famous 'mantra':

'Hare Ram Hare Ram Ram Ram Hare Hare
Hare Krishna Hare Krishna Krishna Krishna Hare Hare'

They receive devotees from all over the world and several Europeans and Americans have become devout Vaishnavites. Visits to Jalpaiguri game sanctuaries, to Alipurduar, Cooch Behar, Murshidabad with its Hazarduari Palace, the old capital of Gaur, the Haldia port, all remain pleasant memories.

In May 1983, when we were in Darjeeling, I suddenly got an invitation from the World Bank at Washington to deliver a keynote address at an international seminar being organized for transport specialists especially from the Third World countries. The report of the National Transport Policy Committee that I had chaired earlier had attracted a great deal of favourable comments in many quarters. The World Bank was greatly appreciative as they were financing a number of transport projects in the developing countries. The Government of India accepted almost all of its important recommendations—I was told that even China had asked for fifty copies. Some Latin American and African countries were also interested. Naturally I was very pleased to receive this invitation some three years later. The Government of India agreed to let me attend the seminar. So I had to make some very hurried preparations in Darjeeling for the speech as also for the journey. I was hoping that I may be able to spend a day or two in England on my way there or back. But just at that time we had the sad news of the sudden death of my cousin, Ghanda, in Nainital. I therefore returned early. It was a sad meeting at Nainital. Ghanda had been like an elder brother to me.

Although I did not then know it, but our stay in Bengal was coming to a close. Some memories and observations regarding the Goverment and its functioning will be in order. An outstanding impression made on me was of the exemplary personal conduct of the ministers and MLAs of the Left Front. No one ever even whispered or cast aspersions on their personal character. The party discipline was strong and whenever anyone was suspected or proved to have been corrupt, he was immediately dismissed from the party. This was in sharp contrast to the reputation of ministers in some other parts of India. The civil servants, I found, were happy in working with the ministry. They were always encouraged to give their frank views and were not taken to task for it. Ministers overruled them whenever they thought necessary. Officers were not transferred whimsically. They were kept in their places for their full tenure. There was no discrimination on grounds of caste. In fact, caste considerations never came up. No one accused another group of such activities. Divisions were on political lines—pro or anti Left Front.

This was one state where I felt that Indian culture and traditions truly survived. Women and the old were given due respect. Even in the most crowded buses, people got up to give a seat to women or the elderly. Women could go about even at night without fear of molestation. There were no instances of chain snatching, bride burning, eve teasing—this was in sharp contrast to the atmosphere in Delhi. Communal trouble, killings or atrocities against Harijans and Tribals were almost non-existent. On the whole, I would consider the government as one of the cleanest and ably run. That is why it has so far survived for nearly nine years without any changes in the ministry, or frequent reshuffling of portfolios which is a common past-time of Congress(I) ministries. As of now it does not look as though the CPI(M)-dominated Left Front Ministry of West Bengal under the leadership of Jyoti Basu will be dislodged from power even in the 1987 election next year.

Public functions, or functions of schools and villages,

receptions in villages and elsewhere were very pleasantly organized and conducted. Invariably, they began with the blowing of conch shells (*shankha-dhoni*) or in the way only Bengali girls can do it, making a similar sound with their hands and fingers (*urhul-dhoni*). Flowers were tastefully decorated. Girls applied kumkum-tilak with the ring finger of the left hand—a custom different from our parts. The proceedings commenced with a Vedic hymn and beautifully rendered songs—Rabindra sangeet or Nazrul Geeti. This was so even when the Marxist ministers were present. I always felt the great contrast between the atmosphere prevalent here and that in Delhi, Uttar Pradesh, Bihar or in the West. These are all pleasant memories.

CHAPTER TEN

Punjab: The Sikhs and the Hindus

It was in October 1983 that I went to Chandigarh as governor of Punjab, for just about nine months. I wanted to write about Punjab while my memories are still fresh, but as I said in the beginning, this account may not be chronologically accurate, nor is it based on documents and records made at the time. It is based on memory only and memory is, very often, deceptive and of course forgetful. I paid no heed to Vice President Justice Hidayatullah's advice which he gave me while I was in Calcutta and more insistently later when I was in Punjab, about keeping notes of all conversations and important developments as they would be useful in the future. But there it is—such contemporary documents are not with me.

*

Let me begin first with my understanding or rather my view of the Punjab problem. This is based on my study of several books and articles and my conversations with Punjabis—Sikhs and Hindus alike.

The story begins sometime around 1849, more than a century ago. After the defeat and subsequent death of Maharaja Ranjit Singh, the Sikhs as a community were left totally disorganized and demoralized. The British allowed a few of the princely states to continue, such as Patiala, Kapurthala, Jind, Faridkot, etc. Ranjit Singh's son and heir, Gulab Singh, had turned a Christian—thus an apostate—and had gone to England where he later died. The Sikhs were left more or less leaderless. The British occupied the rest of Punjab and brought it under their direct rule. This victory of the British, it should be noted, was won by the Bengali and Bihari, that is Eastern Indian soldiers, trained and commanded by the British. Then came the Civil War or Mutiny of 1857, by both the Hindu and Muslim elements of the British Indian Army. At this time, when the British were fighting their last war with the troops of the last Mughal Emperor, they recruited the defeated and demoralized Sikh peasantry and remnants of Ranjit Singh's Army in large numbers. The main reason behind this was the known traditional enmity of the Sikhs against the Muslims. To trace this, one has to go back five centuries to the days of Guru Nanak Deb.

*

When the Muslim empire's rule was advancing over the length and breadth of India during the fourteenth and fifteenth centuries, Hinduism had to fight a new kind of battle for its survival against Islam. Islam preached a formless, supreme God, was against image or idol worship, and all its followers were equal—there was no distinction of caste. As part of their campaign, or holy wars, against the 'non-believers' or infidels, Hindu temples and idols were destroyed and Hindus were forcibly converted to Islam. To counter this attack and save Hinduism, there appeared throughout the length and breadth of India a number of preachers and seers, almost contemporaneously. They all preached the cult of 'Bhakti' or devotion to God and said that all that was required was to have faith in Him, and to recite His name. Worship of idols in temples was not necessary, the orthodox rituals need not be observed, caste distinctions were not ordained by God—all were equal in His eyes and all who had faith and devotion attained salvation. 'Jap'—recitation of His name and 'Sankirtan'—singing His praises, was all that was required of man.

Such preachers appeared in all parts of India and spoke to people in the local language, most often in verse which could be easily remembered and sung. Among these were Chaitanya Mahaprabhu in Bengal and Orissa, Shankardev in Assam, Tulsi Das and Surdas in Uttar Pradesh, Nanak Deb in Punjab, Mira Bai in Rajasthan and Gujarat, Namdeo in Maharashtra and so on. Many appeared in the South too, I do not readily recall their names. This Bhakti cult preached the existence of One Supreme God—a formless God or Nirankar—by not insisting on temple and image worship, removing distinctions of caste and creed, and preaching the unity of mankind, they were successful in resisting the advance of Islam. Perceptive historians have noted that Hinduism, the most ancient living religion in the world, has gone through phases and deep convulsions from time to time, but has had an inner strength to reform and revitalize itself, surviving millenia. Hinduism recognizes the essential unity of all religions, that different paths lead to the same One, that the great preachers of all religions, Buddha, Mohammad, Jesus Christ are all manifestations or 'avatars' of the Divine God to save mankind from sin and affliction.

Guru Nanak Deb in Punjab was one such preacher. He travelled through the length and breadth of India, came to the Himalayas to meditate like other seers of the past and was a Hindu. His direct descendants are still called 'Bedis' or knowers of the 'Ved', the most ancient Hindu revered scripture. A line of his followers still exists in Punjab. They go by the name of Udasins and recite the *Granth Sahib* at many places of worship.

In fact they have an 'akhara', as it is called, in one corner of the Golden Temple complex in Amritsar—the Brahmbuta Akhara. There is another branch of Nanak Deb's followers called Nanak Panthis. They were mainly present in Sind as also in other parts of India. The modern Sikhs do not recognize these groups as true Sikhs. Following Guru Nanak Deb, came several gurus one after the other. They were all Hindus and recognized themselves as such, but they preached the unity of God and absence of caste. The martyrdom of the fifth and ninth gurus, Guru Arjun Deb and Guru Teg Bahadur, needs special mention. They were beheaded by the Mughal Muslim rulers for their insistence on the right to freedom of worship according to their faith, namely Hinduism. In the case of Guru Teg Bahadur, it is said that a party of Kashmiri Hindu Pandits came to him and asked him to fight their cause. They said that their sacred thread was being forcibly cut and their head shaved, with the 'chutiya' being removed by the Muslim invaders in Kashmir. They told Guru Teg Bahadur that they had selected him as their leader because he was a fearless man and known for his intrepid honesty and courage of conviction. This trait of fearlessness, of standing up for their faith, is a recurrent theme in the lives of all the Sikh gurus and later among their followers. Guru Teg Bahadur agreed and came to the Mughal Court at Delhi and asked them to stop this atrocity. He was not heeded and, on the charge of sedition and rebellion against the Emperor, was beheaded at the place where Gurdwara Sisganj in Chandni Chowk Delhi stands today. One of his followers surreptitiously removed his head at night and brought it to Gurdwara Rakabganj in New Delhi and later it was taken to Anandpur Sahib in Punjab where it was finally cremated. Gurdwara Keshgarh Sahib exists at that spot today.

The tenth and last Guru, Guru Govind Singh, then took up the fight. Guru Govind Singh was born in Patna (Bihar).

But it was at Anandpur Sahib on Baisakhi Day, usually the 'Sankrant' day, which falls in mid-April in the year 1699, that Guru Govind Singh formed his 'Khalsa'—the pure. He initiated five of his most devoted followers to take a special oath for the preservation of their religion and formed a special militant sect to fight the Mughals and the Muslim invaders. The special oath involved the keeping of the five 'K's' by the followers all the time. They are the hair (kesh), the comb (kangha), the wrist band (kara), the loin cloth (kutchha) and the sword (kirpan). He also declared that there would be no succession of gurus or preachers, he was the last, and thereafter his followers should consider the recorded preachings of all the past ten gurus, now known as the *Guru Granth Sahib*, as the teaching. But it may be mentioned here that Guru Govind Singh also wrote a version of the Ramayana and also a special prayer to Debi (the Eternal Mother Goddess). In fact, Anandpur Sahib stands at the foot of a hillock at the top of which is a temple of the Goddess.

Guru Govind Singh formed his band of sword-bearing militant followers for the protection of Hinduism, the right of the Hindus to follow their own mode of worship and fight against forcible conversion to Islam. He waged a relentless war with the armies of Emperor Aurangzeb. There were several feelers for peace but nothing came of it. After years of fighting and skirmishes, which took both parties to the Deccan, both died more or less at the same time in 1707—Emperor Aurangzeb in Aurangabad and Guru Govind Singh at Nanded in Maharashtra. But the followers of Guru Govind Singh did not surrender. They kept up the fight. Guru Govind Singh said that his followers formed a special *quom*. This is an Arabic word and can mean many things. It basically means a group of people united together by a common bond. It can be used to describe a nation, a tribe, a caste, a language group. He also said that all members of this common heritage must help one another and be united to preserve their individuality. The Sikh *quom* was formed in this way, somewhat distinct and united by the outwardly observance of the five Ks, the most distinctive being the long unshorn hair of the head and beard; by their method of worship, by the teaching of the *Guru Granth Sahib*, without idols, without distinction of caste, eating their meals together, with simplified forms of marriage, etc. The Sikh guerillas continued to fight the Muslim invaders. When Nadir Shah attacked Delhi and invaded India, they caused a great deal of harassment to Nadir Shah's forces. Twice he demolished the Akal Takht at Amritsar on grounds that it housed the guerillas and was a centre of clandestine activity. But the Sikhs re-built it twice with their own contributions. The name of Baba Jassa Singh Ahluwalia, the founder of the house of Kapurthala, is associated with this rebuilding venture, also known as 'kar sewa'. This was 250 years ago.

In more recent times also, the Sikhs and Hindus have been together on one side and Muslims on the other. This was amply demonstrated in the pre-partition and post-partition communal riots at the time of Independence, during the Great Calcutta Killings of 1946 and the Punjab riots of 1947. The unity between the two communities—Hindu and Sikh—is demonstrated by the free inter-marriages between the Sikhs and Hindus and free and unrestricted dining. Both communities shun beef and observe the same eating habits. Very often the eldest son of a family is Sikh, given over to the service of the Gurus as a vow by the parents, and the younger sons remain Hindu.

*

Aware of this deep-rooted hostility and facing a revolt at the hands of their recruits from Eastern India, the British decided to enlist the demoralized Sikhs in their favour. Having defeated them, the British now recruited them in large numbers. Several of the Sikh Infantry fought with the British against the Mughal and the mutineers of 1857. After their victory, the British rewarded the Sikhs even more. They were declared a martial race and their recruitment into the Indian Army was greatly increased. As they were very good farmers, when new land was colonized in Western Punjab, the ex-servicemen—Sikh soldiers—were given large tracts of land to cultivate under irrigated conditions. The British did not make the mistake of extending the Permanent Settlement of Bengal, instead they dealt directly with the peasant farmer owners. The community and Punjab both prospered. The Sikhs became beholden to the British for their prosperity, and the British had a reliable band of soldiers.

Although generally considered loyal by the British, the Sikhs played a very important part in the struggle for Independence. They first came into prominence at the time of what was called the Gaddar Movement. Many Sikhs were killed by British troops near Budge Budge in Calcutta. Then they suffered greatly at the time of the Jallianwala Bagh Massacre. Although the British compelled the Golden Temple authorities to present a 'saropa' to General Dyer—the man responsible for the massacre—the Sikh nursed such a hatred against this man, and then governor of Punjab, Sir Michael O'Dyer, that almost twenty years later, when he was living in Britain after his retirement, a Sikh youth of Sangrur district shot him dead in England in 1940. He was sentenced to death and hanged, but Punjab, especially Sangrur district, honours his memory even today.

In the cellular jail of the Andaman Islands at Port Blair, where the names of political prisoners sentenced to transportation for life are written, one finds the largest number belonging to either Bengal or Punjab, and includes a large number of Sikhs. Then there is the celebrated martyr Bhagat Singh, who along with his two Hindu colleagues, was cremated at Hussainiwala on the charge of conspiracy of waging war against the King. He had thrown a bomb in the Central Legislative Assembly in 1929. There were other cases too.

While the bonds and closeness of identity between Hindus and Sikhs persisted without a break all these years, the British continued to follow a very well-thought-out policy of separating the two communities. Their colonial policy of 'divide and rule' was applied wherever and whenever possible. In the case of the Sikhs, in about 1880, i.e., a century or so ago, very little distinction seemed to exist between the Sikhs and Hindus. The number of people observing the prominent five tenets was not large. Although members of both communities heard the recitations from the *Guru Granth Sahib* and worshipped it, this time period also saw the control of several gurdwaras taken over by Hindu mahants and idols of Hindu gods and goddesses installed therein. Even the Golden Temple had idols of Hindu gods and goddesses, against the teachings of the Sikh gurus who did not favour idol worship.

To begin with, the British insisted that all Sikhs recruited into the Army must abide by the five tenets, especially the long uncut hair. They were required to take an oath of fidelity on the *Granth Sahib*. The British also appointed special preachers to teach the soldiers about Sikh religion and established special gurdwaras for them. Recruitment was also made in such a manner that the Sikhs formed separate special battalions and regiments of their own like the Sikh Infantry, the Sikh Light Cavalry, the Sikh Rifles, and so on.

The British also commissioned some scholars to write on Sikhism. The first such book was written by a German scholar—I am forgetting his name. He had made a deep study of the *Granth Sahib*. He came to the conclusion that Sikhism was essentially a Hindu reformed sect and not a separate religion as such. This was not to the liking of the British authorities. They next commissioned a British scholar to write on Sikhism. This gentleman, Macauliffe, propounded the theory that Sikhism was a new and separate religion, nearer to Islam than Hinduism. He emphasized the fact that Guru Nanak Deb had visited Mecca and that he preached against idol worship, caste distinctions, and of a formless God, like Muslims. But nowhere in the *Granth Sahib* is there any acceptance of Islam as a religion to be followed to the exclusion of Hindu philosophy. The Sikhs believe in reincarnation as do Hindus, their descriptions of heaven and hell are not like those of Muslims. But this book was very helpful to the British. They immediately got it published in large numbers and ensured that it was widely circulated especially among the Sikh intelligentsia. About the same time they set up the Chief Khalsa Diwan. This was a body of eminent Sikhs, loyal to the British. It was given official patronage and Sikhs were encouraged to recognize themselves as separate from Hindus and were also encouraged to submit petitions to the British Government for special concessions and considerations of their community because of their loyalty and because they were different from Hindus. The Chief Khalsa Diwan was also encouraged to set up a number of educational institutions, especially for members of their community, called Khalsa Colleges.

At about the same time, a reform movement started among the Hindus also—the Arya Samaj. The founder of this movement, Swami Dayanand Saraswati, was a Gujarati and a learned man who had made a special study of Hinduism in Benares. He came to Punjab where he attracted a very large number of followers. He preached that Hindus should go back to their ancient religion as propounded in the Vedas. He denounced the subsequent faith based on the Puranas. Thus he denounced idol and temple worship, he wanted the forms of prayers to be simplified, denied the need of a priestly Brahmin caste, favoured and practised reconversion to Hinduism—which is not accepted in the Sanatan Dharma. He was a great critic of Christianity, Islam, Sikhism (which he said was a nondescript form of Hinduism), Jainism, and Buddhism. In other words, the only true religion, according to him, was the Vedic religion of the Aryas and his followers formed what is today called the Arya Samaj. This movement in Punjab spread rapidly and attracted a large number of adherents. Special stress was laid on education and special institutions called Dayanand Anglo-Vedic (DAV) schools and colleges were set up at many places. As the teachers and the management were devoted Arya Samajis, they attracted a large number of students and in a sense revived and boosted Hinduism.

But a curious historical phenomenon is that this period (1880–1890) also saw the emergence of several other sects in the central part of Punjab, round about the Lahore-Amritsar area. Among the Sikhs three new sects came up—the Nirankaris, Namdharis and the Radhasoamis. These sects accepted the *Granth Sahib* but said that for proper realization of Godhood, the blessings of a living saint or guru are essential. The Nirankaris and Radhasoamis also attracted a large number of Hindus. These groups are not recognized today by the orthodox as true Sikhs.

A new movement started in Islam as well—in the village Qadian by one Ahmed, whose followers were called Ahmediyas. They worshiped the Quran and followed the tenets, but said that this Ahmed was a new and modern prophet sent to revitalize the teachings of the Quran. They are considered heretics by the orthodox Muslims and are not recognized as Muslims. In fact, they are forbidden in Pakistan, for example, from calling themselves Muslims. But this creed also attracted a large number of very educated and well-placed Muslims who occupied important positions in the government and social life. A former judge of the Supreme Court, foreign minister of Pakistan and a judge at the International Court of Justice at the Hague, Zafrullah Khan, was an Ahmediya or Qadiani, who later was not allowed entry into Pakistan.

We thus have a veritable profusion of creeds and sects growing in Punjab from about the end of the last century carrying on to the present one. A rift began to develop between the Nirankaris and the Orthodox Sikhs. The Nirankaris published their own literature and books and the heads of their missions were also called 'gurus', living teachers of the faith, somewhat therefore in defiance of the edict of the tenth Guru Gobind Singh that only the *Granth Sahib* would henceforth be the 'living' guru. In 1978, the Nirankaris held a big congregation (samagam) at Amritsar. This was when the Akali Government was in power in Punjab with Parkash Singh Badal as the chief minister. The Akalis and the more fundamentalist Sikhs began to oppose this gathering. They decided at a meeting (at which Jarnail Singh Bhindranwale was also present) to send a protest demonstration group to this congregation. Jarnail Singh backed out at the last moment and one Fauja Singh, a former Punjab Government official, led this demonstration. Violence was apprehended, but the police did not restrain this group. When they reached near the congregation site there was a clash. Some Nirankaris and some Akalis were killed. A case was filed against the Nirankaris. The trial was held in Haryana as the accused said they would not get justice in Punjab. They were all acquitted on grounds that they had been attacked and had therefore exercised their right to self-defence. The Akalis were dissatisfied with this judgement. The wife of Fauja Singh, Bibi Amarjit Kaur, was the leader of what was called the Akhand Kirtani Jatha. This was a group of trained singers and preachers who would go from village to village or house to house and hold an 'akhand kirtan', a non-stop recitation, of the *Granth Sahib* which usually lasted three days and nights. She decided on vengeance and called Jarnail Singh a coward. At about this time, the five head priests ex-communicated the Nirankaris—'tankhaiyas'. The Nirankaris offered to remove any objectionable portions in their books which the Akali Sikhs considered as derogatory to their gurus. But this offer remains unheeded even today. In the meantime, a fanatical band began killing Nirankaris. They killed their head of mission despite strict guard. They attacked a senior IAS officer of the Punjab Government in the Chandigarh Secretariat and although he escaped unhurt, his brother and guard were killed. At isolated and scattered places, not only in Punjab, but in states like Uttar Pradesh, Madhya Pradesh and elsewhere, over thirty Nirankaris had been killed by gangs of extremists, while I was in Punjab, in 1984. This was one aspect of Punjab terrorism—a desire to score even with the Nirankaris. The feud between these two factions has not yet ended.

Similarly, the orthodox Akali Sikhs do not recognize the Radhasoami sect followers. These people have a very big campus on the banks of the river Beas between Amritsar and Jalandhar. The sect attracts a large number of Hindus and Sikhs and also a number of foreigners, Europeans and Americans. They stress on a good moral life, vegetarian food, simple living and meditation. Most, if not all, prayers are from the *Granth Sahib*. The heads of this mission have, I think, been all Sikhs. Originally this sect was founded at Agra. That became a purely Hindu sect more or less at Dayabagh and now bears no connection with the Beas branch. Some very prominent Radhasoamis whom I had always thought were Sikhs told me (while I was in Punjab), that the orthodox Sikhs did not recognize them as Sikhs. One of them was a very prominent industrialist of Delhi and Punjab, and another a very senior civil servant of the Punjab Government. I was very surprised to learn this and of the divisions that had taken place among the Sikh community on what may be called religious practices and interpretations.

The Sikh reform under the Chief Khalsa Diwan continued side by side. Around 1920, they started removing the Hindu mahants from the control of the gurdwaras. There was a very big agitation in 1921–22, to change the control and administration of Nankana Sahib, one of the most revered of gurdwaras connected with Guru Nanak, that is now in Pakistan. More than 200 Sikhs were killed. The British Government then enacted the Sikh Gurdwara Act. Under this act, the Shiromani Gurdwara Parbandakh Committee (SGPC) was elected from among the Sikh community and placed incharge of what were called the historic gurdwaras of the then undivided Punjab—that included present-day Pakistan (now outside its jurisdiction), Punjab, Haryana, and Himachal Pradesh. The SGPC has, in the last sixty years, become a powerful body with large sums of money at its disposal and it looks after a number of gurdwaras. It has improved the administration of the gurdwaras, removed the powerful mahants and Hindu influences. All donations are collected and utilized and accounted for by the SGPC. It trains priests, singers, publishes books, appoints guards called 'sewadars' to look after the gurdwara property and runs the communal kitchens. The SGPC is thus the controlling body for running and maintaining all the important gurdwaras, especially in Punjab.

At about the same time, in the early 1920s, the Sikhs formed a political party of their own called the Shiromani Akali Dal. As the British had initiated reforms towards self-rule in India, they encouraged the Akali Dal too and gave prominence to the demands of this group for special representation of the Sikhs in the Provincial legislature, reservation of seats and separate constituencies with separate electoral rolls. While the Muslims were given separate special representation in all the Provincial

Assemblies of India, Sikhs were given this representation only in Punjab. This was a special consideration because of their large representation in the Army—then almost 33%—and the special part played by them in the 1914–18 war. This was done through a greatly increased recruitment of Sikhs into the Army. So from that time onwards, the Sikhs were given special representation whenever talks of constitutional reforms took place.

Although the Indian National Congress claimed that it was the representative of all groups, religions, sects of the people of India, it could not prevent the Sikhs from having a special representation in the Round Table Conferences of 1930s or presenting their special points of view to the Cripps Mission or the Cabinet Mission of the early 1940s. In fact, the Indian National Congress, in several of their public statements made by Mahatma Gandhi, Jawaharlal Nehru and others, referred to the fact that the Sikhs would be given special consideration in Independent India. This was because of the great part this community had played in the Independence struggle. Thus in 1946, when Lord Mountbatten declared that India would be independent in August 1947, Master Tara Singh, the leader of the Akali Dal at the time, began to meet and negotiate with the British—Lord Mountbatten, the Muslim League—Mohammed Ali Jinnah, and the Congress—mainly Jawaharlal Nehru. Till almost the very end he was hopeful that along with the partition of India between a Muslim state and a predominantly Hindu state, the Sikhs would be given a separate homeland of their own in Punjab. But when the British clearly refused and told him he would have to opt either for Pakistan or India he started bargaining for the best terms from the leaders of these two parties. There was a fateful meeting with Jinnah in June 1947 who told Master Tara Singh that he would have to join Pakistan without any pre-conditions and that he would give no assurances. A meeting of the Punjab legislature was taking place then in Lahore and, in a very dramatic gesture, Master Tara Singh came out of the Assembly weilding a naked sword in his hand declaring that the Sikhs would go to India—Hindustan.

Then came the Radcliffe Award, drawing the line between India and Pakistan. Even here the Sikhs were hopeful that certain areas especially where their sacred shrines were located like Nankana Sahib would come to India. But this did not happen. The Sikhs were greatly disappointed. One of the greatest migrations in history started at this point wherein millions of people were uprooted. The entire Hindu and Sikh community from Western Pakistan moved to India and equally large numbers of Muslims moved from parts of Haryana, Delhi and Uttar Pradesh to Pakistan. Many were killed or ended up dead. There was hardly a family which was not affected. Hindus were mainly businessmen and lost their wealth. Sikhs were mainly farmers and lost their lands—mainly irrigated lands that had been developed by them with their own hard work and enterprise. In this movement, the Akali Sikhs and the Hindu RSS volunteers worked hand in hand in helping and rescuing the refugees, giving them shelter, protection and so on.

The Indian Government organized the rehabilitation of these refugees on a massive scale. No efforts or funds were spared. New land was reclaimed not only in what is now Punjab or Haryana, but even in Uttar Pradesh, Rajasthan, Madhya Pradesh, and other states. The uprooted Punjabis, both Sikhs and Hindus, were encouraged to settle wherever they liked in India, and in whatever profession they liked—agriculture, industry or business. The Punjabis are an enterprising and hardworking people. Soon they prospered wherever they settled. The Sikhs also did extremely well especially in agriculture, small industries and motor transport—the last almost a monopoly with them—as truck owners, taxi owners and drivers—whether it be in Punjab, Uttar Pradesh, or as far away as Calcutta, Assam or Bombay.

The Sikhs as a community form just about 2% of the population of India. Half of them are in Punjab and the other half spread all over the country. Even in present-day Punjab they constitute a bare majority of 52% against 48% Hindus. Before the present crisis, they were fully assimilated with the rest of the society, were considered good citizens and reliable neighbours and a brave people. But the Sikhs somehow felt that they had not got their due. It is a curious fact that other minorities who remained in India, like the Parsis, the Indian Christians, the Anglo-Indians and the Muslims felt that they would not get justice in a Hindu India. But the fact was that they were getting disproportionate benefits at the hands of the British and at the cost of the majority community. For example, special and extra weightage in the services, in the Army, in the legislatures, etc., were available to them. In contrast to the 2% representation in the country's population, the Sikhs had a 33% representation in the Army.

In the Constitution, under the chapter of Fundamental Rights, protection to the minorities was guaranteed in areas like freedom of worship, running their own schools, and so on. But special protections in services was withdrawn, for example, the Anglo Indians' special privilege of being recruited into the Indian Railways and representation in Parliament and the legislatures. The only exceptions made were for Scheduled Castes and Tribes, because of their social and economic backwardness. At the special request of the British Government, a few seats were nominated for Anglo-Indians. It is a curious historical fact that following Independence, members of several minority groups emigrated from India in fairly large numbers: Parsis and Anglo-Indians to England, Rhodesia, South Africa and Australia, Jews to Israel, Muslims to Pakistan, Sikhs to England, USA and Canada. The most important reason for minorities, other than Muslims, to leave India, was the prospect of better economic prosperity. For Muslims it was the culmination of partition—the fear of majority Hindu rule also played a part, apart from economic incentives to the Muslim community as a whole.

While all representatives of the minority interests signed the Constitution, the two Sikh representatives did not do so. They said that the assurances that the Congress had given before and at the time of Independence of a special status to the Sikhs had not been honoured. It is true that one of the representatives, Sardar Hukum Singh later became an MP, speaker of the Lok Sabha and governor of Rajasthan and on each occasion he took the oath under the Constitution. The other representative, whose name I forget, also became a member of the Punjab Legislature and took oath under the Constitution, but throughout, the Akalis maintained that the Sikhs had not been given what was promised. This fact was of course, and rightly, denied by not only the Congress but all other representatives in the Constituent Assembly. All necessary guarantees were accorded to all minorities including the Sikhs. As a result in a few years the Sikhs had become one of the most prosperous communities in India in all fields. In fact when Akalis raised the cry that the Sikhs were being discriminated against, the Government of India set up a commission under a Supreme Court judge to investigate this charge. No evidence was adduced before this commission and the Akalis boycotted it. The charge of discrimination could not be established. But despite this, Sikhs along with other minorities, especially the Muslims, Anglo-Indians and some others, have continued to harbour an undefined feeling of discrimination. Naturally, the members of the majority community, the Hindus, do not subscribe to this and if they belong to the higher castes, they vehemently resent it. I am reminded here of what I felt when I was in England, of being a member of a minority group. The non-whites in UK have a feeling of being discriminated against despite the equal laws of

England. In the USA, despite every equality of opportunity, the Blacks, the Jews, and the Red Indians remain a disaffected minority. The WASP—White Anglo-Saxon Protestant—is the Brahmin of the American society.

When a few years after Independence, the demand for linguistic states was raised throughout India and a very powerful commission was set up to look into it, there was vehement protest against the non-formation of a Punjabi-speaking state. At this point, the Punjabi Hindus openly opposed the Punjabi Sikhs and the beginning of a rift can be more openly traced to this. The Punjabi Hindus, although they all spoke Punjabi, intermarried, inter-dined and had the same customs, said that Punjabi was only their dialect (boli) but their language (bhasha) was Hindi. The Punjabi Sikhs said that Punjabi was their language as recognized in the Constitution. In fact in the Census of 1951, Hindus en masse recorded Hindi as their language. In fact some people even told me that when a Hindu enumerator came to their houses, even if they said that their language was Punjabi he recorded it as Hindi. So the battle of a Punjabi Suba took a communal tinge unlike that in any other part of India.

Here again there is a curious historical cause to be noted. With the revival (I am using this word deliberately) of Sikhism from the end of the nineteenth century, and especially after the 1920s, Sikhs began to insist on the reading and writing of Punjabi in the Gurmukhi script. Now Gurmukhi is the script in which the *Granth Sahib* is written. It is a simplified and, some would say, a corrupted form of the Devnagri script in which Hindi is written. In any case the alphabet is the same, only the script differs. Moreover, this is one of the most recent regional scripts of Devnagri, being only about three-centuries old compared with say Gujarati, Bengali, Assamese or Oriya. But in Punjab, the state language for official purposes was Urdu, written in the Persian script. Every educated person knew Urdu, primary education started with Urdu, the language of the courts was Urdu and all the vernacular papers were published in Urdu. In fact, Pandit Nehru used to say that the fight for the Punjabi Suba was being fought in the Urdu papers. At the same time, with the spread of the influence of Arya Samaj in Punjab and the establishment of the DAV schools and colleges, teaching of Hindi also spread, especially among the Hindu community. While Hindu menfolk generally were fluent in Urdu, their womenfolk were fluent in Hindi and they read Tulsi Das's *Ramcharitmanas* in Hindi. Among the Sikhs, the position was again, that the men were fluent only in Urdu, women were mostly illiterate and a few of the religious-minded Sikhs and their priests and preachers knew Gurmukhi as they read the *Granth Sahib*. The Muslims of undivided and pre-partition Punjab knew only Urdu. Thus language and script in Punjab was divided on communal lines—Hindi for Hindus, Punjabi (using the Gurmukhi script) for Sikhs and Urdu (using the Persian script) for Muslims.

If the Hindus had declared Punjabi as their language—what a different territory it may have been. But then,
'Of all the words of tongue or pen,
the saddest are these—it might have been'

*

After Partition, the majority of people in Eastern Punjab were Hindus. Sikhs formed a minority. For several years, almost two decades, the chief minister of Punjab was always a Hindu. With the declaration of one's language having taken a communal aspect, and the Sikhs feeling that they would always be in a minority and that Punjabi would never be encouraged, the demand for a Punjabi Suba began to grow. The Centre opposed it, saying that in an important border state this would be militarily dangerous and would affect the security of India. The Sikhs felt this to be a further slur on them. A community which had sacrificed so much for India's Independence, had left their homes in Western Pakistan, had fought in the wars with Pakistan with conspicuous bravery and had sacrificed in the Civil Disobedience movements—was not being given their just demand for a Punjabi Suba. Even their loyalties were being suspected, while all other language groups had been conceded their demand. Andhra, Karnataka, Maharashtra, Gujarat, etc., had all been reorganized and reformed on the basis of the linguistic principle. Only Punjab was being denied this. This gave further ground to the Akalis to agitate.

In 1967, the demand for a Punjabi Suba was conceded. If the Punjabi-speaking Hindus had also declared Punjabi as their language, the boundaries of this state would have been much different and larger than that today. If the communal aspect of the division is taken into account in the new Punjab, the Sikhs were only just a majority, 52% against 48% Hindus. Barring three or four districts, the Sikhs do not form a preponderant majority anywhere in the state. This creation of the new Punjab in 1967 also meant that only about half of the total Sikh population of India would be in Punjab and the rest scattered all over India. The Sikhs, like all communities—despite claims of being a casteless people—are divided among three broad categories. The Jat Sikhs are predominantly land-owning agriculturists, the non-Jat Sikhs are mainly in business and industry, and the Mazhabi Sikhs are mainly Scheduled Caste and therefore generally agricultural labourers. And there is one other classification—those who came from Pakistan and those who had always been part of India. These divisions also divided the Sikhs among different political parties. There was a traditional enmity between the Jats and Mazhabi Sikhs—a landlord-tenant enmity; as also between the agriculturists and non-agriculturists. The Akali Dal had its largest following among the Jat rural agricultural Sikhs. The Congress was able to attract the Mazhabi Sikhs to their fold. The non-Jat was divided. This meant that even in this bare-majority Sikh state, the Akalis could not come to power on their own, or in fact the Sikhs by themselves could not form a government without the support of a substantial section of the Hindus. This became possible in 1967 and 1969 when the Jan Sangh, a Hindu right-wing party—with the support of the small businessmen opposed to the left-oriented Congress policies—joined hands with the Akalis. This combination of Akali and Jan Sangh, for the first time, deprived the Congress of their hold and majority in Punjab.

After Independence, profound social and economic changes began to occur in the Sikh society as indeed in others. For example, among Hindus, the observance of outward forms of caste began to disappear, several social taboos were discarded. Similarly among Muslims, women gave up the purdah, specially the 'burqah'. While the British dominated the scene, the stress was on maintaining one's Indianhood. But with the departure of the British, Western styles and customs began to be freely adopted and Indian society as such became more progressive, more tolerant and permissive in terms of social norms. Among the Sikhs, this took the form of men not flaunting long hair and long beard. Such people were called 'mauna' Sikhs. The Sikhs were widely dispersed; they were becoming economically more prosperous, Punjab was the most prosperous state in India with the highest per capita income, and many had emigrated to Europe and America. This social mobility had its impact. Even women began to flaunt short hair. Both in Hindu and Sikh society, this was formerly a sign of widowhood, but it was now fashionable. Both men and women began to smoke and drink in public. There seemed hardly any outwardly differences between

Hindus and Sikhs and the latter began to get more and more assimilated as Hindus. Sikhs abroad found it more convenient for business and other purposes not to keep long hair. There were some very amusing situations. Once an Indian Sikh officer went to the USA on an Indian passport. His photograph showed him with a beard and turban. On his way back he got a haircut and shaved his beard and so was stopped by the Customs people. He was allowed re-entry after spending a long time pleading, but then the Indian Embassy had to issue him a fresh passport. The grandson of President Zail Singh once came to Calcutta, he had a clipped beard in the fashion of young men with a haircut and without a turban. Even in wayside towns and larger cities of Punjab one could see Sikh youth getting their hair and beard trimmed, and smoking.

Among women too, a great change was being witnessed. With increasing education, including higher education which had rapidly spread to rural areas, the traditional Jat woman who looked after the fields and cattle was not willing to marry an uneducated farmer, no matter if he was rich. Women were taking up jobs in the cities and becoming economically freer and willing to seek a marriage outside their caste. Sikhs settled abroad came in large numbers to get married to modern English-educated Indian girls as they felt that such marriages would make for more stable family life in the Western society.

On the negative side, economically, two factors have come to the forefront—one in agriculture and the other in defence services. The state has made enormous advances in the field of agriculture. The yields of wheat and rice in Punjab are among the highest in the world. Punjab, with a bare 2% of the geographical area of the country, contributes around 50% or more of the total procurement made by the Food Corporation of India for the Public Distribution System. The total purchases made in this state exceed the combined totals of wheat-producing states like

Uttar Pradesh, Haryana, Rajasthan and Madhya Pradesh or in case of paddy those of once surplus states like Madhya Pradesh, Orissa, and Andhra Pradesh. In fact, it was the tremendous increase in foodgrains production in Punjab, which has made India not only self-sufficient, but even surplus in foodgrains. As a result there has been an enormous increase in the wealth and well-being of the Punjab farmer, who is the best nourished, clothed and housed farmer in India. This agricultural revolution has been accompanied by a total change in agricultural methods. Use of fertilizers and improved seeds has multiplied several-fold. Mechanization has come up significantly. Tractors are also being used for ploughing and other operations. In fact, during my entire stay in Punjab, I did not see a single bullock cart nor were bullocks employed for ploughing. Even for harvesting, combine harvesters are being used in increasingly large numbers. Each year, Punjab is creating a new record, both in production and procurement—all operations are taking place on time and without a hitch. While there is prosperity on this account, it has also led to a reduction in the manpower employed and there is, therefore, a certain amount of unemployment among rural agricultural youth.

The traditional means of employment for agricultural youth were the defence services, especially the Army and police. The British Indian Army was recruiting a very large percentage of its personnel from among the Sikhs. This added to their prestige as also financial benefits in the form of pay, perks and later pension. Land grants were also given to them. After Independence, this special privilege was withdrawn and recruitment from other areas which had been declared 'non-martial' for example, Bihar, was opened up. Still later, the Government of India decided that recruitment to the Army would be from all parts of India and quotas were fixed based on the population of each area. This is based on the idea of having a real national army which has people from all parts of the country. Under this dispensation, Punjab's share came to only 2%, i.e., its share in the total population. Thus over the course of years from over 30% this figure had fallen immensely around the early 1980s, with a further fall likely in the future. This further added to the unemployment problem and also gave rise to a source of grievance and discrimination.

Industry could provide jobs for people thus rendered surplus. And Punjab showed great entrepreneurship in this. Small-scale industry especially prospered and Punjab became famous for its machine tools, hand tools, sports goods, woollen knitwear, bicycles and the like. Unlike the national 80:20 ratio between agriculture and industry, Punjab depicts the ratio as 60:40. This also is a favourable development. But then small industry also needs the back-up strength which large and medium industries provide. Here Punjab suffered on account of being a border state, and more importantly, a vulnerable border state with Pakistan. The Government of India's industrial policy did not favour location of industry so close to a vulnerable international border. Punjab considers this attitude or policy also as another example of discrimination. Incidentally, only this year, in 1986, has there been some change in the government's policy in this regard as some big projects are being established in Punjab.

*

Reverting to the political background of the Punjab situation, it is noticeable that every two years or so, the Akalis have launched one agitation after another in Punjab. Sometimes it has been for recognizing the Scheduled Caste Sikhs—the Mazhabis—as being entitled to the benefits that Hindu Scheduled Castes get. Other times it is for recognition of Punjabi language, sometimes for a Punjabi state, or for the right to carry kirpans on domestic air flights, and so on. Then came the fight for

Chandigarh to be given to Punjab instead of Haryana or being made a union territory. Every time they have sought this issue, they have courted imprisonment, organized protests, hartals, demonstrations, etc., to no avail. They have even gone so far as to threaten self-immolation. For example, Sant Fateh Singh had decided to commit self-immolation by throwing himself in a cauldron of boiling oil. All this is to show that the Sikhs have felt that the Government at Delhi, which they call a 'Hindu Government', will not even concede their legitimate rights without a struggle.

Another example comes to mind—when in 1969 the Congress(I) party in the Centre toppled the Akali Government in Punjab. They created a rift and bribed, cajoled or otherwise hired a group of fifteen or so people led by Lachhman Singh Gill to desert the main Akali party and form a government. They promised this group support in the legislature. Lachhman Singh Gill was a man with a deplorable reputation. He was believed and known to be very corrupt, very undependable and was in fact being threatened with expulsion by the main Akali Dal for these reasons. And among his supporters was the now well-known Khalistan protagonist, Dr Jagjit Singh Chauhan, now in England. Several senior and well-respected leaders of the Congress in Punjab went to Delhi to plead against this unholy and unprincipled alliance. Among them was Pt Mohan Lal who told me about this himself and later gave me a book he had written on the Punjab turmoil. Mrs Gandhi turned down the plea of the local leaders. This government of Lachhman Singh Gill did not survive for more than a few months. And in the process was created a champion of Khalistan in the shape of Jagjit Singh Chauhan. He was a member of Lachhman Singh's Cabinet. A very near parallel to this was the ousting of Farooq Abdullah in Kashmir by G.M. Shah with Congress(I) support that resulted in grave consequences for Jammu and Kashmir— apart from corruption, nepotism and rise of communalism.

The consistent setbacks on the political front for the Akalis, a feeling of frustration among the Sikhs as a whole, despite all round prosperity and a growing fear that under the influence of modern movements, Sikhs as a community may lose their identity and become merged with the Hindu masses, gave rise to a Sikh fundamentalism and a growing cry to go back to the tenets of Sikhism propounded by Guru Govind Singh. A hundred years of British propaganda was paying off. Sikh intellectuals, retired and even serving Sikh officers, writers, etc., began to write and talk of preserving and consolidating Sikhism. And among the preachers of this fundamentalism was Jarnail Singh Bhindranwale. This period also saw a rise in Hindu and Muslim fundamentalism. Although I am setting this problem in the context of the Punjab problem, but worldwide also, in places like Iran, Libya and elsewhere, fundamentalism was attracting a growing number of people, especially the young. I think the reason for this was that the young did not see a bright future ahead of them. Instead the future appeared empty and devoid of any light. Annihilation seemed to loom ahead. So what resulted was recourse to blind faith—a faith not based on reason and understanding.

CHAPTER ELEVEN

Punjab: The Anandpur Sahib Resolution

In 1973, the Akali Dal adopted what has now come to be known as the Anandpur Sahib Resolution. It has several versions, but the final version was adopted in 1978 at Jalandhar. It has broadly three parts. The first dealing with the economic development of Punjab, its agriculture, industry, five-year plan investments, etc.; the second dealing with religious issues concerning the Sikhs and their demands, like live-broadcast of the Gurbani from the Harmandir Sahib, Golden Temple, early morning from about 4 a.m. and the enactment of a new All-India Sikh Gurdwara Act so as to bring important gurdwaras outside Punjab also under the control of a Central Managing Committee of Sikhs; and the third dealing with political matters with special reference to centre-state relations, more devolution of powers to states if necessary by revision of the Constitution and a more federal structure of the central government. This resolution was presented to then Prime Minister Morarji Desai when the Akalis were in power in Punjab, in alliance with what is now called the Bhartiya Janata Party. It is said that Prime Minister Morarji Desai dismissed the resolution as not worthy of consideration. Morarji Desai was known for his straight and blunt talk. As a result, this resolution lay dormant and nothing was heard of it for some time.

In 1979, the Janata Party Government at the centre fell, as

did the Charan Singh Government in the subsequent elections. In early 1980, the Congress(I), led by Mrs Gandhi, again came into power after three years in the wilderness. Following the example set by the Janata Government in 1977, the central government dismissed several state governments and ordered fresh elections. Punjab was one such state. The Akali-BJP alliance lost and Congress(I) again came into power with a clear majority in the state legislature. Shri Darbara Singh formed the Congress Government as chief minister. Having lost political power, both at the centre and the state, the Akalis again put forward the Anandpur Sahib Resolution before the central government for consideration. A few more issues were added: namely, the transfer of Chandigarh to Punjab as its capital, the question of redefining the boundaries between Punjab and Haryana on linguistic basis by taking the village as a unit and on the principle of contiguity, and finally a reconsideration of the sharing of the river waters of the Sutlej-Beas-Ravi systems among the concerned states—Punjab, Haryana, and Rajasthan.

A little background on these issues. When the demand for the creation of a Punjabi state on a linguistic basis was conceded in 1966, the question of Chandigarh became important. It was a majority Hindu area, and on the assumption that Hindu and Hindi speaking are one and the same, there were rival claims from Punjab and Haryana. So a commission was set up headed by Chief Justice of the Supreme Court of India, Justice J.C. Shah, with two other members formerly of the ICS, one a Kerala Christian M.M. Philip and the other a Bengali S. Dutt. This commission awarded Chandigarh to Haryana on the ground that it was largely Hindi-speaking and suggested that Punjab build a separate capital of its own. This recommendation of the commission was met with great agitation. All Punjabis were united on the issue that Chandigarh should go to Punjab and Haryana should build a new capital. Not only the Akalis but even Congress(I) wanted this. There were agitations all over Punjab. The argument they made was that Punjab had lost its capital Lahore to Pakistan, and Chandigarh was built as its new capital. So the new Punjabi Suba was entitled to it irrespective of the linguistic or religious composition of its inhabitants. And as Haryana was carved out as a new state it should build its own capital as, for example, Gujarat and Andhra Pradesh had done. Mrs Gandhi's award gave Chandigarh to Punjab as the elections approached closer. But it also provided for a redetermination of the boundaries between Punjab and Haryana on the basis of village (and not tehsil) as a unit—both sides were claiming more villages for themselves. A further provision was made for the Fazilka and Abohar tehsils of Ferozpur district of Punjab to go to Haryana. These were Hindu majority areas. But as this was not contiguous with Haryana, a seven-kilometeres long corridor would be built through Punjab to connect Haryana with Fazilka-Abohar. This again caused great dissatisfaction in Punjab. The Congress(I) State Committee headed by Giani Zail Singh, who was then its president, vehemently opposed it. The idea of a corridor was opposed as being an untenable proposition. Fazilka and Abohar were rich agricultural cotton-growing areas in Punjab and the state opposed its transfer on that ground. Although it was stated that Haryana would build its own capital within five years, no work was started and the provisions of this award remained unimplemented thereafter, so that even by 1980, Chandigarh had not gone to Punjab but remained a union territory.

On the river waters dispute, Punjab's case was that it was not being given due share and that more water was being diverted to Haryana and Rajasthan than they were entitled to. A case had been filed in the high court under the Inter-State River Waters Act that was pending. Several leading legal authorities, including Justice Hidayatullah, former chief justice and vice president of

India, supported Punjab's case. But on coming to power again in 1980, Mrs Gandhi persuaded Chief Minister Darbara Singh to withdraw the case and leave the matter to what had been earlier arbitrated. This gave a larger share of the river waters to Haryana on the grounds that it was more underdeveloped, dry and needed more water.

So soon after, in 1981, the Akali Dal began to agitate on these issues. First came statements and public meetings. Then in 1982, a more aggressive phase started. They elected a dictator, Sant Harchand Singh Longowal, shifted their headquarters for the present agitation to the 'dharamshalas' or places to stay for visitors of the Golden Temple Complex, and said that they were now starting a 'dharam yuddha' or a 'righteous war'. According to the Sikhs there is no difference between their religion and politics. Politics has to be based on moral principles which are found in their religious tenets. In the Golden Temple Complex there are two flags on long poles—'nishans'—one representing the religious tenets with the headquarters (or the highest seat) being at the Harminder Sahib, and the other representing the political creed of the party with the headquarters (or the highest seat) being the Akal Takht. There is, thus, a combination of religion with politics, a situation similar with that of the Muslims. This is in contrast with the Hindus, who would like religion and politics to be kept apart, especially if we are to have a genuine secular state in India. Some other minorities like the Christians and Parsees recognize this, although the Christian church has been known to dabble in politics, for example in the tribal areas, and this is a source of considerable disquiet and trouble in those regions.

One of the consequences of this joining up of political and religious issues, and more importantly, their preaching and indoctrination being carried out in places of religious worship—be it a gurdwara, mosque or church—is to add a difficult dimension to the whole question. First of all, an issue of interest to all communities appears in public eye or in the eye of the community concerned, to be a problem peculiar to them alone. This in a way alienates them from the rest of society. The second problem, that is very difficult for a state to tackle, is if along with religious teaching, sedition is preached. If the police were to enter such a place of worship then cries of freedom, of religious worship being in danger and the sanctity of the place of worship being desecrated would be raised. In such an atmosphere it is very easy to raise tempers of the congregation. India had experienced the dreadful consequences of this combination of religion and politics in the case of the Muslim community which resulted in the partition of India. Similarly, in the mind of the Hindu and that of the majority of Indian citizens, this combination of politics and religion by the Sikhs— by using their gurdwaras for carrying on their preachings, indoctrination and agitation, even when dealing with political problems that concern members of all communities—revived memories of the pre-Partition days. This isolated the Sikhs to a considerable extent and in turn created in their minds a sense of discrimination, of riding roughshod over the interests of a small minority by a powerful and huge majority.

The agitation by the Akalis for the acceptance of their demands took various forms, but it must be stated with emphasis that it was entirely peaceful, conducted with great discipline and was not at any stage communal or directed against any community, least of all the Hindus. The agitation was organized in the form of processions, violation of prohibitory rules, hartals, closure of shops, filling of jails, etc. The filling of jails—called 'jail bharo'—brought forth such large numbers of people to court arrest, that the jails in Punjab could not accommodate them. Temporary jails were created in school compounds, public parks, etc. Those arrested, however, made no effort to escape. They were not tried for any offenses or convicted by any courts, nor were they detained under any preventive detention laws. At best they can be called under-trial prisoners put in jail for violation of prohibitory orders. Except Sant Harchand Singh Longowal, all the leaders were in jail. The Punjab Government found the problem of feeding and housing them to be very difficult. So the question of releasing them was taken up and when the Government of India gave them a vague assurance to discuss their demands, they agreed to come out.

Then they had 'rasta roko', an agitation to close all roads; 'rail roko', an agitation that involved squatting on railway tracks; and 'kaam roko' agitations which constituted surrounding government offices, district courts, offices, etc. They achieved their purpose and show of strength and solidarity on the part of the Akali Sikhs. However, in the case of 'rasta roko' agitation, the government decided to be firm and not allow blockade of roads. Police had to resort to firing at the large crowds that had gathered in many places and some Akali agitators were killed as a result—about fifty or more people lost their lives. In the 'rail roko' or 'kaam roko' agitations, the Darbara Singh Government decided not to try and disperse the crowds, but allow the agitation to continue for a day as planned.

Three incidents of this period need to be mentioned. In the first, a van of the Akhand Kirtani Jatha, while travelling in some villages of Haryana, was attacked and partially burnt. A number of religious books, including copies of the *Granth Sahib* were burnt. This angered the community, especially Bibi Amarjit Kaur, wife of Fauja Singh who had been killed in the Akali-Nirankari clash of 1978. Secondly, the sessions court acquitted all the Nirankaris who were accused of assault, firing and murder while upholding that they were in exercise of their right to self-defence, as the Akalis had attacked the Nirankari sangam. The third incident was that of a bus carrying some agitators to jail that was hit by a train at an unmanned railway crossing that resulted in several people dying. Although this was purely an accident, the community, especially the hotheads among them, were greatly agitated.

Repeated attempts and negotiations were made for the settlement of these issues. Their subsequent failure caused the consequent rise of terrorism and extremism. Meetings were held by the Prime Minister with Sant Longowal and the opposition parties at Delhi, Chandigarh, etc. The question that always cropped up was how do we convince Haryana, Rajasthan and other states. They would say that the matter would be considered further and thereafter negotiators were appointed, like Sardar Swaran Singh, a skilled negotiator and diplomat who had been a minister in the central government for a number of years. After consultation with Sant Longowal, he produced a plan which would form the basis of an agreement with the Akalis. On the one or two occasions that he came to see me I asked him why his efforts had failed. He told me that Mrs Gandhi had asked him if Bhindranwale would agree to his plan. So Sardar Swaran Singh met Bhindranwale in Amritsar and got his agreement. When Swaran Singh came back to Delhi, Mrs Gandhi told him that he was much too pro-Akali and she could not agree to his plans. Thus ended his efforts. Some months later, when things had become even more difficult, he was asked by Mrs Gandhi to try again. He refused.

A second negotiation effort which saw a similar fate was conducted by Amarinder Singh, Congress MP of Patiala and Bir Devinder Singh, MLA deputy speaker, Akali Dal. Both were young and anxious to bring to an end this confrontation. Their formulation was also not accepted by the Government of India.

A third attempt was made by some opposition leaders, prominent among them being Harkishan Singh Surjeet of CPI(M). Meetings were held with Principal Secretary Dr P.C.

Alexander, then Cabinet Secretary Krishnaswamy Rao Sahib, and Home Secretary T.N. Chaturvedi. The Akalis were also present. A draft agreement was finalized and agreed to by everyone. It was decided that the paper would be sent by a special messenger in a special plane to Amritsar to be signed by Sant Longowal and made public the next day. The plane was asked to stand by at Safdarjung Airport and Amritsar Airport was alerted to remain open. It was decided that the Prime Minister would see the final draft before the paper was sent. It was sent to her at about 8 p.m. and the people present in Dr Alexander's house were given to understand that they should wait for her approval which would not take much time. But the Prime Minister did not return the draft with her approval. However, Harkishan Singh Surjeet made a statement late at night that an agreement had been reached. This was published in the papers in the morning. The government vehemently denied this and Surjeet was blamed for premature leakage of news and the consequent failure of their discussions.

At about this time, terrorism began to rear its head. On one hand were the attacks on Nirankaris—the rift between the orthodox Sikhs and Nirankaris was growing. The former referred to certain Nirankari publications which were disrespectful of the Sikh gurus, but more so because the Nirankaris said that the tradition of a living guru had not ended with the tenth guru, Guru Govind Singh. No compromise could be reached on these issues. The priests declared the Nirankaris as 'tankhaiyas'—socially ex-communicated. With the acquittal of the Nirankaris in the 1978 case, they found themselves at the receiving end of terrorist attacks almost simultaneously. Athough no evidence directly linking them was found, these attacks were masterminded by the group led by Bibi Amarjit Kaur of the Akhand Kirtani Jatha. Most, or rather several, of the Nirankaris killed were those who had been acquitted by the courts, but whom these Sikhs held guilty. So this was a case of seeking personal justice through revenge. There were a few cases of attacks on innocent Nirankaris and in one case innocent women and children were killed when a bomb was thrown at a Sunday congregation. The head of the Nirankari sect was also shot and killed at Delhi. A senior Nirankari leader showed me a list from which it appeared that reprisals were mainly being directed at those who were believed to have been in the 1978 clash. When I once asked the Akali Dal party leaders and SGPC leaders why they did not ask the Sikh priests to condemn these attacks, they replied that they had always opposed such killings which were against the Sikh faith and the teachings of their gurus, they had never encouraged or authorized the killings, the Sikh priests had only called for a social boycott so the question of any further hukumnama (command) did not arise.

The other set of terrorist or extremist attacks was related to the political agitation started by the Akali Dal. This group began declaring that the Sikhs would not get justice from the Delhi Government by peaceful means and that they should take up arms for their cause and effectively remove those who stood in the way. The most extreme element of this group were the pro-Khalistan protagonists. They were led by Jagjit Singh Chauhan of England, one Dhillon in USA and various other people—mainly in UK, USA and Canada. They were sending money to India and supporting activities in favour of Khalistan. They were also visiting Pakistan and using that base for their propaganda. Their demand was the creation of a new state, comprising of Punjab, parts of Rajasthan, Haryana, Himachal and even extending to parts of Uttar Pradesh where Sikhs had settled after partition and migration from Western Pakistan. This demand for Khalistan was never supported by the Akali Dal, the SGPC, the moderate sections of the non-political Sikhs or the Congress(I) Sikhs. The Akali Dal always said that

Khalistan is not their demand, they know it will be harmful for the Sikhs as a whole. But a large section of the Indian press and the Congress(I) party at the centre and the states, if not directly then certainly by innuendo, continued to suggest that the Akali Dal and SGPC were in favour of Khalistan, that they were not in agreement to settle the issues with the Government of India because they wanted disturbed conditions in the state which would help with the objective of the creation of Khalistan. It is true that there were some, especially among the youth, who sometimes appeared shouting pro-Khalistan slogans. Some of them belonged to the All-India Sikh Students Federation. Somehow as a result of all this propaganda and the failure to reach an amiable political settlement, a feeling had been created in the minds of a large section of the Hindus that the Sikhs as a whole are pro-Khalistanis and want a dismemberment of India—on the lines of Pakistan. This has created a serious rift in the two communities.

*

One other aspect of this role of extremism is the part played by Jarnail Singh Bhindranwale. Much has been written about him, so I would just like to mention some facts which have left a mark on my memory. He was not a highly educated person, was of village stock and had been trained from a very early age as a preacher of Sikhism. He had a personality which attracted people to him. He was a powerful speaker though somewhat crude. At an early age he was appointed the head of the Chowk Mehta Gurdwara in Amritsar district. It was here that he attracted attention. There is no doubt that among the first people to encourage him, and to use him, was Congress(I) and in particular, Giani Zail Singh. The advantage of having him on one's side was that he could be effective against the Akalis.

Of course, at that time it was not known that he would develop into a megalomaniac. It is all well-corroborated that he sided with the Congress nominees and canvassed for them against the Akali nominees in the SGPC elections. It was the common belief in Punjab that he canvassed for Congress(I) candidates ahead of the Parliamentary elections of 1980. But because of the rifts in the Congress Party, he was not supported by Darbara Singh.

Jarnail Singh Bhindranwale became a preacher of Sikh Fundamentalism. He wanted the youth to become 'amritdharis'* in larger and larger numbers. As I mentioned earlier, the growing apathy of the younger generation to the outward observance of rituals, growing unemployment and education was making a large section of the Sikhs believe that they would in course of time get merged with Hinduism. Bhindranwale started preaching against this. He started asserting the Sikh identity more and more forcefully, and denounced any departure from it. Hence initially his tirade was against Nirankaris. His attack was not frontally, as far as I know, against Hinduism, but he greatly decried Sikhs adopting Hindu customs. He would go to the extent of saying that Hindus are only shaven Sikhs. His name came into prominence in the 1978 Akali-Nirankari clash, but he did not take a prominent enough part to be cited in the criminal cases. However, he did make some enemies, for example, Akhand Kirtani Jatha. But gradually he was becoming more and more militant and strident in his speeches which were mainly confined to gurdwaras. In the earlier part of the 80s, he was considered to be only a good preacher of Sikhism and was even invited by various Police Lines and Army Sikh Regimental Centres to speak to their men on Sikhism. It was as a result of

---

*'Amritdhari' means an initiated Sikh who has taken vows of a cleaner and more disciplined life.

these speeches that he attracted a number of police constables and army jawans to himself. He was also able to convey to his listeners the 'injustices' done to the Sikhs. And with every failure on the part of the Akalis in securing the acceptance of their demands made in the 'dharam yuddha', he began to attract more young followers to his pleas of more militant action. The Akalis did not like his appeals and his talk. Sant Longowal openly criticized him. In fact, there was no love lost between the two sides. But despite this attitude of contempt for the Akali Dal and their peaceful methods, and derision of the Government of India by him, somehow whenever negotiations were taking place, or due to take place, the government wanted to know what Bhindranwale's reaction would be.

The Sikhs, and Bhindranwale in particular, would quote incidents from Guru Govind Singh's life when he was betrayed by Hindus to convey to his listeners the idea that Hindus, and Brahmins, could not be trusted. One of these was the failure of the rulers of the princely states in what is now Himachal Pradesh, to give Guru Gobind Singh a safe refuge in his flight from Anandpur Sahib with the Mughal armies behind him. Another was the betrayal by a Brahmin Hindu, who revealed where his family was hiding to the local Mughal Governor, as a result of which two of his sons were buried alive at what is now known as Gurdwara Fatehgarh Sahib. This all pointed to the futility of talks with a Hindu, Brahmin-dominated Government at Delhi.

Why were the talks with Akalis failing and what were the major differences which could not be resolved? It will be difficult to give an exact and correct account as I never saw any documents on this—I doubt if they exist—and secondly not even the participants were fully aware of why the talks failed. I will now deal with some of the important demands and against each mention what, I think, was the reason for non-acceptance.

I will begin with the case of Chandigarh. The Akalis wanted an immediate implementation of Mrs Gandhi's award transferring Chandigarh to Punjab. This had not been implemented for over a decade. It was said on behalf of the Government of India that Haryana was insisting on a simultaneous transfer of Fazilka-Abohar. Akalis, and in fact all Punjabis, including Congress(I) Punjabis, kept stating that this was not part of the award. Various suggestions were made—like dividing the city itself in a 60:40 ratio between the two states. Objections were raised since the city was not planned or built that it could be divided thus. Mrs Gandhi also accepted that the city could not be divided. The Akalis offered some sixty to hundred villages from the adjoining districts of Ropar and Patiala in Punjab as compensation to Haryana. Also, Punjab Akalis offered cash compensation to Haryana to build its own capital. Sums of the order of Rs 100 crores were mentioned. But none of these suggestions were accepted. To me it appeared that Mrs Gandhi was keen that Fazilka-Abohar go to Haryana, so that contiguity between Punjab and Rajasthan could be broken, which would make the claim for Ganganagar district of Rajasthan becoming a part of Punjab untenable. Not all of Fazilka-Abohar was Hindi speaking and in any case it was not contiguous to Haryana so a corridor was needed. The corridor principle in an extreme situation could be extended to secure the transfer of the city of Jalandhar, a predominantly Hindu and therefore Hindi-speaking area, to Haryana by providing a corridor. The corridor system reminded people of the Pakistani claim to a 1000-mile corridor across India to connect East and West Pakistan. The issue of Chandigarh thus remained hanging.

On the river water distribution issue, Punjab felt it had been deprived of its legitimate share and that an unwilling Darbara Singh had been more or less forced to agree to withdraw Punjab's case pending before the courts. The distribution was clearly in favour of Haryana, which was given an unduly large share. On the question, therefore, of appointing a new commission, various objections were raised by the government, for example Rajasthan's share. Although at one stage the Akalis said that Rajasthan was not a riparian state and thus not entitled to any water, they were prepared to drop this and assure Rajasthan what it had been getting and take up the other question. But this issue was also not settled.

Government's hesitation on the demand for an All-India Sikh Gurdwara Act was clear from the fact that they considered this would make the SGPC an even more powerful body. Even now they had an annual budget of about Rs 10 crores and controlled the important gurdwaras of erstwhile Punjab. The government said that other states were not agreeable and were in fact opposing such an Act—but the question was not put before Parliament, neither was a clear picture before the public. SGPC suspected that the government was not keen to go ahead with this measure.

Lastly, I should mention the Anandpur Sahib Resolution especially with regard to the revision of centre-state relations. For a long time the government did not consider this resolution. As pressure started mounting, not only from the end of the Akalis but also CPI(M), DMK, AIDMK, Telegu Desam etc., a commission headed by Justice Sarkaria was set up to look into it. The Akalis wanted the government to formally refer the Anandpur Sahib Resolution to the Sarkaria Commission on the premise that it had been set up mainly to consider this demand. The government said that Akalis could present their own memoranda before the Sarkaria Commission. This minor difference, along with a few other issues, created a stalemate. The Akalis took no interest in the activities of the Sarkaria Commission and did not submit their case before it. An important point to note, however, is that at no time during the various negotiations, or while making statements concerning the Sarkaria Commission or centre-state relations, was it ever said that the Anandpur Sahib Resolution was seditious, or against the integrity of the country, or was a precursor to the demand for Khalistan. The Akalis consistently and vehemently denied these allegations as meant only to malign them.

At one stage a further rift was caused between the Akalis and the government when Mrs Gandhi, on the advice of some of her people, went to a gurdwara in Delhi—Gurdwara Rakabganj, I think—and made an announcement accepting several of what were called the 'religious demands', like the right to carry a kirpan, banning the sale of liquor near the Golden Temple area, etc. The Akalis ignored these and said that they were not the result of any negotiations, and were rather unilateral announcements that were accepted but not implemented. For instance, the relay of the live Gurbani from Harmandir Sahib (by Jalandhar Radio) was not implemented by SGPC on the grounds that the time allotted was insufficient. The government did ban the sale of liquor near Golden Temple but from an area that was considered too inadequate by the Akalis.

The result of the repeated failed negotiations and a bleak outlook left a sense of deep despondency in the minds of the public at large. It also gave the extremists an opportunity to come out in the open. Bhindranwale also became more strident in his attacks on the government and heaped more ridicule on the Akali tactics and the movement—the 'dharam yuddha'. Even more tragic was the increasing alienation between the two communities, Hindus and Sikhs, that were hitherto, over the last three centuries, knit by bonds of marriage.

*

Some terrorist events in 1982 and 1983 caused the situation in Punjab to deteriorate rapidly. The murder of Ramesh Chandra, the editor of a leading Hindi newspaper in Jalandhar, by a few scooter-riding young men is generally said to be the beginning of terrorism by the people and press. The Hindus were greatly agitated, the Hindi press was up in arms, as was the national press. Ramesh Chandra was a respected man and a journalist of standing. He was an open opponent of the Akali movement and Bhindranwale in particular. This murder made the extremist activities take on a new dimension.

The next case was that of A.S. Atwal, deputy IG of Police. Atwal was a Sikh IPS officer of the Punjab police, incharge of the Jalandhar range. Amritsar falls under it. One day he visited the Golden Temple to offer prayers. He was in uniform as he was supposed to go back to duty thereafter. As he stepped out of the main gate of the Temple complex, he was shot at and died on the spot. There was a furore and great restlessness in the Punjab police as one of their senior officers had been shot by extremists. The local police wanted to enter the Temple complex for a search—as the assassin was most probably hiding there. The shot had been fired from the Temple precincts. But before doing so, they thought it wise to get the approval of the government at Chandigarh. The Chief Minister summoned an urgent meeting of the Cabinet. Darbara Singh was in favour of the police going in, but some suggested he should contact Delhi before doing so. Delhi was contacted and the local Chandigarh version was that Delhi asked Darbara Singh to not allow the police to go in. This incident has remained a mystery to me so far. I hope some historian later is able to ascertain why exactly the Punjab police did not go in. Some think that the terrorists shot Atwal as they thought he was recceing the Temple precincts.

In the Ramesh Chandra murder case, investigations revealed the complicity of Bhindranwale in the murder. It was decided to arrest and interrogate him at length. So a warrant of arrest was obtained against him. At the time, he had gone out of Punjab on one of his lecture tours in Bombay. The Punjab police party left for Bombay. Bhindranwale was tipped off that a warrant for his arrest was out. He hastily left Bombay in a jeep, and by a circuitous route returned to Chowk Mehta Gurdwara, his headquarters. People pointed fingers at the union home ministry for not arresting Bhindranwale while he was in Delhi earlier and for the tip off at Bombay. Some said that the Union Home Minister himself flew to Bombay to tip him off. These are rumours, but whatever be the case, the fact remained that Jarnail Singh Bhindranwale had, at this stage, escaped the police dragnet. Measures to secure his arrest were discussed. Finally, a Sikh Deputy Superintendent of Police (DSP), known to be a friend or admirer of Jarnail Singh and from whom he had even taken 'amrit' or 'initiation', was entrusted the task to secure his arrest. This part of the story I have gathered from the DSP himself. He came to see me once as he had been suspended for dereliction of duty and was undergoing departmental enquiries. He said he had gone to Chowk Mehta and had several talks with Jarnail Singh. He was ultimately able to persuade him to surrender himself to the police. This DSP informed the government of Bhindranwale's decision. A date was fixed for this, as Bhindranwale had said that he would first make a public appearance, speak to the assembled crowd and then surrender himself to the police. Anticipating a large crowd to assemble and violence breaking out, the police also rushed large reinforcements from all the adjoining districts.

On that fateful day, the DSP took Bhindranwale to the Golden Temple early in the morning where he had his bath in the holy tank, then said his prayers and returned to Chowk Mehta. At the appointed hour he came out, spoke to the crowds and then allowed himself to be arrested. He was taken away to Amritsar. As he was leaving, there was a melee, the police started firing and the crowd went into a rampage. A number of people were killed and several shops and police tents were damaged or burnt and some police officers were also injured. There was a great hue and cry over this incident. The police were blamed, as was the Darbara Singh Government, for mishandling the entire fiasco. The Darbara Singh Government appointed a commission under a retired high court judge to enquire and report on the incident. This commission submitted its report after nearly a year and a half and held that the police were not to blame and so exonerated them. However, the extremists among Bhindranwale's followers made several of these exonerated police officers targets for their revenge.

Jarnail Singh Bhindranwale was in police custody for ten days on the charge of conspiracy in the murder of Ramesh Chandra. After ten days of intensive interrogation, the police could not establish any links or secure any evidence. He was discharged from custody. This time he immediately went into the Golden Temple complex, never to come out alive again; a hero among his followers. The fiasco regarding his arrest, the failure on the part of the police to make any charges stick against him apart from the murder conspiracy, for example incitement to violence or communal hatred, emboldened both him and his followers. This was a great setback for the Darbara Singh Government and pushed the Akalis further into public limelight.

Government and police had a similar setback in the case of Bhai Amrik Singh, president of the All India Sikh Students Federation. He was considered to be one of the active and determined instigators of terrorism, but again, he could not be charged on any specific case. Ultimately, he was charged under the Arms Act for being in possession of an unlicensed firearm. However, the Court acquitted him of this charge. He immediately left the Amritsar Court with three or four of his followers and went inside the Golden Temple also not to emerge alive again. Some police officers had been deployed on duty to re-arrest Amrik Singh in case he were acquitted as he came out of the court room. Amrik Singh and his followers gave the police a slip. The police officials were later suspended and charged with dereliction of duty.

All these incidents, one after another, helped to build up the extremists. Bhindranwale became more and more vitriolic as the Akalis had nothing to show to their credit as gains. And these terrorists began to hit out against policemen who had taken part in the Chowk Mehta incident, or the Akhand Kurbani Jatha vehicle incident, or those they considered had tortured Bhindranwale or Amrik Singh during investigations or were suspected to be police informers, or were Nirankaris. The toll grew as did public concern, but in all these cases more Sikhs than Hindus had been killed.

In a futile bid to attract attention, the Akalis announced two programmes to internalize their demands. One was to demonstrate before the large international gathering for the Asian Games—the Asiad, and the other to demonstrate and present a memorandum at the Commonwealth Heads of Government Meeting (CHOGM) in New Delhi. Both these measures were ill-conceived and alienated the Akalis from even their well-wishers. In the case of the CHOGM they sent their memorandum by post, but CHOGM took no notice. What it referred to was the part played by the Sikh soldiers of the British Army or the British Indian Army during the world wars. In both cases, the Sikh soldiers were mercenary soldiers and were no different than any other members of the British Indian Army. However, they also harped on the breach of trust by the British at the time of Independence for not giving the Sikhs a fair deal. People read into this a demand for Khalistan, which the Akalis denied. Later a case was registered against Sant Longowal by the police on this memo. The case never came up for trial and it could not be asserted whether or not the document was seditious in any way.

On the occasion of the Asiad, the Akalis had decided to send 'jathas' or groups of people to demonstrate and thus may be even to disrupt the smooth holding of the games. The Prime Minister issued instructions for the strictest enforcement of all possible security. Any such international meets, whether the Asiad or CHOGM or similar occasions, are always beset with very serious problems of security—international terrorism is taking so many facets and who will be the target and where becomes extremely difficult to predict. So security enforcement was essential. The task of preventing would-be agitators from travelling from Punjab to Delhi fell on Haryana. Haryana mounted a strict guard and search of every Sikh passing through. In the process a former Governor, a Chief Justice of the Punjab Haryana High Court, a retired Lt Gen of the Army, several major generals and others who had retired were stopped, detained for long hours, their cars searched, etc. Although the result of all this was that both the events passed off peacefully and without any incident, to the credit of the Prime Minister and the Government of India, the Sikhs of Punjab—including even the most moderate and loyal elements among them—felt humiliated and hurt at the treatment meted out to them. This left a deep wound and widened the rift between the communities. The Sikhs felt that Haryana, being a predominantly Hindu state had done all this deliberately to humiliate the Sikhs in the eyes of the rest of Indians.

Bhindranwale and the extremists got some more material for their reckless vengeance and the phase of killing innocent people—in no way connected with politics or the police—began. Hindu shopkeepers, petrol pump dealers, liquor vendors, banks, etc., became targets of attack for two purposes—killing and also looting money. Motorcycles and scooters were stolen this way, along with guns, wherever possible. The motorcycles and scooters were used for hit, grab and run crimes. It became difficult to chase them. They ran into bylanes, off the main roads, left vehicles at one place and went to another by bus, and began to take refuge in the gurdwaras, specially the Golden Temple, thinking they would be safe as the police would not enter a place of worship. Usually all these crimes were committed by two or three people. Not a day passed when some incident or the other was not reported with the largest concentration around Amritsar. In this atmosphere, burglaries, armed private disputes over land or property, generation-old feuds—common to Punjab and replete in its history—were lumped with terrorist activities.

It is not as if the Darbara Singh Government was mute witness to all this and did not take effective steps. They got more police from the centre—the CRPF and the BSF, who were deployed on guard, patrol and check duties. Apart from those put on checkpost duties, numerous barriers had been erected on the roads to check vehicles and their passengers, some policemen were employed on patrol duty and over 2500 people were deployed around the Golden Temple to prevent terrorists from going in or coming out of it and to confiscate any arms and ammunition. The deployment was in three rings—the innermost around the temple was usually the CRPF or the BSF, the second ring was also composed of the BSF and the outermost ring constituted the Punjab police. This was due to lack of trust in the Punjab police. The central force—though nominally under the control of Punjab police, the DSP and the IG of police—was actually being monitored and directed from Delhi. Moreover their field officers were directly in touch and in constant communication with Delhi. Often, not even the police control room at Amritsar knew of an event which the central forces had directly reported to Delhi, who in turn rang up Chandigarh, who of course knew nothing of the matter. They in turn had to ask Amritsar police who also came to know of the event thereafter. This happened even though both the forces were just a stones' throw from each other and the Amritsar police control room only a hundred or so metres away from the Temple. Essentially this was based on the lack of trust between the two forces—in fact the central forces had been instructed not to pass any message to the local authorities until it had been cleared by their headquarters. This huge force had not arrested or intercepted a single terrorist for over ten–twelve months. At the check posts, innocent travelers were harassed and sometimes commercial vehicles and taxis made to pay— but terrorists riding on scooters and motorcycles got through with impunity and were not stopped, chased or arrested. None were shot. In a few instances on the other hand, the police at the check barriers were fired at and in some cases even injured or killed. There was a very serious case where the terrorists were being chased by a police party—an alert by wireless had gone to all the checkposts to stop scooters and motorcycles as two of them were going on one vehicle. The terrorists got through a CRPF barrier as the pillion-riding passenger feigned serious illness and the driver said he was taking him to the hospital. The chasing party arrived a few minutes later. By then these people had abandoned the vehicle in a village road, walked across the fields and disappeared into the darkness.

Around the Golden Temple itself, not one person with illicit arms was ever arrested during this entire period nor was any vehicle with illicit arms and ammunition detained. It was commonly believed that arms and ammunition were being smuggled in. But why this failure? There were several reasons. First of all the number of visitors and devotees going to the Temple every day was very large and on special occasions like 'sankranti' or 'amavas' the numbers ran into lakhs. Among them a large number were women. At one stage an attempt was made to search everyone individually at all gates. This took too long, crowds swelled, and protests were raised. The same difficulty was with vehicles. At times, the cars of the SGPC president or the chief priest of the Temple would be detained and they would raise a howl of protest. Trucks carrying large quantities of groceries were going in at regular intervals. Several devices were tried to check these—near the temple, on the outskirts of Amritsar, or at random midway points. Again, the practical difficulties were formidable and none of the searches revealed any arms. Yet intelligence sources said that arms were being put inside milk cans, mixed with firewood, inside wheat and dal bags and what not. Individuals were carrying them folded in bags, inside shawls and so on.

There was yet another difficulty. The Temple Complex is surrounded by houses built close to each other. Sometimes a lane only two-and-a-half-feet wide separates the back walls of the temple and the private houses outside. In some cases they even touch each other. Then there were numerous doors from the Temple complex leading to the lanes surrounding it. I was once told that there were eighty-four such possible openings—doors, windows, etc. Not only this, but one could jump from rooftop to rooftop, or from one house to another and emerge a kilometre away. All this made the deployment of force totally ineffective. When people, after Operation Bluestar, said that the Army should have laid a siege they were not aware of the practical impossibility of it. Moreover, the Temple was always very well stocked with food, fuel and water as almost 10,000 people ate in the communal feeding kitchen (langar) every day—so there were provisions available. I often expressed my dissatisfaction at these deployments as they were not yielding results and asked the police officers, both at the centre and state to come up with better ideas for more effective use of this force, but no more superior and effective strategy could be evolved. And this was not effective.

Another major step taken by Darbara Singh's Government in consultation with the centre was to revamp the police administration. This meant replacing the director general of police and transferring the superintendents and deputy IGs. Sometime in July 1983, a new officer—P.S. Bhinder—was posted. P.S. Bhinder, IPS originally, belonged to the Punjab Cadre, but had later been allotted to Haryana. His home district was Gurdaspur, and his wife was a Congress(I) MP from there. Bhinder had come into prominence during the Emergency years when he was the police commissioner of Delhi. His name got associated in what was called the Sundar murder case. Sundar was a notorious dacoit wanted in several cases of dacoity and murder. One day his body, riddled with bullets, was found in the river Jamuna. It was suspected that he had been murdered by the police on being arrested. After the end of the Emergency and during the Janta regime, P.S. Bhinder had to stand trial in the Sundar murder case. He was, however, acquitted of all charges. Bhinder told me that he had to spend a few lakhs of his own to defend himself and even after his acquittal and the return to power of Mrs Gandhi, he had not been compensated in any form by the government.

Bhinder was however known to be very close to the Gandhi family, especially to Sanjay. During the Janata regime, he told me that he had arranged for Mrs Gandhi's guards by getting people from Punjab to take on that duty. Once when a Congress(I) Sikh worker was killed by the terrorists in Punjab, Bhinder had told me that the man shot had been one of Mrs Gandhi's guards. He had every access to Mrs Gandhi's household and would often go there, sometimes late in the evenings after other visitors had left. There is also no doubt he used to receive direct instructions from the Prime Minister or her closest aides. There was, however, a persistent rumour that he was close to Bhindranwale. Bhinder denied this and once or twice even in the press, but the rumour persisted. It was said that Jarnail Singh had campaigned for his wife's election in 1980 and that she, along with an uncle of P.S. Bhinder, had gone to see Bhindranwale. This uncle was a member of the SGPC as well. Bhinder was also not pro-Darbara Singh, because soon after I joined, Bhinder told me on two or three occasions that I should speak to the Prime Minister to send Darbara Singh out of Punjab, preferably out of India as an ambassador or high commissioner in some country, or at least to Delhi. In Bhinder's view, as long as Darbara Singh remained on the scene, there would be no conclusion to the Punjab problem. His wife was in the anti-Darbara group of the Congress(I) members who often came to see me. At the same time, he was not pro-Zail Singh. But Bhinder was clearly a pro-Mrs Gandhi man and had been specially selected for his loyalty and posted to Punjab.

His posting caused considerable problems for the Punjab police administration. There were several officers, both Hindu and Sikh who were senior to him and could not be superseded on grounds of merit. So the government had to create about half a dozen posts, ex cadre, in the IG's rank and promote these officers. Bhinder was given a free hand in the posting of the district and divisional police chiefs as also other officers. Sometimes his choice was not liked by many. For example, the officer he selected as SP of Amritsar, though known to be a tough police officer was also described by some as a 'dacoit in police uniform'. Another had been a superintendent in the Uttar Pradesh district from where Mrs Gandhi had been elected. His postings, people felt, were at the behest of Mrs Gandhi's household. There were some difficulties which not only Darbara Singh's Government faced, but were hurdles in Bhinder getting the unstinted support of his officers and men. Some months after I joined, I was asked by Dr P.C. Alexander if I would like Bhinder to be moved out. I told him that frequent changes of officers had already done great harm to the Punjab police, and as Bhinder had been especially selected by Mrs Gandhi and the Government of India, there was no point in moving him. It was not going to alter the situation on the ground, nor were it likely to improve the police morale or functioning. So he continued and left at the same time as me.

*

So, I should sum up the Punjab situation at the beginning of October 1983 as one full of frustrations, with no light on the horizon. Peace parleys or talks with Akalis had also ended in failure. Before actual talks—or even rumours of talks—terrorist activities showed an increase. There were attacks on police officials identified by the terrorists for various reasons like torture during interrogation, unjustified firing on crowds. There were also a spate of dacoities with murder for looting cash from banks, from liquor vendors, petrol pump owners, etc., or for stealing motorcycles, scooters or arms. For example, a police armoury had been attacked and over two dozen sten guns stolen. Along with this was the alienation of the Sikh community due to the propaganda in the press and by politicians of all hues, that they were pro-Khalistanis, secessionists, terrorists. The events in Haryana on the eve of the Asiad and CHOGM rankled. In clubs and messes, Hindus and Sikhs sat apart, formed separate foursomes in golf. This alienation was felt more in the intellectual circles and the educated classes than in the rural peasantry or workers in factories. There were also stories of police encounters with terrorists and reports of several being shot. The public took this to be the killing of innocent people just to notch a score as there was no evidence to say that the people thus killed were terrorists. Rarely were arms recovered.

Against this background, in early October, a most dastardly killing took place—the first of its kind. A few terrorists hijacked a Punjab Roadways bus, made the driver go into a side village road and then asked all the passengers to step outside. The Hindus and Sikhs were separated and six Hindus were killed at point-blank range. The terrorists then fled away. This sent shock waves across Punjab and throughout the country. Darbara Singh was asked by the party Congress High Command, the Prime Minister, to submit his resignation to the Governor. As the Congress party was in an absolute majority in the legislature, no alternative party government could be formed. The Congress(I) also did not want to change their leader. As a result, President's rule was proclaimed in Punjab, and it fell to my lot to be sent to Chandigarh from Calcutta at short notice.

CHAPTER TWELVE

Governor, Punjab: 1983–84

It was on the evening of 6 October 1983 that I got a telephone call from Dr P.C. Alexander asking me to come to Delhi immediately. We had been planning a visit to Darjeeling. I took the early morning flight from Dum Dum. The early morning papers carried banner headlines announcing the proclamation of President's rule in Punjab, following the resignation of Darbara Singh. Names of four advisors to the governor were also announced. They were rushed to Chandigarh on the night of October 6 or 7.

I reached the South Block to meet with Dr Alexander. He had rung me up at about 8 p.m. the previous evening to inform me that I had been chosen to replace A.P. Sharma as the governor of Punjab. A.P. Sharma in turn would go to Calcutta in my place. Later that night, Mrs Gandhi had gone to meet President Giani Zail Singh to tell him about these developments and also the names of the advisors. Giani Zail Singh had suggested that a Hindu and a Brahmin, especially a Hindi speaking person from Uttar Pradesh, should not be sent to Punjab, instead the person should be someone from outside the Hindi speaking belt. Thereafter, at about midnight it had been decided that A.N. Banerji from Karnataka should be sent to Punjab. At that stage Dr Alexander thought of asking me not to come to Delhi, but because it was so late he did not do so and thought he decided to tell me in person the next day. He had not yet spoken to Banerji and would do so after he met with the Prime Minister. Soon after, when Mrs Gandhi came to office at 10 a.m., the decision would be reconfirmed. He suggested that I wait for a while.

Around noon, Dr Alexander informed me that the Prime Minister had decided to send me to Punjab and the idea regarding Banerji had been dropped. I went back to Calcutta to get my family and luggage to Chandigarh. I requested for the arrangement of a special plane that could take me to Chandigarh a couple of days later, on October 10.

While in Delhi, I could not meet Mrs Gandhi to find out what her plans or policies were regarding Punjab or what she expected the administration to do. Dr Alexander only said that things in Punjab were not at all happy and I should see what could be done. However, I called on the President in the afternoon before leaving Delhi. He advised me that among the first things I should do was go to Amritsar and visit the Golden Temple, the Durgiana Temple and the Martyr's Memorial at Jallianwala Bagh. He was critical of Darbara Singh's administration. It was common knowledge that Zail Singh and Darbara Singh never got along and were always pulling in different directions. Zail Singh also said that a number of officers had been put in wrong places and that should be changed soon. This referred to not only those in the Secretariat but also the districts. He had uncomplimentary remarks to make about my predecessors, especially Chenna Reddy, and also A.P. Sharma, hinting that the first had a 'roving eye' and the latter was a die-hard Hindu, almost a chauvinist. Later on, I learnt that some of the persons recommended by him did not necessarily have a good reputation, but they had direct access to him and reported to him the developments that took place from time to time in the state. This was one of the problems that Darbara Singh faced—the tales that were carried to the powers that reside in Delhi.

I returned to Calcutta in the evening. Chief Minister Jyoti Basu was away, perhaps at Srinagar, and he issued a strong statement criticizing the move, especially because the Prime Minister had not consulted him about my appointment or that of A.P. Sharma. Next day, while I was recording my farewell speech to the people of Bengal—in English, Hindi and Bengali—Basu called up from Srinagar and a meeting was arranged late at night on October 9 when he returned to Calcutta. The West Bengal Cabinet hosted a farewell dinner at the Great Eastern Hotel on October 9—it was very hurriedly arranged but all the ministers other than Chief Minister himself (who had not yet returned) were present. Jyoti Basu came to see me later in the evening and said he was sorry I was leaving Bengal. He then said he would ask one of the CPI(M) Politbureau members from Punjab, Shri Surjeet, to meet me. Harkishan Singh Surjeet had been active in trying to bring about an accord in the Punjab, but had not succeeded till then.

We left Calcutta on 10 October 1983 in the early morning by a special BSF plane. We flew straight from Calcutta to Chandigarh, arriving at about 11 a.m. or so, and at 4 p.m., I took the oath of office at Chandigarh.

Why was my predecessor, A.P. Sharma, not allowed to continue in Punjab? He was a seasoned politician, former railway trade union leader, and a union cabinet minister for many years. He was very anti-Akali and pro-Hindu, if I may say so. He would have been very tough, but perhaps this was also not wanted. Some people told me after I had joined that a civil war had been averted in Punjab as they feared that A.P. Sharma would have precipitated it. Not that I was able to avert the subsequent developments and the schisms that took place in Punjab!

On the flight from Calcutta to Chandigarh, were my wife Vimla, our son Lalit, daughter Ratna, our grandson Anant, and our fox-terrier, Sheba. During the flight, I wrote out the speech I would make after assuming office of the Governor of Punjab. This speech and the ceremony were widely publicized in the press, on the radio and television. The whole thing finished by about 6 p.m. After the guests had gone and I had retired to the drawing room, people came in groups to see me. One of the first was a group of ex-cabinet ministers of Darbara Singh's Government led by Beant Singh, Dr Kewal Krishna and some others. They promised me full support. Then another group, apparently not wholly pro-Darbara Singh, also came to say the same thing. This was followed by several others. After they had gone, I met the advisors, Chief Secretary and IG of Police.

A little about the advisors. Four of them had been selected and appointed by the Government of India following a special selection. I was not consulted. In fact, I found that throughout my stay in Punjab, when as many as seven or eight advisors were changed, the decisions were made in Delhi. I was simply informed. I would, however, not say that they appointed anyone I objected to, but I was not part of the initial process of selection nor was I asked if I wanted a change. The advisors were frequently called to Delhi, where they met Principal Secretary Dr Alexander, Cabinet Secretary Krishnaswami Rao Sahib, and sometimes the Prime Minister herself. The advisors were briefed by them and information was also sought from them. Based on this, they then made their judgement about the suitability of the advisors. In one or two cases, even the portfolios to be allotted to the advisors were indicated from Delhi. This was not a satisfactory position at all, and sometimes I wondered if some of the advisors were reporting certain matters or decisions somewhat differently to this trinity in Delhi. My own way of working was to be quite frank with them.

I used to have frequent, sometimes daily, meetings to discuss important matters, specially those concerning law and order. I also had separate meetings with each of them. Separate and joint briefings by the Chief Secretary, Home Secretary, IG of Police and IG Intelligence was a daily affair. Despite all this, I must say that I received complete cooperation from all my advisors and officers of the Punjab Government. I also had their trust. In any case, whatever I failed to achieve in Punjab was not due to them—the advisors, officers, all worked towards the same goal—but because some other forces nullified all our efforts.

The first few days I was intensely busy. My working hours started at 8 or 8.30 a.m. in the Raj Bhavan office, clearing papers that had come overnight. Come 9 a.m., I went to the Secretariat. The Punjab Government's working hours were nine to five for five days in the week—all Saturdays and Sundays were holidays. I was usually in the Secretariat until 1 p.m.—meeting with officers and the public took most of my time. This was followed by lunch and a little rest and I was back to the office at 2.30 p.m. From then onwards it could be 8 or 8.30 p.m. before I could leave the office. This was followed by a break for dinner after which I again went through files, intelligence reports and so on till may be 11 p.m. or even midnight. For the first ten days, I did not even see the grounds of the Raj Bhavan or go out for a walk. Later, as I got more acquainted with the situation, the pressure was somewhat eased, but all through my stay in Punjab, the working hours were long.

An important decision that I had to take within a day or so of my joining was whether or not a cricket test match between India and Pakistan, scheduled to take place in a few days time at Amritsar, should take place, given the surcharged and tense atmosphere of the state. As I drove to the Secretariat in the morning at 9 a.m., I decided we should go ahead with the cricket match. I consulted the Chief Secretary and IG of Police and they got in touch with the District Collector and Superintendent of Amritsar. All agreed that it could be held. So we announced the decision in its favour. I also decided to inaugurate the match. This would also be my first public appearance in Punjab. So all of us—Vimla, Lalit, Ratna and Anant—went to Amritsar. In Punjab, I usually travelled by the Punjab Government plane as it was much easier and also better from the security point of view—the police preferred this method as they did not have to make arrangements on the road.

It is expected of a new governor that he would make the round of three places in Amritsar in the following order: the Golden Temple for paying obeisance—'maatha tekna', as it is called, then the Durgiana Temple of the Hindus, and then the Martyrs Memorial at the Jallianwala Bagh, the scene of the infamous massacre in 1921 where hundreds were shot dead. Early morning, the first place we went to was the Golden Temple. A large crowd had gathered outside to see me and at the gates of the temple I was greeted by Shri G.S. Tohra—president of SGPC, Shri Prakash Singh Badal—former chief minister of Punjab, Balwant Singh—former finance minister of Punjab, Kirpal Singh—head of the Chief Khalsa Diwan and several others. We went to the Temple, round the Parikrama, into Harmandir Sahib, the main Golden Temple, to the Akal Takht up its very narrow steep and twisting steps to the room where the *Guru Granth Sahib* is kept every night (it is taken every morning to Harmandir Sahib and brought back at night) and up another storey where the Akhand Path continues uninterruptedly. Outside we were shown the two high banners with golden colour triangular flags signifying, as they stressed, the fact that this Temple and the Akal Takht were the seat of both the state and religion—unifying both. Outside, we were presented with shawls, books, a miniature model of the

Golden Temple and other souvenirs. As we were going around, a large crowd had followed us, comprised of both Hindus and Sikhs. The crowd was well-disciplined. At several places, on the ground, on top of buildings, etc., sewadars of the SGPC were posted. Later, several Hindu officers told me that it was the first time in almost two years that they had entered the Temple precincts, although earlier they used to visit it daily. Police and intelligence officers said that the SGPC authorities had been very worried and had hoped that no gun-toting people would be visible. I did not see any. They must have kept themselves concealed. I did not meet Sant Harchand Singh Longowal nor Jarnail Singh Bhindranwale. The former talked to me over the telephone several times and wrote a few letters also, but with the latter I had no contacts. This visit was widely televised. Several people wrote about the brave front I had put up and the risks I had undertaken! Although there was nothing of the sort, the atmosphere had certainly been vitiated as it is today. However during the visit, the atmosphere in the Temple complex was peaceful, as befitted it. With the leaders, only pleasantries were exchanged and a first acquaintance made.

Then we went to Durgiana temple where I was greeted by large crowds of Hindus, very vociferously. This temple has been built fairly recently and has adopted the same layout style as the Golden Temple. It is smaller and has not yet acquired the halo of the Golden Temple. The crowds were not as disciplined as in the Golden Temple. There was much pushing and jostling and even we had some difficulty in getting a good view of the idols of the gods and goddesses. In fact, the contrast between the discipline, quiet orderly movement of the Sikh devotees in the Golden Temple and the noisy, bustling, pushing disorderliness in the Durgiana Temple, I thought, revealed in a manner the difference between the two communities that had emerged over the years.

Our next visit was to the Jallianwala Bagh. The spots on the walls where the bullets hit were still marked as also the well where a number of people had been drowned. A new memorial in the shape of a flame has been constructed. It recalls the days of the British rule.

At the Golden Temple, I must also mention a visit to their museum of Sikh history. In this museum are portraits of people who had been martyred in the cause of their religion. There are scenes of torture inflicted on them. The whole thing leaves an indelible impression on the mind—a long history of sacrifice, struggle, and martyrdom. This is deeply embedded in the mind of every Sikh, especially the youth, from early childhood. However, more noteworthy were the additions of photographs or paintings of people who had died in the recent past—for example, those involved in the Akali-Nirankari clash, or those who had died as a result of police firing and had been extolled as heroes and given a place in this historical museum.

One of the few orders that I had issued to the police soon after was that I did not like 'fake' encounters and that I would like the police to follow up terrorists based on good intelligence and then deal with them. The general charge and complaint with respect to the 'fake' encounters was that often innocent people were killed, it was not known if those killed were really criminals or terrorists. Often the result of this was counter-productive and created a greater gulf between the police and the people. However, just as I arrived at Amritsar, a few miles outside, the police had engaged a party of terrorists who were hiding in a sugarcane field. After a night-long encounter, the police were able to close in at midday. Three or four terrorists were killed, arms and ammunitions recovered. Unlike on other occasions, there was widespread public support for this action and the police were applauded. This raised the morale of the police and I publicly applauded them for the good work they had done. Unfortunately, there were not many similar favourable encounters in the future. The police were most often outwitted and failed to get timely or accurate intelligence in advance. There were some very brilliant arrests of wanted terrorists or murderers, but several remained unapprehended. And of course, more were joining the fold, and fingers were always being pointed at the Golden Temple and in particular at Bhindranwale on grounds that he was enlisting or encouraging more and more of the young men to his fold and way of thinking.

After doing the round of these three places, we went to the cricket grounds, reaching there, I think, at 9.30 a.m. The stands were fairly full. I inaugurated the match and spent an hour or so there. The games went off without any incident and were well patronized. Everyone and, to some extent, the general depressing picture, was somewhat relieved. Though not for long.

At the cricket ground, from where we were seated, I noticed larger crowds in two separate galleries at the other end of the pavilion. As I could not see very clearly that far, I enquired about it and was told that it was the students' enclosure, with special cheap rates—one stall was for boys and another for girls. I was surprised at this separation and asked why this had been done. People told me that in a mixed stall there is always apprehension of trouble—eve teasing or similar indecent behaviour. The contrast between Bengal and Punjab in this regard was very great. In Bengal, boys and girls sat together in the same enclosure, together in classes in schools and colleges, at dramas, concerts, etc. There never was any indecency. The boys were always well-behaved. In Punjab, this could not even be contemplated, though Punjabi youth is, shall I say, more westernized in this respect—but curiously it has not imbibed a freer mixing of the two sexes. Yet another curious custom.

Everyone understands that when you enter a gurdwara, you should have your head covered. So women also have their head covered with the 'dupatta'. But generally, as is happening everywhere in India, most women are nowadays going about with their hair uncovered—whether they be wearing sarees or salwar kameez. Even in Punjab one saw them going about with uncovered heads. But on Jalandhar TV, it was taboo for a woman to appear without her head covered. This I consider an example of the throwback to the fundamentalism that is taking place among the Sikhs, specially in Punjab, and an unconscious mannerism by which they could assert their identity and prevent absorption in the Hindu fold. Similarly, most Punjabi Hindu women would now wear sarees, Punjabi Sikh ladies would appear in salwar kameez—specially in Punjab. In Delhi and elsewhere, they would be seen in sarees like other Indian women.

Yet another curious feeling and experience—not just felt by me, but by everyone in our family and by many others—was that from a distance, especially from Delhi, and after reading the national dailies and hearing or seeing the news on the radio and television, Punjab appeared aflame. It appeared that walking about was most unsafe—one did not know who would be killed, when and where. All life appeared to be at a standstill with business, industry and agriculture collapsing and Hindus and Sikhs killing each other. But when one came to Chandigarh, one found life normal as in any other part of India, in fact with less police publicly deployed than in Delhi. I have known people who, living in Delhi, were even afraid of coming to Chandigarh. Then from Chandigarh if one went to the real Punjab—Amritsar—the biggest and most populous city, or Jalandhar, or Ludhiana, one would find similar normalcy. Driving through the countryside, all was peaceful, with farming going on normally. The cities were bustling with activity. Shops were open as usual doing brisk business. Factories were working normally with no strikes or lockouts. Streets were crowded. Schools and colleges were functioning normally. Hindus and Sikhs were walking together, visiting each other's shops, riding together on bicycles, scooters, etc. The contrast from what one anticipated and what one actually experienced was vivid. Over the months, as I visited one district headquarter after another, as I saw more and more of the interior, I could not help but emphasize on this otherwise peaceful atmosphere.

Some months earlier, when I was in Calcutta, Brij Bhushan Mehra, the speaker of the Punjab Assembly, had come with his family to see me. He was a resident of Amritsar and had been elected from there. When I asked him what life in Amritsar was like, he said absolutely normal, just like in Calcutta. He had said that all the stories that were being published in the papers were wildly exaggerated and were only causing nervousness in an otherwise unruffled scene. I had not wholly believed him then, but now I did, after my own experiences in the city. A former director of the Intelligence Bureau and a very experienced police officer, B.N. Malik, had come to Punjab. He too came to see me. He had planned to visit a Devi temple and was visiting some districts of Punjab on his way. I asked him to look around, talk with people and tell me his observations. He had found life normal and relations between the two communities cordial and peaceful. In another example, a team of five or six had come from Kerala to give an award to a Punjabi poet. They had gone to Amritsar where the function was being held. The award was presented to the poets' wife as the poet himself was out of India. When they came and saw me, I asked them what their impression was. They said the same thing. This goes to show the effects of the continuous propaganda against Punjab and the Sikhs, in a veiled way, that had spread all over the country.

Year after year, people have been saying that life in Punjab is totally disrupted. Yet Punjab is achieving higher and higher production of foodgrains, all operations are going on peacefully, more contribution is being made to the public distribution system every year. In industry, there are no strikes, or lockouts, or more importantly, no mandays are lost on account of civil disturbances. In fact, Punjab has the best record in comparison to other states in this respect. This also refers to labour relations. The same is the picture in industrial production. All sectors have registered a growth. Once, in a meeting with an industrialist who complained of the disturbed conditions, I asked for specific information regarding exports. He was dealing in sports goods. He said that his production and export had increased by nearly Rs 5 crores from Rs 24 crores to Rs 29 crores. When I asked how that was bad, he said that if things in Punjab were peaceful, it would have been better as more buyers would have come. This was true. But as I said before, the atmosphere and propaganda was totally anti-Punjab.

My financial advisor was once taken to task by some journalists when he said that he had no evidence of a decline in industrial production, on the contrary there was an increase as was evidenced by larger sales tax revenues and increased octroi income of the bigger municipal corporations like Amritsar, Jalandhar, etc. This was irrefutable and based on firm evidence—but they would not accept this as it went against their pre-conceived notion that Punjab must be badly off—every activity must be disrupted!

Between October and December 1983, many new industrial ventures were licensed totaling over Rs 100 crores in investment. Similarly, in the first three months of 1984 too, many new industrial ventures were licensed. A 200 MW thermal station was set up and energized in record time, the best in India so far, in less than twenty-four months. The thermal plant at Bhatinda got the all-India first prize for best performance. The contrast between this plant and those in Bengal had to be seen to be believed. The efficiency here was so much higher.

There was a great deal of talk and publicity about industries moving out of Punjab and to Haryana. And among one of the most important to do so, I was told, was the Hero Honda company which was to manufacture their mopeds in Haryana. I met the proprietor of Hero cycles at a big function of industrialists of Punjab at Ludhiana to which the Union Industries Minister Shri N.D. Tiwari had also been invited. The proprietor is a resident of Ludhiana and one of the largest manufacturers of bicycles—the Hero Majestic—in India. He has a work force of nearly 8000 in his factory at Ludhiana. I asked him quietly as to what the facts were. He said his Ludhiana factory was working to full capacity, he had no problems with his labour, Sikh or Hindu. But almost a decade earlier when he decided to go into the moped business, he had decided to set up a separate plant and like all industrialists he had decided not to put all his eggs in one basket and had therefore acquired land in Haryana for the moped plant. Work there had been going on the last four or five years and now the factory was nearing completion. This decision of his was prior to, and had nothing to do with, the present disturbances in Punjab.

In January 1984, I met the press in Chandigarh and gave them the crime figures in Punjab for the previous year, i.e., 1983. These included murders, bank robberies, terrorist crimes, thefts, etc. While there was some increase in crimes like bank robberies, all others had come down markedly over the previous year. And if figures of Punjab were to be compared with those of Haryana, Rajasthan, Delhi and Uttar Pradesh, on the uniform basis of per 100,000 of the population, the figures for Punjab were the lowest in this region. In other words, there was more crime outside of Punjab than in Punjab. And yet not a day passed, or passes, when the Punjab police is not condemned for its inefficiency. I will come to that later.

In respect of the much publicized twenty-point programme, on which the Prime Minister laid great stress and which was especially monitored every month by the Planning Commission, and on the performance of which the Congress(I) chief ministers thought that their survival in office depended, Punjab stood first in the country, month after month, on each item of the programme. How could this be achieved if conditions were not favourable? In some cases Punjab was not first. And this was because in that field, for example—electrification of villages, connecting villages with pucca roads, etc., Punjab had already achieved 100% coverage and further improvement was not possible. Furthermore, these items were taken out by the Planning Commission from its computation as further progress was not apparent from the monthly statistical returns.

Punjab led the way in the small savings scheme, women's education, adult education and was even winning Red Cross awards at the national level.

Then why this unending propaganda that Punjab is in flames, that Punjab is going down, that progress is halted? Incidentally, Punjab has the highest per capita income among the states of India—people are best fed, best clothed, best housed! This fake reporting is mostly carried out by the Hindu owned national press. I think it is a kind of death wish and I fervently pray that the most dreaded consequence of this subtle and sustained propaganda against Punjab, Punjabi Sikhs, and Sikhs does not fructify. Our leaders are doing all that is possible in this direction and there is nothing to restrain them. They do not see the writing on the wall. The worst offenders are the Hindu chauvinists and I would put the neo-fascist types on top, like the Hindu Shiv Sena of Punjab with backing from reactionary and political forces.

A few days after stepping in as the governor and my visit to Amritsar, I went to Delhi to meet the Prime Minister for the first time since I had taken over at Chandigarh. The meeting was pleasant enough and I reviewed the situation in Punjab. Mrs Gandhi however stressed her determination to stamp out these terrorists and said that all measures must be taken to do that. Moreover, she added that she would not hesitate to bomb the Golden Temple if she had to. I listened to this somewhat spellbound as I could not believe that she would go to such lengths. I realized that she was quite serious and was willing to take the harshest measures necessary. I felt greatly disturbed at the thought and the consequences if such actions ever became imperative.

Thoughts concerning Mrs Gandhi's character flash through one's mind. Even though one acknowledged her remarkable sense of political astuteness and timing, there was an element of ruthlessness in facing or removing her adversaries. For example, in the 1969 Congress Party split, she faced and routed the stalwarts of the party—people like Kamaraj Nadar, Nijalingappa, Atulya Ghosh, S.K. Patil, N. Sanjiva Reddy, Morarji Desai, and others. Again during the 1971 Pakistan-Bangladesh war, she did not hesitate to take the sternest action. She calculated and played her cards well. Even threats from the US Navy's seventh fleet did not daunt her. She thought of herself as the Indian 'Jean d' Arc' come to liberate India. She introduced what may be called the amoral theory in Indian politics. Power had to be seized and retained—the measures adopted did not really matter. Thus money collection for the party elections became important. It did not matter how the money was collected. People like L.N. Mishra and A.R. Antulay came into prominence—they knew how to collect money. And anyone who could not deliver the money was out. What I am trying to say is that Mrs Gandhi could not and would not tolerate anyone or any party standing up to her. And the Akalis were one such party. They were prepared for any sacrifices and were quite willing to fight and die for their cause. So it was a bitter head-on struggle. During the Emergency, the Akalis had not supported her, but all its leaders had gone to jail or were detained. And even now, since they had started their agitation, they were not willing to compromise.

After my meeting with Mrs Gandhi, I felt that there was going to be a clash in our approach to the Punjab problem. So far all the years that I had been in Delhi, even as cabinet secretary and later as governor of West Bengal, this had not happened as somehow, in the end, the policy adopted was one not very different from the one I myself would have advocated. For example, the Marxist Government of West Bengal was not removed and President's rule imposed, as that would have spelled trouble. In Punjab, however, even though her own party men, opposition leaders, independent observers, non-party leaders of public opinion all suggested a political settlement of the Akali problem while dealing at the same time with the terrorists, she did not want a political settlement as that would have given the Akalis strength independent of Indira Gandhi in Punjab. Sensing this difficulty, I wrote out an undated letter of resignation and when I went to see P.C. Alexander later, I gave it to him. I told him that whenever Mrs Gandhi decided I should go, all he needed to do was to fill in the date in my letter and hand it over to her. I would leave Punjab instantly. He did not take the letter and said it should not be necessary. However, there were, I remember, three distinct occasions—apart from the final one—when I offered to resign. One was when the question of foreign, especially Pakistani, hand in the Punjab terrorism arose. The other two related to administrative or police failures in Punjab. In the first case, I rang up Dr Alexander and told him to tell the Prime Minister that I was ready to go.

He said it was not necessary. On the second occasion I spoke repeatedly to Cabinet Secretary Krishnaswamy Rao Sahib for a couple of days and on the third instance it was to the Home Secretary T.N. Chaturvedi when he had come to Punjab for discussions. I am mentioning this as it appeared repeatedly to me that the Mrs Gandhi and I were not on the same wavelength and that our approach to the very difficult problem of terrorism was not similar.

It was not my practice to go to Delhi every few days to meet the Prime Minister and obtain instructions from her. I would go only if there was an important conference or meeting to attend, or when I was called by her. Dr Alexander would ring up and say that I had not been to Delhi for sometime and would I go. In such cases, I often went in the morning, spent a few hours and returned by the afternoon. The flight from Chandigarh to Delhi by the state plane used to take forty-five minutes only.

I want to say something about the Punjab police. The continuous propaganda by the politicians of all hues and the press—both, the extremely biased vernacular press of Jalandhar and English and other language newspapers—have been at the forefront of the campaign against the police. What has been essentially a failure on the political front, has been bandied about as a failure of the police. It is true that the police are demoralized as a result of this continuous propaganda not only in Punjab but all over the country. There is interference at all stages in the police work. Even the process of selection has been interfered with. The senior police officers are not allowed to select men on merit after verification of their antecedents, and criminal and political links if any. In some cases it has been known that ministers or even MLAs have been given a quota, i.e., a number of posts have been filled by a candidate of their choice, in the district police. The policemen cadre has been made a district cadre, which means men are selected only from within the district and not transferred out of it. The cadre is not even a deputy inspector general (DIG) range cadre. Then to make matters worse, the candidates recommended are not those who are deserving or qualified—it is because they have paid money to be selected. In Punjab, it was said that a constable had to pay Rs 15,000, and this amount went on increasing according to rank, so that a DSP had to pay between Rs 50,000 to even a lakh—no one was immune from this cancer of corruption. Having paid this money and been recruited into the force, the constable owed allegiance to the political boss and not to the official boss—the DSP. There was interference even in the posting of constables. Certainly, no superintendent was free to post a sub-inspector or assistant sub-inspector to a particular thana without the consent of the local political party chief. It was clear to me that this would happen every time some ex-Ministers of the Congress party would come to me asking for the posting of some minor functionary, like a school teacher, an inspector of the co-op department, a police sub-inspector, etc., to their constituencies, or a specific block, or village. When I would ask what the special reason for this request was, they would tell me frankly that these officers would help them with or during the elections. Assuming that I was a Congress(I) man, and must have been sent to help the Congress interests and that I would be familiar with the political imperatives, they did not hesitate to tell me this.

Not only did the politicians interfere with postings, they even did so with police investigations, in the filing of the charge sheet and the subsequent trial. Whenever they wanted it, the trial would be delayed, or the case manipulated. As a last resort, in important cases, the government even withdrew the cases from court saying that it was in the national interest. In my knowledge, there were at least two instances in Punjab—once before I joined and once while I was there—that recruitment was not carried out because the political nominees had not been selected. When I was there, the Inspector General pointed out that there were 15,000 vacancies and no recruitment had been made for five or six years and he was extremely handicapped for want of essential manpower. I ordered for these vacancies to be immediately filled in. Applications were invited. A special selection team of three officers including two superintendents from other districts was constituted. Rigorous physical tests were prescribed and after completing two preliminary rounds for elimination, a final selection was to take place. To the consternation of the Congress(I) people, their recommendations had been disregarded—the selection had been made on merit. I was approached to cancel it or postpone it until a popular ministry was sworn in. I did not agree. So the union home ministry was approached, and lo and behold, the Home Secretary rang up the Punjab Home Secretary and IG of Police and asked them to hold up the recruitment. That was the end of it. The manpower requirements of the state thus could not be filled up. That such interference took place in other cases was again vividly brought to my attention when the question of appointment of some assistant registrars of the co-op department came up. The Punjab Public Service had apparently sent some names. Normally, the recommendation would have been processed by the department and appointments approved by the advisor. I do not know whose candidate was not recommended but I got a ring from the Prime Minister's house that the list should not be approved because it had several irregularities. At first I took no notice. I received a similar call again after two days and yet again later. So I had to ask the Advisor to look into the matter. Later he was told not to proceed with the selection and, as far as I am aware, the selections were not made and the posts remained vacant.

Yet another charge against the Punjab police was that it was predominantly Sikh and the Hindus were in a minority. The fact was that the Hindus did not come forward for enlistment as constables. The Hindus of Punjab are essentially town dwellers, businessmen and money lenders. In the villages, they are the food grain merchants, grocery shop owners, brick kiln owners and the like. They are not farmers or agriculturalists. The sturdy, well-built farmers are the Jat Sikhs. They have a tradition of joining the Army and police. They surpass their Hindu counterparts on the basis of their physique alone. So that whenever a physical ability test is made, the Sikh Jat farmer comes ahead. The Hindu businessman does not volunteer nor does he qualify. There is however the Hindu Scheduled Caste who qualifies because he is also essentially of rural stock— generally a landless agricultural labourer. He qualifies along with his Sikh caste brethren, the Mazhabi Sikhs. These two together constitute nearly 33% of the Punjab police, 50% or more are Jat Sikhs and only the remainder are Hindus. But this composition is not the result of any bias against the Hindus or in favour of the Sikhs.

The political interference in recruitment was started by the Congress, kept up by the Akalis during their rule in 1967–1969 and '71, again continued by the Congress during Zail Singh's time between 1972 and 1977, and later upheld by the Akalis from 1977 to 1980. So all political parties have been playing this game. This is not the case only in Punjab. In West Bengal, Congress(I) was accusing CPI(M) of putting their men in the force. In Bihar, Uttar Pradesh and elsewhere, caste is said to be the main factor in making recruitments. In these two states, for example, it is alleged that communal consideration, i.e., an anti-Muslim bias, is displayed in the selections and whenever a Hindu-Muslim riot occurs, the Muslims blame the police for being communal, i.e., pro-Hindu and anti-Muslim, even though this may not be the case.

In Punjab, this took another turn. Because the CRPF was recruited on an all-India basis it had more Hindus naturally. So, the Hindus began to ask for the CRPF to be posted for their protection, and the Sikhs, the Punjab police. Most unfortunately, this bias and the generally vicious atmosphere created differences even between the two forces. The CRPF local commanders, did not even trust or share information with the local police heads if they happened to be Sikh, which was often the case. There were two very serious incidents of firing between the forces that could only be quelled by a great deal of tact and directions from Delhi to the CRPF. Once a Sikh Punjab police constable was shot dead by the CRPF. A revolt almost rose in the Punjab police, but fortunately it was checked and controlled in time. But this alienation was very visible and palpable.

The Hindus however did appear and qualify for the higher police service, the IPS, as this examination was held on an all-India basis and concentrated more on academic distinctions wherein the Hindus were able to score. The physical test was minimal—so that quite a good number of Punjabi Hindus qualified for the IPS. Even in this service, because of the generally vitiated atmosphere, the Hindu and Sikh members of the IPS did not see eye to eye on many matters.

Let me recount what I think must have been only a specimen but was a most blatant example of political interference and police complicity therein. I refer to what came to be known as the 'Payal murder case'. Three or four people, including a rich young man in a Fiat car, were murdered. The police said that this had been an encounter by some terrorists or dacoits. But the local people were not satisfied. They said that the police officials—including the Senior Superintendent of Police (SSP) and other policemen—at the behest of Beant Singh, a Minister in Darbara Singh's Government, had got these people murdered in cold blood because of a land dispute. This incident occurred when the Darbara Singh ministry was still in power. When I joined, Sardarni Nirlep Kaur MP came to see me and said that this was a cold-blooded murder. She submitted a petition on behalf of the family of the victims and urged that I get a CBI probe ordered into the matter. The facts were convincing enough. So I asked the Home Secretary to write to the union home ministry for a CBI probe. There was considerable effort both in Punjab and in Delhi to prevent this from happening. It took me some months before I could get the CBI to take up the case. After more than a year of investigation, the CBI have recently filed a charge sheet against then Senior Superintendent of Police and several other police officers for murder and they are now standing trial. Beant Singh, however, is the present president of the Punjab Provincial Congress Committee.

This is a very glaring example of political interference in and misuse of police functioning. I was told that Darbara Singh could not take action, because an important minister of his, Beant Singh, was involved and he had threatened a revolt in the government and the party.

The charge that the Punjab police is not effective and that it does precious little to suppress terrorism is totally false. In fact, if any arrests have been made, terrorists nabbed in encounters or killed in action, it has all been the work of the Punjab police. The CRPF and BSF do not have even a fraction of such success to their credit. BSF however does catch smugglers on the border, but they are the only force there and anyone moving in suspicious circumstances is apprehended. Throughout the period, till the end of 1984, more policemen—among them a large number of Sikhs—had been the victims of attacks by terrorists. Several high-ranking police officals, inspectors, sub-inspectors and constables on patrol duty, etc., posted as security guards to VIPs or people in the hit-list, had been killed by terrorists. But this has not dampened the spirit of the Punjab police to deal with terrorists. Many police intelligence men and informers have been killed, yet they have kept up a very good intelligence system. Whenever an incident occurred, the Punjab police intelligence was blamed, even though they had supplied advance information. For example, they had alerted the Delhi police in advance before some major murders took place, like the killing of the Nirankari Chief or the Delhi SGPC Chief Manchanda. They had even sent an alert when a number of railway stations were attacked.

The most exemplary case was at the time of Operation Bluestar. When the white paper issued by government was being prepared, I came to know that some adverse comment was going to be incorporated regarding the lack of supply of intelligence by the Punjab police. The white paper mentioned the number and kinds of arms recovered from the Golden Temple by the Army authorities post Operation Bluestar. I sent my Advisor (law and order) Surendra Nath to Delhi to ensure it had no such comments otherwise I would publicly denounce it.

Some six weeks ago the Punjab police (intelligence) had furnished the Director of the Intelligence Bureau, the home ministry, and the Government of India with exact details of all arms inside the temple. The difference between the list furnished by the Punjab police and that by the Criminal Investigation Department (CID) was that of only one firearm! And it was said, and continues to be said, that the Punjab police had failed in its duties. I strongly refuted this whenever I had an opportunity in the meetings in Delhi. But then, the proverb is so true—give a dog a bad name and then hang him!

It is interesting to note here that the Punjab Government was not consulted during the preparation, drafting or editing of the white paper presented to the Parliament.

No amount of change of police personnel is going to solve

the Punjab problem. The police personnel and their ammunition can only be effective if the political issues are resolved and political interference in the working of the police at all stages is stopped.

This is not to say that some Sikh members of the force are not affected. There was one DIG, S.S. Mann IPS, who was rabid, one can almost say so, in his belief that Sikhs are being discriminated against. And he was very highly connected. Mann was so outspoken in his criticism that during Darbara Singh's time he was transferred out of Punjab to the CISF and posted in Bombay. Charges were drawn up against him. I saw one of his replies to the charge which ran across several pages and was full of vituperative attacks on the government and its policy regarding the Sikhs. He was finally dismissed after Indira Gandhi's murder. Many enquiries were made to see if he had any links to the case. But nothing could be found against him even though he is still under detention.

But several havildars and constables had become followers of Bhindranwale and some of the dismissed men featured in the list of terrorists. Some would possibly be sympathizers as a number of people, specially Sikhs in the service, were sympathetic to the Akali demands, even though they would be against the extremists, or the demand for Khalistan or for violence in any form.

Central Government's interference in the Punjab administration went beyond all of this. The President expressed his dissatisfaction with some of the Punjab officers several times and even hinted that I consider replacing them. What had happened was that his favourite or preferred officers had been shunted out by Darbara Singh or sent away to Delhi. I made almost no changes in the postings as I found them. For example, I did not replace the Chief Secretary K. Vasudev whom I considered to be a good officer, even though Zail Singh had spoken about him in disparaging terms a couple times. Whenever I went to meet Zail Singh at Rashtrapati Bhavan, his Deputy Secretary or Press Advisor would meet me before or after the meeting and comment about the posting of some officer or the other and say that it was the President's desire that they be removed. His son-in-law and granddaughter met me several times in Chandigarh in connection with the transfer or specific postings of some of their family friends. My inability to oblige in such cases had been perhaps a source of some disappointment or dissatisfaction to the President, especially because I did not consult him or act on his advice. Here the views of the Prime Minister and her Secretariat were diagonally different from that of the President. They saw to it that no officer known to be pro-Zail Singh was posted to Punjab.

I had another open rift in the case of the transfer of the Commissioner and Deputy Commissioner of Ferozepur. After observing their work for several months, witnessing no drive or zeal on their part coupled with the reports against them, I decided to replace them. The reports were of two kinds, first that they were afraid of the terrorists, had built a fort around their houses and would not move out whenever there was trouble in their charge, not even in the town. This was true. The second was about their integrity—always difficult to prove. Before the transfer orders were issued I was told by the Chief Secretary that I might consult Dr Balram Jakhar, speaker of the Lok Sabha, in this matter as Ferozepur was his constituency. I did not see the necessity of doing so and ordered for their reliefs to take charge immediately. So this was done at once. The officers went to Delhi and met Jakhar. He first rang up Home Minister P.C. Sethi, who in turn rang me up to cancel the transfers. I said it had already been done. Then he asked me to explain the position to Dr Balram Jakhar who was also on the line. I told him the same thing. But the matter did not stop there. He went to Mrs Gandhi and asked her to speak to me. She did and I told her the same thing and refused to cancel or modify the orders. Although this was not to the liking of the authorities at Delhi, it was clear how the postings of officers were done to suit certain important people. And these officers then helped the politicians at the time of their elections and were perhaps rewarded in return. But my insistence and my resistance to oblige the people at Delhi was certainly not liked. Questions regarding the Punjab Government's functioning were raised. And it was on these grounds that I had offered to resign thrice.

In fact, not only the police, but even the other departments in Punjab were well-administered when compared to many other states. It had to be shown that administrative failures were responsible for the deterioration in the Punjab situation. This was why, just after I left, a high-powered committee was set up in Delhi under R.V. Subramaniam to recommend changes in the administrative structure, including that of the police. The recommendations were nothing to write home about and in any case were soon forgotten. The purpose of temporarily influencing public and press attention had been achieved, though I do not think anyone was deceived by the farce.

*

The first month of my tenure in October 1983 proved to be very busy and tiring. Long hours of work, meetings, conferences, visitors of all shades and importance, visits to some district headquarters had been quite tedious. As November approached, the staff—the Secretary and Deputy Secretary—suggested that I go to Simla for a long weekend and relax a little. The change would be good, besides Simla would start getting colder and it would then be difficult to go. The Punjab Governor has a small but very nice Raj Bhavan on the outskirts of Simla at Mashobra.

As this lay outside the limits of Simla it did not come under the Himachal Government and remained with Punjab. So one Saturday in early November, we all left for Simla, reaching there at about 4 or 4.30 p.m. The sight of the hills and the Himalayas was immensely satisfying.

CHAPTER THIRTEEN

Punjab: 1984

[Written on 9 May 1986]

Early in the morning on 6 November 1983, I received an urgent telephone call from Chandigarh. I was informed by the Chief Secretary that news of a passenger bus being hijacked by some terrorists had just been received. The bus had been taken onto a side road where the passengers were asked to get down. Some three or four Sikh terrorist youths shot five or six Hindus dead. One Hindu was saved because a Nihang Sikh protected him, saying that this Hindu was his brother and the terrorists would have to shoot him first. This person was later praised for his courage and honoured by the Punjab Government at many public functions.

On receiving this news, I decided to immediately return to Chandigarh from Simla to see what could be done. This was the biggest terrorist activity following the declaration of President's rule and was similar to the outrage which had compelled Darbara Singh to resign. I decided to call in the Army. So, a little later in the morning, I called Lt Gen Sundarji, then general officer commanding-in-chief (GOC-in-C) Western Command, and requested him to come and see me as early as possible and also arrange for a helicopter to take me from Simla to Chandigarh. Thus my only visit to Simla as governor of Punjab was suddenly cut short.

Lt Gen Sundarji arrived at about 9 a.m. He had arranged for the helicopter. I told him that I intended to call in the Army as soon as I got back to Chandigarh and that he should be prepared for the next course of action. He said that although he would be duty-bound to send the Army if I called for it, he would prefer that I did not do so, and strongly advised me against it. He mentioned two reasons when I asked him the reason for this. The first was that in his opinion the Army would not succeed in suppressing the terrorism, especially from his experience in the North East. He believed that the Army would not do any better than the Punjab police or the paramilitary. In any case the terrorism was also connected to political issues. Secondly, he had a large number of Sikh officers who would not like to be involved. In fact he was not too sure of how they would react. Therefore he wanted the Army to be kept out of the Punjab imbroglio as he feared unpleasant consequences. I took his advice and held off the idea of calling in the Army in the immediate future.

I left for Chandigarh at about 10 a.m. and thereafter for Amritsar to have discussions with the concerned officers. Despite the very large deployment of police, increasing its mobility, improving the communication system and so on, the terrorists remained at an advantage. They had a wide option of targets to choose from—often it was just random. They could come any way they liked, by car, motorcycle, scooter, bicycle or even on foot, could hide anywhere—in the gurdwaras, private houses, fields, and could just merge with the general population. After committing a crime at one place they could get several miles away within a short time because of the good connectivity of roads and buses. The police were thus greatly handicapped. Even when they got intelligence that a group was out to go after a particular VIP or attack some particular targets like banks, railway stations, they could not pinpoint the target because of these reasons. The police knew that some railway stations were to be attacked. While precautions were taken at all the important ones, wayside flag stations or halts could still be attacked.

*

This brings one to the question of how terrorism is to be tackled. It took more than twenty-five years to bring peace to Nagaland. More than twenty years have passed, there is no peace in Mizoram. The same is the situation in Manipur. Talks had to be held with extremists in both Nagaland and Mizoram. A settlement could be reached in Nagaland, but not in Mizoram and Manipur so far. Looking beyond India, Northern Ireland has faced terrorism for some seventy years now and more recently the IRA has succeeded in killing Lord Mountbatten, with Mrs Thatcher just managing to escape the Brighton hotel bombing. Explosions have occurred in London streets. Even Palestine has seen unabated terrorism for the last forty years.

The Government of India, especially Mrs Indira Gandhi, repeatedly said that Pakistan was encouraging and helping the terrorists in Punjab. It is true that ever since the creation of Pakistan there have been all kinds of clandestine activity across the huge land barrier. There has been smuggling of gold, narcotics, opium, arms, and more. Hindus, Muslims, Sikhs have all taken part in it. Smuggling activity continues at our borders with Nepal, Bangladesh, Sri Lanka and even across the seas from the Gulf Countries. So gunrunning is no new thing.

Amidst questions surrounding Pakistan's involvement, I asked several intelligence people, the Punjab police, Central Intelligence Bureau, BSF, Army Intelligence and others if they had any firm evidence of this. None of them could provide any specific evidence except point out suspicions. These suspicions related to training camps at places which are known to be Pakistani cantonments, like Kasur just across Ferozepur. But these were simply suspicions that could even be part of a propaganda point. Pakistan, for example, is accusing India of fomenting trouble in Sind and Baluchistan and that it is conniving with the USSR and Afghanistan to create trouble in the North-West Frontier Province (NWFP). In fact, Pakistan seems to be so convinced that India and the USSR intend to crush Pakistan as in a vice, that they have succeeded in convincing America in turn of such a possibility and have as a result acquired enormous quantities of arms from the USA.

Even Nepal, with whom we share such friendly ties, feels that India is intent on destabilizing the Monarchy's rule there. The 1953 collapse of the Rana regime in Nepal was due to Indian intervention and the champions of democratic rule in Nepal live in India, especially Varanasi. So the Nepalese fear that India may upset them politically. Therefore, they have sought close relations with China although ethnically, culturally, economically, and in all other ways, Nepal and India are much closer to each other.

Sri Lanka presents the same problem. For the last ten years there has been trouble in the Northeastern part of Sri Lanka because the Tamils are demanding a separate state. The Sri Lankan President, Prime Minister and others openly blame India for encouraging this secessionist activity. In fact all the leaders of the Tamil liberation movement, whether moderates or extremists, are living in India and operating from Indian bases. India says that they have only been given sanctuary and they are not permitted to operate from their bases here. It has been difficult to understand how the militants in Sri Lanka are getting sophisticated arms and explosives—India is the nearest geographical source of supply. I think India feels that Sri Lanka is drifting or drawing closer to the USA like Pakistan. USA also has a large naval base in Diego Garcia. It is possible that at some juncture Sri Lanka permits USA the use of the Trincomalee harbour in eastern Sri Lanka. This would threaten India's independence.

The above reflections were only in the context of Pakistan's involvement in the Punjab problem. It is of course always done to divert attention to an outside agency but the fact of the internal intensity of the Sikh problem is completely overlooked. Most of the arms, including sophisticated weapons like sten guns, used by the terrorists were obtained within the country, stolen from police armouries, seized from police or paramilitary guards. Several among them were country-made pistols and revolvers. Ammunition was also mostly local. The hand grenades most often used or found were HE36 ones made in Indian ordinance factories. I know of two cases where Sikh Army men coming to Punjab on home leave had their luggage searched on suspicion. Ammunition like hand grenades were retrieved. Similarly in some Army units there were thefts and unaccounted ammunition said to have been used up in firing practices. Ofcourse, all such cases that were detected were followed by court martials. But the point I am making is that the terrorists were getting supplies from their sympathizers in the Indian Army and police, and from clandestine manufacturing centres like those discovered in Rajasthan.

Pakistan was also being blamed about training terrorists but there were several ex-servicemen and ex-politicians who were responsible for this training. The most important among them was Major General (cashiered) Shabeg Singh, who joined up with Bhindranwale. He had been responsible for training the Mukti Bahini at the time of the Bangladesh war. He was an expert in guerilla warfare and had many Army decorations to his credit. However, after the Bangladesh war, it was found that he had been corrupt and had embezzled funds, and he was court-martialled and stripped of his rank. This perhaps had made him an enemy of the government and he began to flirt with and later joined the ranks of the disgruntled. There were several such ex-officers—brigadiers, colonels and the like, some such men in the police too. So Lt Gen Sundarji was right when he said that in such circumstances the Army should not be used. Once, President Zia-ul-Haq of Pakistan was asked about training the terrorists. He is supposed to have replied that he did not have officers as competent as Major General Shabeg Singh so why should the Sikh militants come to him.

*

I have written long on this subject, because once when some press correspondents pressed me to say something about Pakistan's involvement, I said there was strong suspicion but not enough evidence to prosecute anyone in court. Questions were raised in Parliament. The Prime Minister said more or less the same thing, while adding that it was not in the public interest to share the information with the public. P.C. Alexander rang me up on the matter and I was asked to issue a statement adding that although we had suspicions we could not share them with the public. I then sent a long letter to Dr Alexander underlining the statements made by me and those by the Prime Minister and pointing out that there was practically no difference even in the wording. I also added that I was prepared to resign. He said I should not do so, and that the matter may now be treated as closed. The basic difference in approach, in retrospect, was on the assessment of the situation. I felt then and even now that the Sikh resentment was growing out of an estrangement and a feeling of neglect, which I have dealt with earlier. The Prime Minister was emphasizing more on the external aspects of the situation, the involvement of Pakistan, indirectly hinting at CIA involvement via the Sikhs settled in the USA and like those in Canada and the UK. True, the Sikhs in these countries were involved—that I think was due to a crisis of culture—they had been culturally uprooted even though voluntarily from India, and had not been absorbed culturally into Western society, where despite their material success they continued to be second class citizens. And moreover they were rapidly losing their religious and cultural identity in their second generation. This was a very deep wound to their psyche.

I now come to the process of negotiations with the Akalis during my time.

But before this, sometime in November 1983, I went to Delhi and told Mrs Gandhi that Lt Gen Sundarji was not in favour of calling out the Army and instead preferred the problem be dealt with by the police and paramilitary forces. I also informed the senior officers, i.e. P.C. Alexander, Krishnaswamy Rao Sahib and T.N. Chaturvedi about the same. Consultations with all possible experts—of the police, Army, BSF and CRPF, about the methodology to be adopted in dealing with the terrorists were also carried out. Several strategies were adopted as suggested from time to time. Surendra Nath, an IPS officer originally from Punjab was sent as an advisor. He had been chief secretary of Mizoram and had experience dealing with terrorists. Among the methods adopted was strengthening the guards in the banks and introducing a warning system. This did not always succeed, as the banks or the employees would not activate the alarm even in cases where the police station was hardly a couple hundred metres away. We introduced mobile patrols. Districts were divided into various zones and an SP was made to take full charge of each zone. We strengthened the wireless communication networks.

Two interesting incidents resulted from this, that caused anxiety but fortunately no adverse consequences. A wireless set belonging to an airforce jawan on duty just outside Amritsar airport was taken away by some terrorists. This put the whole airforce network into confusion because the terrorists could hear all conversations and gain information about movement of aircraft. Fortunately, the wireless set was recovered a few days later by the Punjab police. But the theft was a warning of the havoc that could result if such sets fell into the hands of terrorists. Several months later we experienced a tremendous fraud. This was sometime in June 1984. The Chief Minister of Rajasthan, Shiv Chandra Mathur, was going to attend a function in Himachal Pradesh. On his way he decided to visit the site of the breached Bhakra canal. The Punjab police had provided him with a pilot and escort car under a DSP. I suddenly got a call from Chief Minister Vir Bhadra Singh informing me of a message received from their police wireless control room at Kasauli that Shiv Chandra Mathur had stopped in a wayside village, gone to a house and that he or some of his companions had been attacked by terrorists. This was followed by a telephone call from the Chief Secretary, Himachal Pradesh. We were in a terrible quandary in Chandigarh. The police force rushed to the reported site. The Post Graduate Institute of Medical Sciences at Chandigarh was alerted to receive any injured and an ambulance was also despatched. Frantic messages were sent to the District Collector (DC) and SSP Ropar. After a few hours, a message was received from the DSP of the escort party, informing us that the Shiv Chandra Mathur and his party had reached Manali comfortably and without any problems, and he was now returning. By then the DC and SSP Ropar had sent all clear reports and the IG also came back. I informed Vir Bhadra Singh of the same. The whole incident had been a hoax. Someone had got hold of one of the wireless sets tuned to the Punjab police network and had sent the message to Kasauli which was the control room for relaying all Punjab police network.

Similarly, while we provided more motorcycles and sophisticated arms to the police, we also had instances of them being attacked and their arms being taken away. Nevertheless, this was the only way that terrorists could be tackled. Several encounters also took place and at other instances terrorists were chased and arrested or killed.

One very serious difficulty was that the majority of these terrorists had no past criminal records. They were mostly young men, between sixteen and thirty years of age, some who were students and others just out of college. Some of them belonged to well-to-do families and were well connected, so getting information about them was difficult.

During my visits to Delhi, Mrs Gandhi and Dr Alexander continuously remarked that the administrative measures should be tightened and the police strengthened. I told them that we had consulted everyone who could advise on this matter. All suggestions from past experiences of experts were being adopted. The greatest difficulty was that the people did not cooperate fully. They were afraid of furnishing information for fear of retaliation or were sympathetic because of non-fulfilment of what they felt were their legitimate grievances.

A couple months after my conversation with Lt Gen Sundarji, the Chief of Army Staff General Vaidya came to see me at Chandigarh and told me that the Army would be willing and prepared to come to the assistance of the civil authorities whenever I so desired. Apparently after my talk there had been many discussions, and consultations about the deployment of the Army, its possible consequences, etc. And ultimately General Vaidya had agreed and he conveyed this to me. After Operation Bluestar and several months thereafter, some fairly senior Army officers continued to express the view that any other chief of army staff would have refused to permit the deployment of the Army for Operation Bluestar. But this was also clear that such an operation could not have been performed by the paramilitary forces. The consequences have however been far reaching and are still not clear in the event of an Emergency, say with Pakistan.

The negotiations on the Punjab problem makes for another story of repeated failures, the cause for which is difficult to say, but I will give my own views as the narrative proceeds. I have already given the background impressions I had gained about the position before I came to Punjab.

Soon after I came to Punjab, leading members of all political parties, except the Akali Dal, came to see me in a group. They gave me their background assessment of the situation and said that something should be done to solve the impasse. All political parties, Congress(I), CPI(M), CPI, BJP, supported the Akali Dal demands relating to Chandigarh, territorial disputes and sharing of river waters. They said that it was unfortunate that the Akali Dal was fighting for these causes as if it was of interest only to them, they should have really widened their base to get support from the other parties also. In fact, in the negotiation with the centre, whenever the Government of India involved the Opposition along with the Akalis, they all supported the Akali stand. So, the Prime Minister said that the Opposition parties only complicate the issues and should therefore be kept out of the negotiations. The Akalis, as a party, could not take non-Sikhs as members because their constitution says that only Sikhs can be members of the party. So despite the support from the Opposition, the impression conveyed to the people outside Punjab, to the rest of the communities in India, specially Hindus, and to the outside world, was that all this was a fight of the Sikhs against the rest of them and did not get projected as an all-Punjab issue.

The Akali leaders came to see me a little later and initially somewhat tentatively. Their district leaders would meet me whenever I visited any district and give their point of view. This, however, was done separately and rarely jointly with other political parties. Prakash Singh Badal came to call on us as a courtesy call with his wife and the former Akali Agriculture Minister. Badal asked me to tell my staff and others that they had come to see me to discuss about relief to agriculturists and some waterlogging problems, not any political problems. He however did say that the Akalis would like an early political settlement and would appreciate it if I could do something in this regard. Thereafter, Surjit Singh Barnala, Balwant Singh, Gurcharan Singh Tohra all came to see me one after the other, separately. They all had long talks with me, all urging some solution to the impasse, and all condemning the murders and violence and saying that their own agitation had been entirely peaceful.

The points that all of them urged, even though differently, led to the same conclusions. Their terms or conditions for settlement were somewhat as follows:

a. Chandigarh should go to Punjab unconditionally. This had already been conceded by the Prime Minister some fourteen years earlier and its implementation was unnecessarily being delayed. On the question of compensating Haryana, their suggestion was to transfer several villages on the border, mainly in Patiala district, to Haryana. Mrs Gandhi once told me that the Akalis were talking only of about half a dozen villages in compensation. When I asked the Akalis, they led me to understand the number could vary between sixty and a hundred and twenty, as may be determined by a commission presided over by a Supreme Court judge and taking the village as a unit, and contiguity as a principle, apart from being Hindi speaking. They also said that in addition, cash compensation amounting to even Rs 100 crores could be paid by Punjab to Haryana to build its own capital.

b. They were most strongly opposed to the transfer of Fazilka-Abohar to Haryana as it was not contiguous to that state. In fact the Prime Minister's award of 1970 also recognized this and had provided for a 7-kms long corridor through Punjab villages. The idea of a corridor was wholly abhorrent and had not been recognized anywhere. The Akalis said that if a corridor principle was to be accepted then Jalandhar city, which was in the heart of Punjab, could also be given to Haryana as it was an overwhemingly Hindu city.* The other question which the Akalis asked that appealed to me the most, was—why should they ask for the retention of Abohar-Fazilka if they were communal, as they were represented to be. With Chandigarh and Abohar-Fazilka both forming parts of Punjab, the number of Hindu MLAs in the Assembly would increase from six to eight. The percentage of Hindus to Sikhs would increase and to that extent formation of a purely Sikh state would become more difficult. I conveyed this point very strongly to the Prime Minister. In fact, on my own I urged that at any cost the Hindus should not be allowed to decrease in number, rather their percentages should be increased. The ratio of Hindus to Sikhs then was 48:52, and with the amalgamation of Chandigarh this would turn to 49:51 or close. Even today I am convinced that the only way to prevent Khalistan is to prevent a movement of the population on communal lines and

---

* The only corridor I could remember was the Polish corridor to connect the port town of Gdansk after WWI and which in itself was one of the causes of WWII as it had separated German speaking territories.

in fact to see that the Hindu population of Punjab increases rather than decreases. The Prime Minister on the other hand was most insistent that Abohar-Fazilka go to Haryana simultaneously with the transfer of Chandigarh to Punjab. My own assessment is that this was to drive a wedge between Punjab and Rajasthan, so that at a later date Punjab, and especially the Sikhs, may not ask for Ganganagar district of Rajasthan to be added to Punjab. Ganganagar is a majority Sikh district inhabited by residents originally from Punjab, who had immigrated to Ganganagar (then part of Bikaner state) at the invitation of Maharaja Ganga Singh, the then ruler of Bikaner, after the Ganga canal was built. The Punjabi Sikhs were efficient cultivators of canal irrigated lands.

c. The distribution of the river water at the Supreme Court's arbitration. The Akalis were insistent on this as they were convinced that they had suffered injustice on this front. The Prime Minister's award was definitely weighted in favour of Haryana and I think she felt that any judicial award may reduce the extra weightage given to Haryana.

d. The setting up of a commission for a fresh delimitation of the boundaries between Punjab, Haryana and Himachal Pradesh, taking the village as a unit, was one of the points demanded by the Akalis but would have been treated by them as of somewhat lesser importance. In any case, there were no emotional overtones on this issue.

e. The next important issue was the enactment of an All India Sikh Gurdwara Act. G.S. Tohra who was the President of the SGPC laid great stress on this and said that he could not understand how this demand was an anti-national demand. They could not go West, to Pakistan, even if one of their most important shrines, Nankana Sahib, lay there. And when they wanted the historic gurdwaras, i.e., those associated with their gurus, the important among them being Nanded Sahib in Maharashtra, Patna Gurdwara and one or two in Calcutta and Assam, they were only tying themselves more strongly with the rest of India and not confining themselves to Punjab. The objections to such an All-India Act was that it would only make the SGPC stronger and the Sikh community more united. It would place more funds at the disposal of the SGPC for political activity and therefore the government had obtained, especially from Patna and perhaps Nanded too, resolutions to the effect that they did not want to come under the purview of an All India SGPC Act. However, these views were never made public or stated in Parliament.

f. The last point concerned the Anandpur Sahib Resolution. After the formation of the Sarkaria Commission, no real differences remained. The Akalis only urged that since the Commission had been appointed and they had already agreed to abide by its decision they only wanted the resolution as such to be referred to the Commission. This was not a major issue and not referred to as such even by the Prime Minister or the Akalis in my conversations with them.

The Akali leaders all urged that they would like to have the next round of negotiations directly with Mrs Gandhi. They did not want the Opposition parties to be associated and even suggested that the Prime Minister and Sant Longowal should meet alone and settle the issue. I conveyed these suggestions repeatedly to Mrs Gandhi whenever I met her and also to the team of officers earlier referred to by me. I urged that the earlier this was done, the better and easier it would be to settle the law and order problems in Punjab. Towards the end of January 1984, it looked as if some progress was being made and some talks and soundings had been initiated with the Akalis. A change in the atmosphere was discernible. An example of this was the 'Lohri' celebration. People urged me to hold it at the Raj Bhavan. We decided to do so and a number of people responded to the invitation. Mrs Prakash Singh Badal came even though Mr Badal himself did not come. When she was leaving, Mrs Badal told my wife that Punjab would soon be celebrating the ushering of peace, hinting that some political solution seemed to be round the corner. In early February 1984, I think it was the 7th, I had gone to Delhi. Dr Alexander came to see me late in the evening at Kapurthala House and said that my troubles would soon be over and that an agreement had been reached. It only needed to be formalized. I was very happy to hear this but kept my own counsel as there had been so many failures in the past.

Finally, it was announced that the next round of talks with the Akalis would take place on either 12 or 14 February 1984 at New Delhi. As it always happened whenever any talks were announced, there was a spurt in terrorist activity. This was to frighten both parties—to make the moderates feel that they were in danger and the government that any agreement with the moderates would not be binding on the extremists. But the government generally ignored these threats and negotiations were held. This time there was an additional element. In Patiala, a militant Hindu group had come forward under the name of Hindu Shiv Sena or Hindu Suraksha Dal under the leadership of one Pawan Kumar Sharma. They were trying to get some support in other towns like Jalandhar and Ludhiana. A few days before the talks, Pawan Kumar Sharma made some very intemperate speeches and openly invited Hindus to attack Sikhs in their houses and shops. Patiala had witnessed two serious incidents of communal rioting wherein Hindu and Sikh mobs had clashed and ended up with considerable injuries accompanied with cases of arson. These kinds of riots had not been observed in other parts of Punjab. So it was necessary that this mischief be nipped in the bud. The Deputy Commissioner of Patiala, a Hindu, arrested Pawan Kumar and placed him under detention. This helped to put down any further trouble in Punjab. But the interesting thing was that I began to get telephone calls for the release of Pawan Kumar. Haryana Chief Minister Bhajan Lal asked why he had been arrested. Later P.C. Sethi, who was then home minister, also rang me up and asked me to release Pawan Kumar. I refused as this would create problems for us and the situation in Patiala may deteriorate. The point that I am trying to drive home is that these extreme Hindu communalists were being helped by the highest Congress(I) circles in Delhi and elsewhere.

The meeting opened in Delhi. It was not between the government and the Akalis alone, but the Opposition leaders had also been invited. The Union Home Minister started by asking the Akalis if they had reconsidered the whole matter and what were their suggestions now. The Akalis said that they had no new proposals to make. The meeting started and ended in a fiasco. All that P.C. Alexander had said about an agreement having been reached and so on, evaporated into thin air. P.C. Sethi did not make any positive moves for a settlement. I got the suspicion that once again the whole thing had been ditched and the Prime Minister did not want any settlement. The meeting did not last even an hour and the Akalis were preparing to return to Chandigarh and Punjab. However, some Opposition people, especially the CPI(M), persuaded them to stay on for another day to see if some progress could be made.

A few hours later, news was received from Haryana regarding Hindu mobs at various places that had started attacking Sikhs—in buses, cars, Sikh shops and gurdwaras. This went on for a full two days. Gurdwaras were set on fire. Sikhs had their turbans thrown out, hair and beards cut. Women had their dresses and hair tresses cut. The Chief Minister of Haryana was then in Delhi to watch the progress of the negotiations with the Akalis. It was only after two days that the Prime Minister ordered him to return immediately to Haryana and see that the trouble was stopped. These incidents were taking place all along GT Road. A day or two later, calm was restored, but at the expense of a great gloom that had already been cast.

Meanwhile in Punjab, tension mounted. The failure of the talks had been received with great disappointment. Men and women came to Punjab to share stories of their harassment in Haryana, showing as proof their cut hair. This also angered the public. Some attempts were made to take out protest demonstrations, but worse were riotous Hindu mobs, specially in Amritsar and Batala. In Amritsar, a mob went to the railway station and smashed the model of the Golden Temple kept there. In Batala also, a Hindu mob went on a rampage. In both cases, the police and the intelligence and public reports were that the mobs were led by Congress(I) Hindu MLAs of the area.

Then in the third week of February 1984, bands of terrorists went on a killing spree. There were perhaps four or five groups of two or three terrorists each. They struck at five or six places almost simultaneously. They came on scooters or motorcycles, some even on foot and started spraying bullets indiscriminately against Hindus. This happened at a few places in Gurdaspur and Amritsar districts. In Amritsar, two brothers—one Sikh and the other a mauna Sikh—were travelling together. The mauna Sikh was killed despite protests of his brother. He was the editor of a famous Punjabi magazine *Preet Lari* started in the 1930s by his father, a famous Punjabi writer. He had also established a colony between Lahore and Amritsar in a village—Lopoke—which today lies very near the border on the Indian side. The idea was to have some kind of a commune. This young man had married a Hindu girl. Later, the Punjab Government gave a substantial grant for the continued publication of the magazine, also a sum for the rehabilitation of the widow. In another village in Amritsar, a Sikh sarpanch fired his gun at the terrorists and made them flee. Soon after these incidents, I visited several of these villagers and talked to them. They all said that the local Sikh neighbours helped them in every way but the attackers were from outside. In the villages along the Amritsar border, there was panic among some Hindu residents who were businessmen. Some even thought of moving out to Haryana. We provided special police protection and more patrolling in such villages. A few people who moved out to their relatives came back. I recall an incident during this tour of mine. As I moved from Gurdaspur district via Batala to Amritsar, a bomb exploded in the main bazaar of Batala. This happened some five minutes after I had crossed Batala. I learnt of this only after reaching Amritsar. As I had come by a different route through Batala city, this bomb explosion was not in my direct path. Some policemen, specially the SSP Gurdaspur, thought that the bomb might have been intended for me but the attempt misfired.

At the end of February, there was darkness all round. Negotiations had collapsed and there was no hope or possibility of their revival in this atmosphere. Extra police force, modernization of their telecommunication equipment, more intelligence, and even more patrolling was yielding no results. Some suspected terrorists were being arrested. The police from time to time claimed to have solved some murders. But these were all uncorroborated confessions meant either to mislead the police or to save themselves from further torture. None of those apprehended could be prosecuted in court for any serious crime. The most they could be charged with was for being in illegal possession of arms under the Arms Act. The courts awarded sentences usually for six months or a year, most of it already undergone by the time the case ended, so these people were released. To my knowledge there were no convictions for any serious crime, no death or transportation sentences either. Many accused even got away scot free as nothing could be proven against them. Some people were killed in encounters, but their antecedents were not known. The picture was mostly gloomy and disheartening.

Two or three incidents of that time come to mind. A famous Sikh saint, Baba, died of old age. He was cremated on the banks of the Sutlej near Nangal, a place considered to be as holy as Haridwar. One of the saint's followers was Darbara Singh. He went to attend the funeral ceremony. Just when the pyre was lit, some rifle shots went off. Darbara Singh, who was standing near a parapet, ducked. A man standing some distance away with a gun was promptly arrested. He was an employee of the State Agriculture Department. The man was arrested for attempting to murder Darbara Singh. A few days later, the IG, P.S. Bhinder, told me that there had been no attempt to murder Darbara Singh. This man had openly fired a shot in the air as is the custom when the pyre is lit and some famous man's last remains are consigned to flames. This is just a way of saluting the departed soul. But there had been much publicity and when I told Surendra Nath, the advisor, he said this would not do. So they had a further confabulation. A case was registered and a missing Nihang came into the picture who was supposed to have supplied the firearm. But to my knowledge the case never came up for trial to this day. I do not know what the truth was.

Relations between the communities were getting strained. The continuous media propaganda in the Punjab vernacular papers and even the national dailies was adding to this estrangement. At this time two young Sikh girls, about eighteen or twenty years of age reading in a famous DAV-run college for girls in Jalandhar, ran away from the hostel. The college was run by a Hindu Board of Management and had a Hindu principal. All kinds of rumours of scandal began to circulate. The Hindu principal, teachers and wardens were said to be in league with undesirable people and were making girls available to them. One of the girls was the daughter of a senior service man, perhaps retired, and the other of a Kuwaiti businessman. They were getting considerable money from their parents. For a full week after their disappearance the case was not reported to the police. When it was finally reported, their photographs were not supplied as the parents thought that the police were defaming their daughters. The parents did not cooperate and instead began attacking the Hindu management and the Hindu teachers. Several were suspended. The Prime Minister, Home Minister and I were approached. At long last, after a fortnight, the police succeeded in obtaining their photographs. The Jalandhar police, who had all along suspected that the girls had run away for fun, sent a man to Bombay, who got their pictures to broadcast on televsion. A cafe owner of Goa saw the pictures and recognized the girls. He informed the police who promptly informed those at Jalandhar. The girls' statements were recorded by the Goa magistrates. It was clear that the girls had run away—they had gone to Agra, Bombay and Goa and then running short of cash had started working at the café in Goa. The promptness with which the Punjab police succeeded in solving the mystery was creditable to them, but the Sikhs and Hindus for their own ulterior motives went on attacking them. The Sikhs wanted to discredit the college, and the Hindus, the Sikh-dominated Punjab police.

I addressed a passing out parade at the police training

college in Phillaur. In my speech there, I said that circumstances very similar to the pre-partition days of 1947 were developing and if nothing was done we might see a recap of that terrible history with all the carnage accompanying it.

The Akalis started yet another agitation, this time for the repeal of Article 25(2) of the Constitution, or rather its amendment, whereby the word 'Sikh' would be deleted and not clubbed with Buddhists, Jains along with Hindus.* They said that they would tear or burn a page of the Constitution or the article itself which contained Article 25(2) if their demand was not met. They also announced their intention to do this publicly, at various places in Delhi, Chandigarh and Punjab. Prakash Singh Badal was to show this form of disapproval at Delhi. Orders had been received from the government that all these leaders should be prevented from going to Delhi and were to be arrested if they showed disrespect to the Constitution. However, Badal, posing as a truck driver's assistant, managed to reach Gurdwara Rakabganj in Delhi and on the appointed date they all tore out the page of the Constitution. They were all arrested and the question of prosecuting them came up.

Some of the Akalis who came to see me said that their legal advisors had told them that they could not be convicted as they had shown no disrespect to the Constitution nor were they violating it. They only wanted to express their desire for an amendment. Be that as it may, the matter could never be decided judiciously as the cases never came up for trial. After keeping the Akali leaders in jail for some weeks, they were all unconditionally released by the government, who agreed to examine their points and obtain Sikh opinion throughout the country. But nothing more has been done about this. Perhaps

---

*'the reference to Hindus shall be construed as including a reference to persons professing the Sikh, Jaina or Buddhist religion, and the reference to Hindu religious institutions shall be construed accordingly.'

the Sikhs are also not so keen to pursue it. The issue was only to attract attention.

During their period of detention on these charges, Prakash Singh Badal's daughter got married to the grandson of Pratap Singh Kairon, the former chief minister of Punjab. The government wanted Badal to apply for temporary release or bail to attend the marriage. He refused to do so. The government could not order his release on its own. So the marriage was celebrated without Badal. This also left a bad taste among the Sikhs as they all felt that the government had been unnecesarily vindictive and mean in this matter. They could have just released him. But it was so difficult to understand what was going on in the minds of the powers at Delhi.

Despite these setbacks, Mrs Gandhi initiated some public measures to restart a political dialogue. Shri P. Shiv Shankar, then minister for petroleum, was asked to revive diplomatic efforts. He had studied in Amritsar for four years and knew Punjab well although he came from Andhra Pradesh. He visited Punjab several times but failed to establish any contact with Sant Longowal or a rapport with the other leaders. Shri K.P. Singh Deo was minister of state for defence and Arun Singh, a mauna Sikh, was a close confidant of Rajiv Gandhi. They also visited Punjab several times to see what they could do. Y.B. Chavan and Shankar Dayal Sharma were deputed to Punjab and Haryana respectively to meet the local political leaders and to directly report their assessments and suggestions to the Prime Minister. Yet another group of three people was sent to make secret contacts among which were Patwant Singh, the writer living in Delhi, and Gurbachan Singh, a retired Foreign Service officer.

All these were just hares started off to run in different directions to distract public opinion or to divert it. There was no seriousness in all these moves. The Akalis were certainly not taken in by them.

From time to time, meetings were held in Delhi to review the course of action. In one such meeting, it was discovered that a group of commandos under RAW were being trained to storm the Akal Takht. Helicopters had been flying over the Golden Temple possibly to take photographs. The CRPF was trying to come as near to the Temple complex as possible although, as I have said earlier, they could not catch any terrorists coming in or going out. In one meeting where R.N. Kao, Krishnaswami Rao Sahib and P.C. Alexander were present, I asked openly if their intention was to storm the Golden Temple. They said that Zail Singh stood in the way and his reaction was not predictable. I said that attacking the Golden Temple will mean a point of no return and the Sikh community will be totally alienated for generations to come. But perhaps only Zail Singh's reaction was a stumbling block. The Army was being prepared. The outlook began to look gloomier and I was sadder than ever.

Sometime in early November 1983, the question of elections to Panchayati Raj Institutions came up. The Gram Panchayat elections had been held during Darbara Singh's time and the Congress(I) had claimed an overwhelming victory. The schedule for the next higher body elections had also been fixed. The question that came up was whether they should be held or not. Purely from a law and order point of view, as also to help restoration of normal processes, I was in favour of holding the elections. However, both my Advisor and I decided that this was a political question and we should first find out what the government thought about it. So I rang up P.C. Sethi and requested him to let me know if the elections should be held as per schedule or not. Home Secretary T.N. Chaturvedi was also asked to make his own assessment. Two or three days later they rang up to say I could go ahead with the elections. One or two days before the actual issue of notification, I again rang up P.C. Sethi to enquire if he had consulted Mrs Gandhi and got her approval. He said that it was all right. So on the due date we issued the notifications. A few days thereafter I got a call from P.C. Alexander informing me that the Prime Minister wanted the elections to be postponed indefinitely. It was precisely to avoid the embarassment of issuing a cancellation that I had asked for prior approval. The fact was that the Congress was not sure of winning the elections and realized that it would be a loss of face to them as under President's rule there was less likelihood of tampering with votes. A few days later, on grounds that the law and order situation was not conducive to the holding of the elections, we called off the election notification. But I decidedly informed Delhi that even when I had given them enough time to think and come to a conclusion, they had caused me embarassment by such last-minute changes in their attitude.

The law and order situation for normal activities was not disturbed even though terrorist attacks continued. Unfortunately, what was considered to be normal crime in other states, became terrorist and secessionist activity in Punjab. The press and the public continued to play up to what I often said to myself was a death wish of the nation or at least of the political parties. An example of this was when we had the Punjab Public Service examinations. They had been postponed for quite some time for one reason or the other. But now the Public Service Commission wanted to hold the exam, or at least the Chairman did. The Chairman was a Harijan lady who had been appointed a member, by Zail Singh. By virtue of being the seniormost member she became the Chairman. There were complaints against the commission as a whole and also the Chairman of corruption though nothing could be proved. But I found this lady to be a bold and certainly fairly good at her job and keeping control over her staff. She decided that the written examinations would be held at the centres fixed. We agreed—as far as the government was concerned. The members said it was fraught with danger and should be postponed. Some guardians also sent representations. A group of examinees came forward saying that it was dangerous and we should postpone the examination. I said that if they were afraid of taking the examination they were not fit to join the civil service. We did not want cowards. The examinations were held. There were no incidents and no trouble of any kind. What was most depressing was the atmosphere of cowardliness, especially among the educated classes. The high school and Intermediate or higher secondary examinations were also held as per schedule. Even when there was a curfew in one or two towns for a day or two, there was no difficulty experienced.

However, we had difficulty later in holding the university examinations in May 1984. This was principally because then the AISSF had been declared a banned organisation and some of their leaders—those who were not inside the Golden Temple or other gurdwaras—had been arrested. They threatened to disrupt the exams. All the Vice Chancellors took this threat seriously as also the university faculties and their staff. They all urged postponement—the staff threatened non-cooperation if the exams were held. So these had to be postponed. They could be held only after Operation Bluestar. The sympathy of a large number of teachers with the AISSF and the Akali party was very obvious.

Sometime in February 1984, I think, having received instructions from Delhi, orders had been issued that the police could enter the gurdwaras in 'hot chase' and should not consider that there was a blanket ban on their entry. However, the police should act with circumspection and, in the case of the Golden Temple, they should still take prior permission. However, in no instance did the police actually enter any gurdwara or apprehend any suspects or anyone therein. But we faced a very serious situation sometime later in Moga. This sector was under BSF control and on one occasion they suspected that some terrorists had gone inside some gurdwaras after having shot some people dead in the Moga market. There were three gurdwaras and the BSF surrounded and sealed all three. After a day or so, some eight people attempted to come out, they were chased and shot. Among them was a sarpanch of a neighbouring village. All the eight bodies were cremated by the police. The cordon around the gurdwaras was tightened. Water and electricity supply were cut off and a strict curfew enforced. Some women and children were also inside. Yet the BSF would not enter to flush out the terrorists if there were any. An emergency meeting was held in Chandigarh. The BSF Inspector General was also present. The Akali Dal announced that if the siege was not lifted, villagers in thousands would march to Moga. Sant Longowal had also been ringing me up about this. The BSF, despite reinforcements, were not confident of being able to control the situation and wanted to start a dialogue with the Akali jathedars and others to defuse the situation which had turned very tricky. And unless a solution was found much bloodshed was expected. It was therefore decided at this meeting that Dr S.S. Sidhu, one of the advisors and a Jat Sikh belonging to a neighbouring area, should accompany IG, P.S. Bhinder and the BSF Inspector General to see what could be done. Prolonged discussions were held and ultimately a suitable compromise was reached. It was agreed that the villagers would not march to the town. Food would be allowed to be sent in to the people inside the gurdwaras. Water and electricity would be restored. The people inside would come out one by one. Their names and addresses would be noted and they would be sent to their villages. Only those who were suspected of criminal activity would be taken to the police lock-up and then produced before the magistrate. People would be searched for arms before being allowed to come out and board the bus—the Deputy Commissioner and SSP would then enter the gurdwara and search the places for unlicensed arms and ammunition. All operations went off peacefully and everyone heaved a sigh of relief.

Now an interesting outcome—when the gurdwaras were searched, no illicit arms or ammunitions were found, except a few licensed guns in one of the gurdwaras. Bhinder rang me up from Moga about this. I said this would not do, and they must use metal detectors and dig up the courtyards. After a further search, some arms in a gunny bag and a few hand grenades were recovered. But this incident became a kind of rehearsal of the difficulties that would be faced if any attempt was made to lay siege to the gurdwaras. It also revealed the difficulties in regards to police entry, and further, the difficulty of catching any terrorists, let alone prosecuting anyone.

But the Sikhs as a community were losing sympathy among the Hindus within and outside Punjab. A very interesting incident took place one evening in Chandigarh. There was a local Kumaon Parishad and they were keen to invite me to a function. I agreed to attend a cultural programme one evening. Towards the end, one of their members began to tell some humorous stories. In India, jokes concerning the Sikhs are endless. Some of the stories are invented by the Sikhs themselves, but others are spread by people of other communities. I do not recall any other community about whom there are so many jokes. Now the story that this man said about the Sikhs was not so much of a joke as a dig at them. The story was that four or five people of different religions were in a boat—Hindu, Sikh, Christian and Muslim. The boat began to leak and sink. Each person on board said a prayer to their god and then jumped when their turn came. In the end only two people were left—a Sikh and someone else. The Sikhs's turn came. He offered a prayer to his God and then instead of jumping himself as all the others had done, he pushed the other person out of the boat. The story, instead of being humorous, was intended to convey that the Sikhs were treacherous and could not be trusted. I was very angry at this story and its narration and told the organizers about it and left soon after. The story was recited in Kumaoni dialect and so not many may have understood. But this showed the growing feeling of other communities towards the Sikhs, even as far away as Kumaon. That such a feeling exists, is bound to and has in fact, percolated to the Sikhs also and they feel even more estranged and isolated losing all hopes of getting justice at the hand of what they describe as a 'Hindu Government in Delhi'.

*

I have already dealt with the growth of the terrorist movement in Punjab. I have mentioned that several of those arrested have been very young, of good families, with no past criminal records, frustrated or fired by fundamentalism—difficult to explain. I have also written about the foreign hand and my own interpretation thereof, especially about the role of Pakistan. Whatever be the role of the USA and UK, there is no doubt that a large section of the Sikhs settled and working in these countries and in Canada are definitely helping the terrorists in India by sending them money and arms. They were and are sending more money to the SGPC and the Akali Dal for Punjab's development, it is true. But they also seem to be anti-Indian and what may be called pro-Khalistan—and this was even before Operation Bluestar. But why? The several thousand Sikhs working or settled abroad are economically well off and are unlikely to return to India. Their support of the secessionist cause is working against the Sikhs who are outside Punjab and who are getting more and more isolated from the surrounding people, with whom they once shared friendly terms. What can be the cause of this? I have found it difficult to find an answer. I feel that the overseas Sikh is on the one hand getting further and further away from the land of his forefathers, getting more and more alienated and his roots getting weaker. On the other hand, his children are giving up his religion and that of his forefathers—specially the external forms of this religion. The internal form is also lacking in an alien culture. The overseas Sikh thus feels even more strongly in his heart that perhaps he will not survive as part of a distinct community. If his children do not keep long hair, and instead smoke and intermarry, what will be left of them as a community. So they will do anything to keep their identity intact anywhere—be it only in Punjab. The nearest parallel to the overseas Sikh behaviour, according to me, is the behaviour of the Western European and American Jew in regards to Israel. The American Jew will not go and settle in Israel. Life in America is much better. But he will do all he can to help Israel. He will send money, visit sometimes and be happy seeing the ancient religion, the taboos and the customs kept intact as in the days of the Old Testament and the prophets. He himself, however, will be one of the advanced guards of the Western American civilization. The same is, I think, true of the overseas Sikh. His role is a very important one in the present continued unrest in Punjab. It is also playing havoc with the Indian society in Western Europe and America and Canada by sowing seeds of antagonism among each other. It must be remembered in this connection that Dr Jagjit Singh Chauhan, the self-proclaimed leader of the Khalistan movement in Britain, was a minister in the renegade Akali Government under Lachhman Singh Gill which came into power and continued in office with the active support of Congress(I). Such were the persons supported by Congress(I).

*

My story relating to Punjab is coming to an end. Terrorist killings continued to mount. Political discussions and negotiations were at an end. It is true that the Prime Minister continued to say that the doors for negotiations were always open. Some clandestine talks were also going on. But mainly the purpose of these was to divert attention. Some of the Akali leaders came to see me, specially G.S. Tohra. I told him that the Akalis should negotiate and end the stalemate. He and the others said that the government had no intention to settle the issue.

We, that is my advisors and I, told the Government of India that before any Army action was taken it was necessary to ensure the safety of Hindus in the villages, so for this purpose there should be a heavy deployment in the rural areas. Secondly, there was a possibility of large numbers of Sikhs marching to the Golden Temple as unarmed death squads for the defence of the Temple. They were called 'mar jwaras'. They had to be prevented from coming to Amritsar. They would be dressed in white, like corpses prepared for cremation. So one urged that in all calculations these aspects be kept in mind.

The Army, for some time, had been holding discussions with our officers especially from the CID, and collecting as much information as possible. It is also known that the specially trained units of the SSF were practising assault exercises. Helicopters had flown over the Temple area to take photographs and study the layout. So inevitably and inexorably, events were moving towards a climax.

CHAPTER FOURTEEN

Punjab: 1984 and After

I had gone to Delhi on 28 May 1984 to attend a special law and order meeting being hosted in the Cabinet Secretary's room. R.N. Kao and P.C. Alexander were also present. P.C. Alexander informed me of their decision to call out the Army to flush out the terrorists. He also said that the Army Commander Lt Gen Sundarji would get in touch with me regarding the details, timing, etc. One interesting thing that they said was that the Director, Intelligence Bureau, was joining us in a few minutes, but that I should not speak about this in his presence. That such an operation was taking place without taking the Intelligence Bureau into confidence, was quite odd and significant. Then I asked whether I could inform my officers, especially the Advisor (Home), IG Police, IG CID and the Chief Secretary. They said I could do so after the Army Commander had met me.

Soon thereafter, Army units began to move into Punjab in very large numbers. In the beginning we said that these movements were in reply to Pakistan's troop movements across the borders. The next day, as soon as some preparations had been made, the Army Commander accompanied by Lt Gen Ranjit Singh Dyal, a Sikh officer and chief of staff Western Command, came to see me. Later, after a talk with them, perhaps on May 31 or June 1, a meeting with our officers, the Chief Secretary, Advisor (Home) Surendra Nath, IG Bhinder,

IG CID and the Army officers was held. Special telephones were set up in my bedroom. At one time, I think, I had as many as a dozen telephones with sacrophones in my room which would ring at all hours of the day.

My grandchildren had come to stay with us then. Since we were already discussing going to Simla for a few days, I told my wife to proceed on the afternoon of June 2 itself with the children. They all left, except Lalit who stayed on with me. There was an urgent telephone call from Delhi informing me that Dr S.S. Sidhu, the only surviving advisor from the original team, should return to Delhi and step in as secretary to Government of India in the Cabinet Secretariat. I informed Sidhu of this, telling him he had to leave on June 3 and since he had his old mother with him he could use the government plane and leave before the curfew was imposed.

On 2 June 1984, the Prime Minister was to make a broadcast and also speak about the induction of the Army. The broadcast kept being postponed and was aired quite late, perhaps at around 8.30 p.m. Throughout the speech, there was no reference made to the Army. It only spoke about the government's desire for talks. The Army Commander and others met soon after in the Raj Bhavan where I gave them the written order requesting the Army to come to the aid of civil authorities. Lt Gen R.S. Dyal was appointed advisor (security) to the governor. Next morning, on June 3, an indefinite curfew was imposed all over Punjab including Chandigarh.

The original date for the Army's entry into the Temple was fixed for June 3. But this got postponed by forty-eight hours mainly because they were not ready. They told me that they had been given little notice, so it had taken time to gather and move in all the troops required. The date chosen was somewhat surprising. June 3 was Guru Arjun Deb's martyrdom day and large numbers of pilgrims including women and children had come to the various gurdwaras. Several of them got trapped in because of the subsequent curfew. Later someone told me that the date had been fixed because of some intelligence reports received, specially from Soviet Intelligence, which reported that Khalistan would be proclaimed from the Golden Temple and simultaneously from other gurdwaras on June 7 or 8, so preemptive action had to be taken. The Akali Dal had announced another programme of civil disobedience from June 3 aimed at preventing flow of wheat into the markets and export from Punjab. This, the administration had said, they could manage. Delhi talked of this as the immediate reason for calling in of the Army.

On June 5, the Army entered all gurdwaras, some mosques, churches and Hindu temples simultaneously, in order to not be charged with discrimination only against the Sikhs. But they found great resistance from the Golden Temple and this was unexpected. The first few attacks were repulsed with heavy losses to the Army. Commando units suffered very heavy casualties. What was expected to be an operation not lasting beyond a few minutes or at most hours had gone on for the whole night and yet not concluded. At about 1 a.m., Sant Longowal and G.S. Tohra were rescued from the Temple premises along with several others and taken into Army custody. Morning dawned and operations had to be suspended. They were resumed the next night using light tanks and armoured personnel carriers.

Bhajan Lal, then chief minister of Haryana, kept on ringing me up to get the operations expedited and brought to a close early. I said that the Army was taking adequate action and was trying their best.

On the night of June 6, the operations were terminated. On the morning of June 7, the bodies of Jarnail Singh Bhindranwale, Shabeg Singh, and Amrik Singh were found in a cellar of the Akal Takht. The toll had been heavy. The Army lost over eighty men including some officers. Those killed among the terrorists and civilians numbered over 1200. An attempt was made to photograph the dead and carry out postmortems but all the resources available could not complete the task. It was very hot and the bodies were rotting rapidly. Originally the Army tried to dispose the bodies by mass cremation, but even the soldiers could not carry on this task. So the Amritsar municipal scavenging staff were pressed into duty. Among the dead were several women and children who had got trapped inside the Temple. They had come for Arjun Singh's martyrdom day. Several pyres were lit and bodies thrown in one after the other. We had to ensure that a consistent figure of casualties was given. This was put at about 750. The municipal staff were also paid accordingly.

Another great loss within the Temple premises was in the library which had caught fire. Valuable manuscripts were destroyed. Some articles kept in the Akal Takht were also damaged, though the *Granth Sahib* was safe. A bullet pierced through some pages of the *Granth Sahib* kept in the upper storey of Harminder Sahib. Some damage was also suffered by several buildings though not the main Harminder Sahib.

On the morning of June 7, Lt Gen Sundarji and Lt Gen R.S. Dyal came to see me and informed me that the operation had been completed. They said that as soldiers, they took their hats off to the terrorists who fought extremely well. This was a compliment, they said, as professional soldiers.

Cleaning up operations went on for some time. There was resistance at some other gurdwaras also, especially Dukhniwaran Sahib at Patiala.

I told the Army Generals that, as per the information received, despite the curfew and patrolling and the action, some 200 terrorists had got out of the gurdwaras and were in the countryside in small groups, and a sustained search and mopping up operation would have to be carried out for some days. And lo and behold, on June 7 itself, the main Bhakra Canal was breached a few kilometres from Ropar. The job had been done professionally. The water flew into a stream so that fields or villages were not flooded, but supply of water specially to Haryana and Rajasthan was cut off. It was a major sabotage. It took six weeks and over Rs 1 crore to set it right again. And yet again in July, after I had come away, the canal was breached again. Terrorists still continued to be about. The lesson of the action in Amritsar had not been driven home.

President Zail Singh decided to visit Amritsar on June 8. So special efforts had to be made to remove all the corpses from the Temple precincts and clean the place. I had also gone to Amritsar then. I was a little late in reaching Amritsar myself as the time of the President's arrival was being constantly changed. But this enabled me to fly two or three times over the Temple surroundings before landing. Many private houses in the vicinity were still smouldering. I could see some big funeral pyres burning. Inside the Temple and the neighbourhood, the stink of rotten corpses still persisted. I saw two or three dead bodies still floating in the tank.

The President naturally was very upset at all that he saw. When he was taking off, he said to me that this was all due to the failure of the Punjab administration. I had to accept it as I had no reply. Although through the years, since 1981, so many governors and advisors had changed, so many deputy and inspector generals of police had been replaced, all kinds of deployments and re-deployments had been made, the police force, BSF and CRPF had been modernized, with arms and communication links, yet terrorism still continues and has not been contained.

The impact of Army entry into the Golden Temple, now popularly known as Operation Bluestar, which was the Army's secret code for this operation, but subsequently gained widespread currency, was very great and profound on the entire Sikh community. Even those who strongly opposed Bhindranwale, condemned terrorism and were against Khalistan, did not support the Government of India's actions. There was widespread resentment among them, some expressed it, others mostly remained silent. But for generations to come, a great divide had taken place. The Hindus and Sikhs would never be the same again.

As Sundarji had predicted and forewarned me in November, there were revolts and desertions among several Army units in as far away as Hazaribagh, Maharashtra, Rajasthan and so on. A Punjabi Hindu Brigadier of a Sikh regiment in Hazaribagh, previously honoured by Sikh soldiers, was shot dead by the mutineers. Several others were killed. The mutinies were contained but after heavy loss of lives. Several Sikh civilians returned their awards to the President. The erstwhile Maharaja of Patiala and a Congress(I) MP, Amarinder Singh, resigned from his seat in the Lok Sabha and also from the Congress party. Bhajan Lal however congratulated me and sent his Chief Secretary Caprihans to convey this personally. He also said that the Jat, specially the Sikh, understands only the lathi and so things should be all right. One or two other Sikhs came to see me—not wholly in politics, who said that the Sikhs have been, for the time being, dealt a heavy blow, but they would recover. One should watch out for 1999, which was the 300th anniversary of the founding of the Khalsa and the Panth by Guru Govind Singh—Baisakhi day in 1699.

Some propaganda during this period—post-Operation Bluestar—badly misfired. The Army authorities gave out that in their searches inside the Golden Temple a large haul of narcotics, money and gems had been made. This was to discredit Bhindranwale and his men. Later these stories had to be denied as no such recoveries had been made. This was again a mistake.

After Operation Bluestar, the Prime Minister began validating the inevitability of it following the Anandpur Sahib Resolution. For the first time in so many years, it was now being dubbed as secessionary and anti-constitutional. This went on for almost a year. But, unfortunately, at no time since 1973, when the Resolution was first made public, was anyone prosecuted in court. Although cases were lodged against Sant Longowal and so many other leaders of the Akali party and many terrorists or suspects, none were tried for sedition or any such activity all these years. Special laws had been framed, special courts set up, yet none of the so-called 'known terrorists' could be sentenced for any anti-national crime except illegal possession of arms. But even this charge could not be laid in respect of those arrested after Operation Bluestar. This is a very sad commentary on our judicial system.

On 23 June 1984, the Prime Minister visited Amritsar amidst very tight security. Chief of Army Staff Gen Vaidya had consulted me a few days earlier. I was not in favour of the visit as the atmosphere was not conducive. So I suggested Mrs Gandhi defer her visit for some time longer. There had been talks of a 'soothing balm' and 'healing touch' after Operation Bluestar— although it did not signify much. I said that when Mrs Gandhi does come she should also address a public meeting and make some announcements about Punjab's future. However, the visit was fixed for the 23rd. I had also gone to meet her. She visited the Temple, then the Military Hospital and was also given a briefing by the Army. Thereafter there was a more general meeting. Buta Singh and K.P. Singh Deo had also come along with her. There was talk about the reconstruction of the Akal Takht and other damaged buildings. Another question that cropped up was that of what should be done around the Temple complex. At one stage it was suggested that all buildings for a width of 50 or 100 yards from the Temple perimeter should be demolished to retain some open space. Many suggestions were made. I had only a few words with Prime Minister separately, in which I told her that despite the Army operation and the flushing that was going on in the rural areas, terrorists were still out.

Since June 6 or 7, several Akali and SGPC leaders had been arrested and placed under detention, mainly in Rajasthan and Madhya Pradesh. Parkash Singh Badal and Surjit Singh Barnala were out of Punjab. When they returned, they made condemnatory speeches across Chandigarh's gurdwaras. They were also arrested and placed under detention. Only one of the more prominent leaders was not arrested—Balwant Singh, the former and present finance minister of the Akali Government. He came to see me and said that he supported Operation Bluestar and all his attempts at reconciliation had failed. He had tried to bring Longowal and Bhindranwale together but again had failed. He said that the government should keep at least one channel open for talks and, to that end, offered his services. I rang up the Cabinet Secretary in Delhi and told him about this conversation, suggesting that it would be good if Balwant Singh was not arrested. This was accepted and later he was to play an important part in the Rajiv-Longowal Accord.

Late on June 27 or on the morning of June 28, I got a call from Dr Alexander informing me that the Prime Minister wanted to meet me along with P.S. Bhinder the next day. I agreed and asked Bhinder to get ready and come along. I got a little upset at both of us having been asked to come together. On reaching Delhi, I waited for a call from the Prime Minister's Office. I was asked to come and see Mrs Gandhi at 2.30 p.m. at her residence. I was with her for about fifteen minutes. At first she talked about general things and then on the need to revamp the Punjab administration. I suggested that they start with me as I took the prime responsibility. She agreed and said that was the intention. I told her that I would be sending across my resignation immediately upon my return to Chandigarh. In fact, on all my previous visits, I had always brought my letter of resignation with me, but this time I had come in a hurry and left the letter behind. I also asked her if I could tell the President about my resignation since I was to meet him after this. She thought a little and then said yes. So I came away after bidding her goodbye.

I was to see Dr Alexander thereafter. I reached his office at about 3 p.m. He asked me about my meeting with Mrs Gandhi and I told him that I had decided to hand in my resignation. He asked me if I would like to go back to Calcutta but I declined. Before I could have any further discussion with him and ascertain some more background news, Jagmohan, the new Governor of Jammu and Kashmir, came in and our conversation was interrupted.

I met the President at 4.30 p.m. and told him about my forthcoming resignation. I said the formal letter would reach him the next day. I felt sad that Punjab was in such a state and I saw no light on the horizon.

I returned to Chandigarh about 7 p.m. Bhinder had stayed behind. He came to see me before I left and said that he had been told that he would be transferred back to Delhi immediately. He said that it was all right by him.

On reaching Chandigarh I informed Vimla and Lalit about this development and decided to start packing the very next morning. That night we had dinner at Surendra Nath's place—we had decided to make no mention of this matter and credit goes to all three of us for not letting the news escape that night.

I dictated my letter of resignation and asked my staff to arrange for a special car and messenger who left at about 10 a.m. for Delhi. At about 10.30 a.m on June 29, I was invited to release a book at the Chandigarh Secretariat. Some senior officers, like the Chief Secretary and other secretaries to government, were also present at this event, as also the press. At the close of the function I let them know that this was my last public function in Punjab and I wished everyone well. It took some time for the news to sink in. The Chief Secretary later approached and asked me if I had resigned and I told him that I indeed had. The Information Officer wanted to know if he could release the information to the rest of the press. I gave him my go-ahead. After discussions with Vimla and Lalit, we decided to leave Chandigarh for Almora on Tuesday, July 3. While the event at the Secretariat was still on, I received a call from Dr Alexander informing me that the Prime Minister wanted me to hold back my decision regarding the resignation. I told him that I had already sent it through a special messenger and had also announced it to the press at Chandigarh so it must already be on the PTI and other tickers. It was announced during the 2 p.m. news on the radio that P.S. Bhinder and I had resigned. Later Bhinder's resignation news was contradicted and substituted by a transfer to Delhi.

We started packing and making arrangements for leaving for Almora. I had decided to travel by the Punjab Government plane from Chandigarh to Pantnagar and then proceed to Almora by car. After the news of my resignation spread, many people invited us to dinner. Lt Gen Sundarji and Gen Dyal wanted me to come one evening but I declined. The advisors and officers also wanted me to attend a dinner but I refused. In fact I did not accept any invitation. So after making a farewell speech at 8 a.m. and saying goodbye to a number of people who had come to see us off, we left for the airport. We took off at 8.30 a.m. and reached Pantnagar at about 9.15 a.m., had breakfast with the wife of the Vice Chancellor and left at 10 a.m., reaching Almora at about 1.30 p.m. the same day. We stayed at the Circuit House for a few days. Our luggage came by truck early the next morning. Lalit had set about clearing the house the same afternoon, and a few days later we moved into our own house. And that was the end of my stay and experience in Punjab and my short gubernatorial tenure of less than three years.

*

The second anniversary of Operation Bluestar is drawing near. So I add a postscript. A great deal has happened in the interim. On 31 October 1984, at about 9 a.m., Indira Gandhi was assassinated by two of her Sikh bodyguards. She was riddled with bullets and died on the spot. One of the murderers was killed by other guards. The other one along with two other people has been sentenced to death by the sessions court. The appeal and confirmation is pending in the high court. The same evening, her son Rajiv Gandhi was sworn in as prime minister and obtained the support of the Congress party.

The nation was stunned by the murder of Indira Gandhi. On November 1, word went around that the Sikhs had to be taught a lesson. Riots broke out in many places, especially in Delhi. According to eye witnesses and popular belief, the mobs were instigated and sometimes led by Congressmen. In Delhi alone, 2500 Sikhs were killed. A similar number were killed in Kanpur, Bokaro and other cities. Property of the Sikhs that was burnt, destroyed and looted ran into crores of rupees. With the inclusion of Operation Bluestar, the total number of Sikhs who lost their lives due to Army action and mob violence was around 7000—far exceeding the casualties by terrorist action or the number of Hindus killed in Punjab from 1982 till date. There was violence even in Almora where I had gone to attend a condolence meeting on November 1. Towards the end of the meeting, a Congress youth leader gave a provocative anti-Sikh speech. That night, shops of seven Sikhs were looted by mobs. These were the only shops owned by Sikhs and withstanding since the last thirty-seven years since Partition.

Winning the election in December 1984 on a sympathy vote, denouncing the Anandpur Sahib Resolution and playing to the fear of the Hindus, the Congress—led by Rajiv Gandhi—came to power in Delhi and several other states. And a few months later there was a sea-change—a complete roundabout turn. Rajiv Gandhi signed an accord with Sant Longowal conceding all Akali demands and stating that the Anandpur Sahib Resolution was not secessionary and would thereafter be referred to as the Saharia Commission. General elections were held in Punjab, but only after the Sikh extremists killed Sant Longowal who had been preaching communal harmony, condemning terrorism and working for peace. The state elections were held, with the Akali Dal securing an absolute majority in the state assembly. Surjit Singh Barnala became chief minister and also president of the Akali Dal. However Badal and Tohra remained somewhat aloof. They continued to distrust Delhi and the Congress. Tohra later resigned from the SGPC.

The first failure to implement the Rajiv-Longowal Accord came about when Chandigarh was not transferred to Punjab on 26 January 1986. The extremists thus became further emboldened. Some of them entered the Golden Temple and proclaimed the formation of a state of Khalistan and then disappeared. S.S. Barnala ordered the police to enter the Temple complex and look for the extremists. They escaped, but this led to a split in the Akali Dal, with a minority, but about one-third, withdrawing support to Barnala. They were led by Badal. Amrinder Singh of Patiala was one among them. The terrorists still continue to mount attacks.

But in all this turmoil, a fact always overlooked is that the Sikh masses have not gone berserk. In fact, they have kept their calm and, as a mob, never attacked the Hindus, unlike the Hindu mobs in Haryana, Delhi and Uttar Pradesh. The Sikh masses and the Akali Dal have always stood for Hindu-Sikh unity. Will the Hindu majority act with restraint and forbearance? I have my doubts. They are led by self-seeking political leaders who will stoop to any lengths to get votes. They, and the press, continue to sow seeds of bitterness against the Sikhs.

What of the future? Some of what has happened and is happening is reminiscent of the pre-partition days of 1947. Khalistan would be a tragedy and the rest of India will not permit it. The majority of the Sikhs also do not want it. If the Sikhs are not driven to desperation, this could be prevented peacefully—otherwise there could be tremendous loss of life and property, especially for the Sikhs. The other way out is for the majority community to act with patience, not to get hysterical but stay calm. To ignore the isolated acts of terrorism committed by frustrated youths and to go about their general livelihood and work normally. If they do so, and if the press and leaders behave sanely and with circumspection and a sense of balance, in a few years—yes it will take a few years—the old amities can be restored. In a seminar on terrorism organized by the Army here in Chaubatta (Ranikhet) in February 1986, I said that the people of India have to behave like the British in this matter. When a hotel in Brighton was bombed by the IRA at 3 a.m. and Margaret Thatcher and her colleagues narrowly escaped, the British press and public did not go into hysterics and did not start killing the Irish wherever they found them. Instead at 9 a.m. the same day, the Conservative Party Conference had opened as scheduled and Margaret Thatcher delivered her speech—as if nothing had happened. Business was as usual. The police continued their investigations. We in India, especially the majority community and the national press, have to learn and adopt this attitude to terrorism. Help the police and not decry them. The Punjab police is not at all demoralized and nor is it inefficient. The common Punjabi, specially the rustic Sikh, the Jat farmer, is going about his business as usual. Agriculture continues to improve year after year, so does business and industry. This is the greatest hope. For them, business is as usual.

On vacation during his Christ's College days, September 1937
(B.D. Pande on extreme left)

In office at Muzaffarpur, c. 1953

Ministry of Agriculture and Fisheries:
Junior Grade of the Administrative Class, Thomas Douglas Taylor Marriner, John Anson Payne, Ratcliffe John Eric Taylor 21st.

Clerk-Shorthand-Typists, Elsie Tobias Hinsley 2nd, Vera Powers 18th, Linnie Betty Thomas 19th.

Clerk-Typist, Kathleen Joyce Wilson 30th.

Air Ministry:
Junior Grade of the Administrative Class, Arthur Lucius Michael Cary, Ronald Clive Kent 21st.

Burma Civil Service (Class I): Maurice Alfred Maybury, Robert Stevenson Rennie 2nd.

Consular Service, Philip George Doyne Adams, Charles Martin Anderson, Ronald William Bailey, Peers Lee Carter, Donovan Harold Clibborn, Peter Richard Connellan Solly-Flood, John Amory Forrest Gethin, Walter Crowhurst Hacon, Alexander Henry Baxter Hermann, Horas Tristram Kennedy, John Vernon Rob 22nd, Kenneth Albert Geary, Alfred Cedric Maby, Leonard Pickles 26th.

Customs and Excise Department: Junior Grade of the Administrative Class, Basil Mark Fisher 21st.

Departmental Clerical Class, Edward George Batt, Thelma Mary Anderson Keeble, Marion Joyce Lupton, Kenneth Frank Mitchell 7th, Constance Allnatt, Doreen Hodgson Alpe, Margaret Gertrude Darby, Betty Catherine Holley, Mollie Myers, Irene Maud Oakley 14th, William James Russell 22nd.

Male Assistant Preventive Officers, Desmond Booker, Cyril Frederick Horrocks 1st, Arthur Houghton, Frederick James Kippin 2nd, James Gordon Parker 5th, Kenneth William Buttenshaw 7th, Harry Brown 11th, Vermand Ross Simpson 13th, John Young 15th, William Rhydwen Benson, Robert Catnach, George Trevor Spark 20th, Robert Nelson Lamb 22nd.

Forestry Commission: Shorthand - Typist, Isabella Mackie Colquhoun 22nd.
Typist, Vera Ruby Leete 1st.

Ministry of Health: Junior Grade of the Administrative Class, Alfred Robert Walter Bavin, Michael Roland Paget Gregson, Digby Lowry Turner 21st.

Assistant Inspectors in the Insurance Department, Ronald Kenneth Meatyard 5th, William George Wilson 6th, Charles Ernest Chambers, Sidney Charles Pearce, Ian Shepherd 8th, Walter Tony Cotton, Douglas Francis, Marjorie Wostenholm 14th, Richard Arthur Sidwell 15th, Macdonald Emslie 18th, James Gordon 19th.

Department of Health for Scotland: Junior Grade of the Administrative Class, Nigel David Walker 21st.

Home Office: Junior Grade of the Administrative Class, Lancelot Errington, Ronald James Guppy, Donald Alexander Campbell Morrison, Cyril Stanley Pickard 21st.

Clerk-Shorthand-Typists in the Offices of Inspectors of Factories, Nancy Mary Thornhill 13th, Mary Clayton 25th.

Clerk-Typists in the Offices of Inspectors of Factories, Mary Carnegie Palmer 18th, Annie Bates 23rd.

Indian Civil Service: James Dallaway Banks, Ronald Harry Belcher, John Henry Butter, Ian Peter Macgillivray Cargill, Richard Vincent Fenton, Charles Howard Gordon, Roland Charles Colin Hunt, Raghu Pati Kapur, Duncan Cameron Murray, Laxmikant Madhavrao Nadkarni, Savak Dinshaw Nargolwala, Ronald Carlton Vivian Piedade Noronha, Bhairab Datt Pande, Rameshwara Prasad, Yogendra Krishna Puri, Ronald Walter Radford, Del John Samuel, Samarendranath Sen, Janardan Datt Shukla, Felix Lucien Sheldon, John Ashton Clarence Smith, Robert Swinney Swann, Thomas Stuart Tull, Andrew McMillan Webster, George Colville Wyndham 2nd.

Snippet of a page in the *The London Gazette*, October 1939, listing new entrants to the Indian Civil Service

As leader of Indian cooperative delegation to Yugoslavia and Israel at Skopje, Macedonia, c. 1959

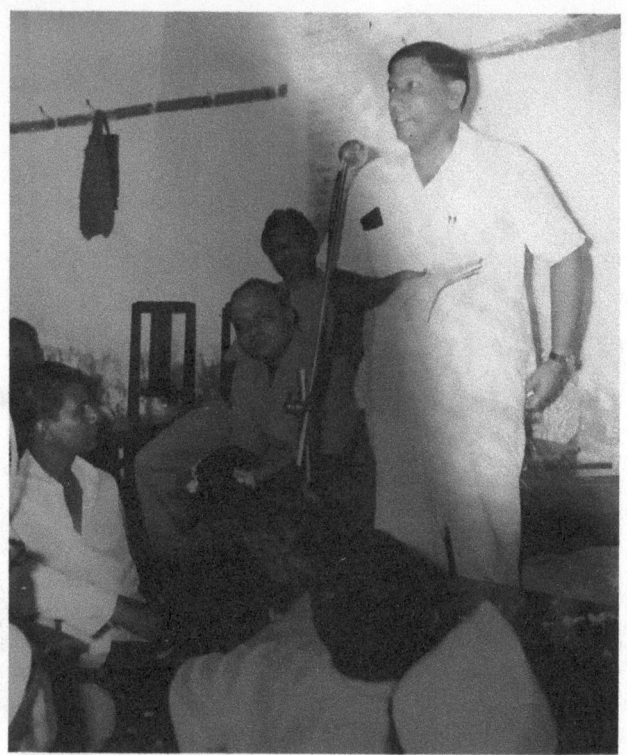

Addressing a meeting with goldsmiths as Gold Control Administrator in Rajkot, Gujarat, September 1964

B.D. Pande (centre-right) with Golda Meir, then Foreign Minister of Israel, at the Indian cooperative delegation in Israel, c. 1960

Driving a tractor on his visit to Escorts factory as Secretary, Heavy Industries, c. 1969

Raising Day of the Special Frontier Force in 1976 with Vimla

At home in Patna, c. 1951. (Left to right: Vimla Pande, Lalit Pande, B.D. Pande, Arvind Pande)

Entering the Raj Bhavan, Calcutta, September 1981

Taking the oath of office as Governor, West Bengal, September 1981

In conversation with Jyoti Basu, Chief Minister of West Bengal, September 1981

With Indira Gandhi (right) and Vimla Pande (left) in 1983

At the Golden Temple, Amritsar in 1983

At Uttarakhand Seva Nidhi workshop on the Seventh Five-Year Plan for the Kumaon Hills, Nainital

Visit to the museum in District Sangrur, December 1983

With a group of Bhangra dancers on a visit to District Sangrur, December 1983

The Pande family on the day of Vimla and B.D. Pande's golden anniversary in May 1990, Almora
(Standing L to R: Mrinal, Arvind, Lalit, Ratna, Sudarshan)
(Seated L to R: Radhika, Aditya, Vimla Pande, B.D. Pande, Anant, Rohini)

Receiving the Padma Vibhushan at the Rashtrapati Bhavan at the hands of President K.R. Narayanan in 2000

Meeting with school teachers and community workers at Uttarakhand Seva Nidhi, Almora, November 1998

Vimla and B.D. Pande at home in Almora, 2005

हम निम्न लिखित पुरुष इस बात का प्रण करते हैं कि हमको पण्डित भोलानाथ पांडे बी. एस. सी. जो कि कृषिविद्या सीख के हाल में भारत वर्ष आये हैं समाज में ले लेने को कुछ भी प्रतिकूलता नहीं है. वह विदेशयात्रा से पहिले जिसप्रकार समाज में गिनेजाते थे वैसेही समझे जायँगे जब तक वह कोई ऐसा समाज-विरुद्ध आचरण न करें जिससे हिन्दू समाज को ग्लानि हो जिन महाशयों ने प्रायश्चित्तादि के पश्चात् उन से खान पानादि किया हो या करें वह सर्वतः प्रसंशनीय हैं और श्रेणि में उनका पद उसीप्रकार रहेगा जैसा पहिले था. इसमें किसीप्रकार की आचरण की विरुद्धता स्वीकृत न होगी ॥

Document recognizing 'prayaschit' of Bholanath Pande

ANNEXURE I

Epilogue—20 April 1994, Ram Navami Day

[This section is based on old papers found in the library of the Purana Ghar, Champanaula]

I finished the previous chapters some time in 1986. Over the last several years, I have come to the conclusion that nothing is fixed or stable. Day succeeds night succeeds day—this applies to happiness, sadness, pleasure, pain, all dualities.

There are various documents which I had found in the old papers from my great-grandfather's time. I have finished reading and sorting these to some extent. Some interesting information has come to light.

The oldest document among these papers is a registered deed executed on a one-rupee stamped paper dated June 1, 1833 at Lohaghat. The registration officers seal says 'Buddhi Ballabh' and 'KaliKumaon'. It relates to the purchase of six nalis of land in Almora town by my great-grandfather, Bhawani Datt 'Simultiya' Pande, for Rs 30, from one Mohana Bhikari Padimaran. There is another deed according to which Bhawani Datt Pande purchased another six nalis of land in Almora for Rs 30. The sale deed was registered at Haval Bagh on 'this nineteenth day of February 1838'. This deed is also on a one-rupee stamped paper. This land was purchased from one Desnidhi Tewari. I think both these relate to the land where our houses now stand at Champanaula in Almora.

ANNEXURE I

There is a document from my grandfather's time relating to Holi festivities. And there are papers relating to the time when the first Brahmin from Kumaon ventured abroad for a few years.

Among my grandfather's papers I found some nine books of accounts, some service papers and letters of correspondence. One book of accounts from 1881–84 is particularly interesting. The first half contains some accounts, but in the other half are drafts of letters written to the Executive Engineer Kumaon Division and Controller of Accounts Allahabad—people under whom my grandfather, Manortah Pande, had served as head clerk-cum-accountant. From these I gather that he was born in 1838 (exact date not available) and died in 1885, aged forty-seven. My grandmother passed away in May 1883. They had seven children—four sons and three daughters. My father was the youngest of them having been born in 1878. My grandfather insists, in one such letter, that he is in great difficulty looking after his motherless, small children. The writing is in pencil and starts with a firm hand but gradually becomes irregular and disjointed. He is on long leave of over a year and writes that he is suffering from paralysis. It is difficult to make out what examinations he passed but his English is good and so is his handwriting—very clear and legible. The accounts refer to payments made to coolies as wages, for spades, etc. It is also clear from these papers that all work here was done departmentally and not through contractors.

Towards the end of 1872, my grandfather was drawing a salary of Rs 70 per month. Later, from 16 May 1885, he was sanctioned an invalid pension of Rs 48/9 (forty-eight rupees and nine annas) by a government order no 3460/XP343 dated 4 August 1885. However, he did not live long thereafter. By the end of 1884 his eldest son, Jai Datt, was employed in Nainital and his second son, Hari Datt, on the government road project (Ranikhet to Almora).

There are several documents, some on stamped paper, some registered, in the nature of promissory notes, mortgage documents for loans of various amounts ranging from Rs 10 to Rs 500. The stamped papers bear the denomination written in English, Bengali and Urdu and vary in value from one anna to five rupees. The documents are spread over a period of fifteen years, from about 1867, and are perhaps indicative of money lending business also.

My eldest uncle Jai Datt would have been born around 1860 or so. He was in service in 1883 when grandfather became seriously ill. He became head clerk of the district office and of the office of the commissioner of Kumaon division and died in March 1917. He had no children.

Jai Datt built what we call our 'new house' in Almora, sometime in 1904. It is said that this was out of some money left by my grandmother—a thousand rupees or so, which was then invested in the house. But the house, even then, was valued at about Rs 5000 so the rest of the money came from my eldest uncle.

Uncle Hari Datt came after him. He did not do very well in life. While he started working soon after 1885, he was in temporary jobs, then went to Kashmir (and according to a letter from him, he was then heavily in debt) and later was in the Uttar Pradesh Public Works Department (PWD) and served in Garhwal, Pauri, Dehra Dun and Nainital. After his retirement, he came to Almora in 1928 or so and passed away in 1937. He also had no children.

Uncle Jwala Datt was probably born in 1874. He got a temporary job as a clerk in 1893 on Rs 20 per month. He got married but died soon after, leaving an only child—my cousin Padma Datt—who was most probably born in 1895. Padma Datt's mother lived long and died in 1960. Uncle Jai Datt, and later my father, brought up Padma Datt.

My father, Chandra Datt, the youngest of four brothers, was born in 1878. He passed the entrance examination of the Allahabad University at age fourteen, getting a second division therein. He went on to complete his MA in 1900, in the second division, from the Muir Central College Allahabad. Then he took up a job as a teacher in the Almora Zila School at Rs 30 per month. He was soon transferred to Amroha Zila School as a teacher at Rs 40 per month. In 1902, he qualified the entrance exam for the postal service as head clerk to the superintendent of post offices—probably at Rs 70 per month. He received some criticism from the family after completing his MA—as he was the first from our immediate family to have completed this level of education—he should have been able to secure a better job. But in 1905, he became post master at Dehradun. For a long time he was personal assistant to the post master general, Uttar Pradesh, at Lucknow and later, superintendent of post offices Kumaon at Meerut. He retired as officiating deputy director general posts and substantive assistant director general in 1931.

Relations between my eldest uncles Jai Datt and Hari Datt and their wives were none too friendly. Hari Datt complains in a letter dated 1908 to my father that he stayed in Almora for three days and was not treated well. In a letter dated 1923, he says he has not visited Almora for twelve years as he does not find it congenial to go there.

Changing social norms: Crossing the Black Waters

A big social upheaval took place in our immediate family as also in the old Almora Brahmin society in 1911. One Bholanath Pande, of Patiya and Jhijhar, Almora, had gone to Japan and then to America to study agriculture in 1905. He returned home in 1910. He was charged with crossing the 'black waters' and flouting the customs of Brahmins. The community decided to excommunicate him. There was one group opposed to this step. They said he had gone for higher studies and in the interest of the country, and therefore if he performed the necessary purificatory rites, 'prayaschit', he should be welcomed in the community. So with the approval of the Maharaja of Benares and the pundits of Benares and Haridwar, Bholanath Pande performed the necessary rites and ceremonies at Haridwar. But then an orthodox group said that 'prayaschit' was not sufficient and he could not be accepted back in society. In this respect, it appears that we were more than a century behind Bengal—Raja Ram Mohan Roy had already gone abroad by then.

Opinions were sharply divided—in Almora and elsewhere. Inter-dining was considered taboo by the orthodox and yet the 'reformists' were seen inter-dining with Bholanath Pande and his immediate family. In our immediate family this took a sharper turn. My uncle Jai Datt's wife was closely related to Bholanath's family. His nephew came to stay at our house in Almora. My granduncle, Tara Datt, belonged to the orthodox camp and asked my uncle to send the boy away but he refused. Tara Datt said there will be no inter-dining with our family. My father was on the side of Uncle Jai Datt. My father seems to even have distributed pamphlets and written to nearly 200 of the prominent people in our community at the time to openly declare their stand in this controversy. Some sat on the fence, but the majority seemed to have been with the reformists, because the controversy subsided in 1912.

Three years later, in 1914, the First World War broke out. Hundreds and thousands of Kumaoni soldiers went overseas to Europe, Mesopotamia, etc., and by the time they returned all question of 'prayaschit' or penance was forgotten or made into a minor formality—with the mere sprinkling of a few drops of Ganga jal.

Of Marriages

Yet another controversy came up in the last quarter of 1939. My eldest maternal uncle, Girish Chandra Joshi, who had been a childless widower since many years, decided to marry one Miss Isa Mukund—an Indian Christian lady who was a teacher—perhaps at Lucknow. This caused a furore—my maternal grandfather was alive and did not like this, neither did my father and several others. But this time there was no open opposition. Soon Aunt Isa was admitted to weddings and festivals in the family. She became the first woman in our family to qualify and join the IAS and retired in the rank of a commissioner. She looked after uncle well, even through his terminal illness.

Over the years all these taboos have more or less disappeared. There are now any number of intercaste, interstate, interreligious marriages. Many are going abroad and the community is advancing.

*

Thus ends this story.

I am suddenly feeling tired and want to stop writing. I have been going through the old papers but though it is interesting to read I am not feeling enthusiastic enough to cull out any interesting details from them. Firstly, I am recovering from a mild attack of flu. Secondly, there is a high number of policemen round the house. After Gen Vaidya's murder by some extremists, the government has ordered tighter security around those connected even remotely with Punjab affairs, specially Operation Bluestar. My requests to the government—about not wanting guards as they in any case are unable to protect anyone—are of no avail. They have made it difficult for me to walk about in the town also as two or three of them always accompany me, thus making me all the more conspicuous. I hope they will be withdrawn after some time at least.

Om tatsat

ANNEXURE II

Uttarakhand Paryavaran Shiksha Kendra (Uttarakhand Environment Education Centre)

It was in October 1984 that Khan Saheb, as we call Chandrashekhar Pande, son of Sukhdeo Pande (Shri Sukdeo Pande, Padma Shri, of Pilani fame, also known as Sukhda), came to see me at Almora. Sukhda, after his retirement from Pilani and return to Nainital, had founded a trust—the Uttarakhand Sewa Nidhi (UKSN), in 1967. The corpus of this Trust was formed out of his personal savings. After his death, my cousin Ghanda,* who was the founder trustee, became the chairman. After Ghanda's death, Khan Saheb became the chairman. Khan informed me that since I was living in Almora and was near to Nainital, all the trustees were of the opinion that I become the chairman. He himself would be a co-chair as he was living far away in Calcutta. Upon his persuasion, I agreed.

At a meeting of the trustees in early 1985, a decision was

---

*Ghanda—Dr Ghananand Pande—was my second cousin who, as a civil engineer from Roorkee, had joined the Indian Railways—at first the East Indian Railway. He had risen to be chairman of the Railway Board. After retirement, he did a three-year spell as chairman, Hindustan Steel Ltd. (the predecessor of SAIL) and then a full term as vice-chancellor of Roorkee University, when the President conferred on him the 'Padma Vibhushan' award for his services as an outstanding engineer and educationist.

made to hold a seminar in Nainital on the Five-Year plans that were just being announced for Kumaon. This meeting could not be held in 1985 and was held later in May 1986. Madhava Ashish of Mirtola Ashram was one of the attendees.

Then suddenly on the afternoon of 15 August 1986, a number of people came to see me. They were led by Additional Secretary Anil Bordia, Department of Education. He was accompanied by Principal Secretary J.C. Pant, Department of Education and a number of other officers of the Education Department in Uttar Pradesh. They said they had come straight from Mirtola where a meeting of a subcommittee on education, set up by the Planning Commission, was held. One of its important recommendations was to set up an innovative programme of environmental education through local NGOs. One such programme was intended to be set up in the hill districts of Uttar Pradesh.

Bordia and J.C. Pant proposed that the Uttarakhand Sewa Nidhi take up this education programme and act as a nodal agency. I had reservations, but after consulting Lalit and the trustees, agreed to the proposal. That same year in early October, P.V. Narasimha Rao, then minister for human resource development, visited Almora as a special guest at the Kumaon University convocation. I was previously aquainted with him and met him over lunch. He said he was glad that I had agreed to take up the environmental education programme. Apparently Bordia had briefed him on the scheme.

I visited Delhi in early November and gave Bordia the outlines of a scheme that had been prepared in consultation with Madhava Ashish, Dr M. G. Jackson, Lalit, and a number of NGOs and school principals who had met in Almora. Bordia and I took the scheme to P.V. Narasimha Rao in the Parliament House, where the minister approved the proposal. Later, Lalit went to Delhi and had a few meetings with Bordia.

In March 1987, we got formal approval for the proposal. A special executive committee of the UKSN had been formed with Lalit as its honorary secretary and headquarters at Almora for the implementation of the scheme. Lalit travelled by bus and on foot to remote parts of Uttarakhand to meet local villagers and NGOs. High level review committees were set up by the Government of India and they found the work satisfactory, and recommended extension and enlargement of the scheme. In October 1991, the second review committee headed by Anil Bordia came and spent four days visiting several areas. On the last day of their visit, Anil Bordia said to me that they wanted to place the scheme on a somewhat more permanent basis by setting up a research-cum-resource centre for environmental orientation to education at Almora with Lalit as its first director. This came as quite a surprise as we had not mooted any such idea. In May 1992, the report of the review committee was received followed by the formal sanction in late March 1993. Effective from 1 April 1993, Lalit was formally designated as director.

Now all these developments took place at some one else's initiative, without our knowledge and with no effort on our side. Clearly, a higher and unseen power was at work. Soon, Anuradha Bhatt joined as the first of the regular staff, and in 1994 she and Lalit were married.

ANNEXURE III

Epilogue: September 1999

Several years have passed and many things have happened. To begin with, we are both alive—Vimla (74) and myself (82). As of now we are both in fairly good health and it seems that we may perhaps see the coming of the year 2000, which in today's world is a great event. This is because the world is ruled by White Western and Christian powers. If Buddhism, Hinduism or Islam had been the ruling civilization, 2000 AD would not have been of such great importance. But the more significant date for us both will be May 19, 2000—the day we complete sixty years of our married life together.

My life has taken so many twists and turns. Every time I think that life will go along a particular route, the road suddenly takes a sharp, unprecedented turn. Although I often repeat the famous Sufi saying, 'This too shall pass', I keep forgetting it myself. For instance, I never thought I would spend the last years of my life at Almora. I have lived here for over twenty-two years, and without a break for the last fifteen years, perhaps the longest time anyone has lived in this house since my grandfather lived here. I give many reasons as to why I chose to come to Almora after my retirement—I talk of my love of the mountains and so on. While this is true in itself, but the fact remains that I had nowhere else to go. I had no land or house built during my service days or even at the time of my retirement. The credit for our successful move to Almora goes to Vimla, who never complained and went through life without demur.

On the personal front, Lalit now has two boys; Raja resigned from the IAS to join the Steel Authority of India and is now its chairman; Radhika, his older daughter, is specializing in oncology in America, is married and has a daughter; Rohini got a Rhodes Scholarship to Balliol, completed her PhD from the London School of Economics and is joining Columbia University as an associate professor; Ratna's marriage to Sudarshan has come apart and she now works at National Council of Applied Economic Research, her two sons are with her.

No one knows what the future has in store. But on the whole, life and God have been kind to me and, I suppose, to Vimla too.

I recall a famous Sufi tale. A king once asked his advisors, why was it that while he had everything he could ask for, a kingdom, queen, etc., he never felt wholly satisfied. The wise men got together and thought. Then they gave him a ring—on which were inscribed the words 'This too shall pass'. They advised him to keep looking at it and think of the ephemeral nature of life. Nothing remains the same. Everything changes and what is now, may not be a moment later.

Om shanti shanti shanti

Timeline

Born 17 March 1917 in Haldwani
Schooling: Lucknow, Delhi, Almora

1933–35:	BSc Allahabad University
1935–36:	MA (Previous) Allahabad University
1936–39:	Cambridge, England
1938:	Start of ICS probation
1939:	Assistant Magistrate, Gaya

Married 19 May 1940

1940:	Assistant Magistrate, Aurangabad
1941:	Sub-Divisional Officer, Khunti, Ranchi district
1942:	Sub-Divisional Officer, Bihar Sharief
1943:	Regional Grain Supply Officer, Darbhanga
	Regional Grain Supply Officer, Monghyr
1945:	Food Controller and Deputy Secretary, Patna
	Joint Secretary, then Secretary to Government in Supply Department
1949:	Finance Secretary, Bihar
1951–53:	Finance Secretary and Food Commissioner, Bihar
1953–54:	Commissioner, Tirhut Division, Muzaffarpur
	Commissioner, Bhagalpur
1954–56:	Land Reforms Commissioner; Officer on Special Duty to rewrite the Famine Code of 1885; to

	recommend the office reorganization of DMs and SDOs of 1901; to recommend re-drawing of district and sub divisional boundaries in Bihar
1956–60:	Development Commissioner, Bihar
1960:	Joint Secretary, Minstry of Community Development and Co-operation, Delhi
	Joint Secretary, Ministry of Economic and Defence Co-ordination (Department of Supply)
	Additional Secretary, Ministry of Finance, Department of Revenue and Gold Control Administrator
	Chairman of Central Board of Revenue
1965:	Chairman, Life Insurance Corporation, Bombay
1967:	Commissioner General cum Chief Secretary, Bihar
1967:	Secretary, Planning Commission
1970:	Secretary, Department of Heavy Industries
1970:	Secretary, Industrial Development
1971:	Finance Secretary
1972:	Cabinet Secretary
	Retired 1977
1978:	Chairman, National Transport Policy Committee (part time)
1980:	(Dec 1980–mid Feb 1981) Director, Rajaji International Institute of Public Affairs and Administration
1981:	Chairman, Railway Reforms Committee
1981:	Governor, West Bengal
1983:	Governor, Punjab
1984–2007:	Chairman, Uttarakhand Seva Nidhi
2000:	Awarded Padma Vibhushan

Died April 2 2009

www.ingramcontent.com/pod-product-compliance
Ingram Content Group UK Ltd.
Pitfield, Milton Keynes, MK11 3LW, UK
UKHW020747271224

UKWH00006B/64

9 789354 471582

This text of the 1912 edition was published by
MAUNSEL & COMPANY, LTD. DUBLIN AND LONDON

Publisher's Note to this 2012 Edition.

I have published this Centenary edition March 2012 in order to raise charitable donations for the Andrews Memorial Primary School, Comber, County Down, Northern Ireland , UK and the Royal National Lifeboat Institution in memory of Thomas Andrews and those who lost their lives.

I will split the whole profits of the sale of this book equally between the school and the RNLI.

(The RNLI is a charity which provides one of the most effective sea rescue services in the world saving lives around the coasts of Britain and Ireland , the Isle of Man and the Channel Islands. The RNLI provide this vital service with volunteer crews and is funded entirely by public donations, at no cost to taxpayers or the UK Government.)

Thank you for supporting the RNLI and the Comber Primary School by purchasing this book.

Simon Andrews

1912 Dedication

TO THE MEN WITH WHOM THOMAS ANDREWS WORKED WHO KNEW AND LOVED HIM I DEDICATE THIS BRIEF STORY OF HIS LIFE

- Shan F Bullock

2012 Centenary Introduction

In 1912 the RMS 'Titanic' tragically sank on her maiden voyage to New York after striking an iceberg on a clear, still and very cold April night. She sank sailing over the Grand Banks in the North West Atlantic 375 miles south of Newfoundland. Approximately 1502 people lost their lives in the disaster and about 705 survived. Many died on board going down with the ship and those who were in the water died quickly of hypothermia in the icy cold.

This book is the story of one man Thomas 'Tommy' Andrews who described himself as a 'Shipbuilder', he was a Naval Architect and leader of the design and build team of the 'Titanic' at Harland and Wolff Ltd. Shipyards, Belfast.

Tommy is remembered in two major films 'A Night to Remember' (1958) in which he was played by Michael Goodliffe and 'Titanic' (1997) by Victor Garber but neither of these accounts described fully what he did in his last hours helping others survive as does this book which was commissioned in 1912 by our family. Although it is written in a style common at the time which seems outdated to us now, it is possible even through the 1900's Edwardian style 'hype' to still see something of the man he was and hear his story. The world has changed much since then but human character and the qualities of honour, love, selflessness, self control and of courage have not.

This account has mostly been supported by subsequent evidence but when this book was written in 1912 by Shan Bullock there was much less information available about the events of the sinking than there is now. It was written and published prior to the completion of the American and British Inquiries and the sunken wreck had not been inspected some of the facts recorded are as a result inaccurate or incomplete, it is also to be remembered that

Tommy came from a wealthy linen mill owning family in Comber, County Down about eight miles from Belfast. He was one of four boys, one of whom later became Lord Chief Justice of Northern Ireland and another of whom became Prime Minister of Northern Ireland in WW2. They all played cricket along with my great grandfather at North Downs Cricket Club where the photo at page 55 still hangs –there were so many Andrewses that they could make up a whole cricket team. They were a large and close-knit family.

By 1912, Tommy was 39 years of age and had married Helen nee Barbour, 'Nellie' in 1908.The couple had settled into a town house in Windsor Avenue, Belfast and had had a daughter 'Elba' who was 18 months old. Thomas was back in Comber and County Down visiting his family regularly and he returned there at weekends to play cricket at NDCC or to sail on Strangford Lough.

The last time Tommy saw his Belfast home was on the morning of April 2nd 1912. He was picked up by a driver in a horse and carriage - motor cars being rare in those days - and taken to the shipyard where he went aboard 'Titanic' with the 'Guarantee' team from Harland and Wolff. 'Titanic' was to undergo her final sea trials that evening before departing for Southampton to set off on her fateful maiden transatlantic voyage to New York. He was devoted to his wife and wrote to her regularly during the early part of the 'Titanic's' maiden voyage.

In Comber in County Down, Northern Ireland where he came from there exists to this day the Andrews Memorial Primary School and because he died saving the lives of mainly children and women and gave up a chance of his own survival in favour of others I want to split all the whole profits of the sale of this book in donations equally shared between the school and the Royal National Lifeboat Institution.

(The RNLI is the charity which provides one of the most effective sea rescue services in the world saving lives around the coasts of Britain and Ireland, the Isle of Man and the Channel Islands. It provides this vital service with volunteer crews and is funded entirely by public donations, at no cost to taxpayers or the UK Government.)

The 'Titanic' was built in Belfast at Harland and Wolff for its owners the White Star Line whose offices were in Liverpool, England where the ship was therefore registered. It was the first ship for which Tommy was wholly responsible from start to finish, having taken over the RMS 'Olympic' project from Alexander Carlisle when he stepped aside as chief designer, reportedly in a fall-out with Lord Pirrie over the number of lifeboats which should be put on the 'Olympic'.

Tommy was quite a young man to have risen to such a responsible role at 39 years age especially in those hierarchical days. Accounts of him as a manager and as a boss portray him as a fair, concerned man who cared about his workers as comes out in this book. As the nephew of the shipyard chairman, Lord Pirrie, it has also been thought that he would probably have been seen as the natural successor to take control of the company on his uncle's retirement.

The 'Olympic' was launched in 1911 and after modifications after the loss of the 'Titanic' was ready for service in 1914 and continued working until 1935 having been for a time the largest and most prestigious passenger liner in the world. He also designed the 'Britannic' which was laid down in November 1910 and finally launched as the third 'sister' in 1914. The last remaining ship afloat that he designed is the 'Nomadic' which was the tender for first and second class passengers embarking onto the 'Titanic' at Cherbourg for the maiden voyage and she is currently undergoing restoration in Belfast.

The 'Olympic' was refitted and modified and given a double hull after the 'Titanic' disaster and bulkheads which had only extended 10 feet above sea level in 'Titanic' were extended to deck level to make the compartments fully watertight as Tommy had originally designed them. Also enough lifeboats were added to the 'Olympic' for all passengers as Tommy had pushed for but was overruled on for the 'Titanic' – this became mandatory internationally following the lessons learnt in the unforeseen scale of the disaster that befell the 'Titanic' as it hit the iceberg that night.

The safety of ships travelling our seas was made much greater as a result of the lessons learnt in 'Titanic' with many improvements in davits (onboard cranes) and other arrangements for lifeboats, lifeboat drills and 24 hour radio usage on ships at sea also became mandatory. International Ice Patrols were also instituted soon after the disaster and have continued since. After the enquiries into the disaster in America and Britain new international maritime laws were established in 1914 with the first International Convention for the Safety of Life at Sea (SOLAS) which still governs maritime safety today.

None of us knows how we would react in a crisis of this magnitude and it is a lasting tribute to the human spirit that Tommy Andrews and many like him caught up in the events of the night of the 14th April 1912 showed remarkably selfless generosity by not seeking their own safety but helping as many other people survive as they could. That so many survived despite all the odds against them is a tribute to the character and courage of these people and their sacrificial final acts.

Tommy searched the staterooms telling the passengers to put on lifejackets and to go up on deck and went about encouraging the reluctant to head towards the lifeboats. He used his technical expertise in the disaster and among other things helped the crew in the Engine Room so as to keep the lights on as long as possible and advised the crew launching the lifeboats. As this book relates one of the last sightings of Tommy was of him throwing deck chairs to people in the sea for them to cling on to.

Another later eyewitness account by John Stewart, a steward on the ship was that Tommy was last seen staring at a painting, "Plymouth Harbour", above the fireplace in the first-class smoking room, his lifejacket lying on a nearby table and that when asked if he would make a try for a lifeboat place, he did not answer and appeared stunned.

Tommy in those moments must have faced the fact that he would never see his beloved wife Nellie and daughter Elba or his family again. We cannot know what Tommy was thinking as he went about his task of helping others survive or his motivations and thoughts as he was doing so and why he stayed with the sinking ship. It may be that in doing so he was somehow taking his part of the responsibility for the loss of the 'Titanic' he had so lovingly brought into life with the shipyard workers he once described to his wife as his friends and too for the people who were endangered and thereby in some way making such remedy as he felt he could .

Let us note finally what his cousin James Montgomery said in his telegram of 19th April 1912 to the Andrews family from New York *'Interviewed Titanic's officers. All unanimous Andrews heroic unto death, thinking only safety others....'*

Simon Andrews, Ormskirk, Lancashire. 2012

LIST OF ILLUSTRATIONS

		Page
PORTRAIT OF THOMAS ANDREWS	frontispiece	5
(Photo by Abernethy)		
ARDARA, COMBER	page	15
(Photo by R. Welch)		
HARLAND & WOLFF'S TURBINE ERECTING SHOP	"	18
(Photo by R. Welch)		
THE TURNING SHOP	"	25
(Photo by R. Welch)		
THE "TITANIC" AND "OLYMPIC" BUILDING IN THE LARGEST GANTRY IN THE WORLD	"	34
(Photo by R. Welch)		
THE "TITANIC" LEAVING BELFAST	"	38
(Photo by R. Welch)		
Additional 2012 edition photos	pages	50-59

1912 Introduction

MR. SHAN BULLOCK, who needs no introduction to those who read Irish books, has done no better work than in this tribute to one of the noblest Irishmen Ulster has produced in modern times. I refer not only to the literary merits of Thomas Andrews, Shipbuilder, which speak for themselves, but rather to the true insight with which he has fulfilled the precise purpose held in view by those who asked him to write this little memorial volume. What that purpose was must be known in order that the story itself, and the manner of the telling, may be fully appreciated.

The book was written at the request of a few Irishmen, myself among them, who work together in a movement which seeks to develop agriculture, and generally to improve the condition of our rural communities.

We are deeply interested in the great achievements of Ulster industry, because we hold strongly that the prosperity of our country depends largely upon the mutual understanding and the coordination of effort between the two great economic interests into which the Irish, in common with most civilised peoples, are divided.

For this consummation Ireland needs, in our opinion, industrial leaders with a broader conception of the life of the country as a whole.For such leaders we naturally look, more especially those of us whose eyes are turning towards the westering sun, to the younger men. Among these none seemed to us so ideally fitted to give practical expression to our hopes as Thomas Andrews. Thus it was the sense of the great loss the country had sustained which set us thinking how the life of the shipbuilder who had died so nobly could be given its due place in the history of our times--how the lesson of that life could be handed down to the builders of ships and of other things in the Ireland of our dreams.

The project having so originated, the proper treatment of the subject had to be determined. Unquestionably Thomas Andrews was a hero. The wise Bishop Berkeley has said: "Every man, by consulting his own heart, may easily know whether he is or is not a patriot, but it is not easy for the bystander." A man cannot thus know whether he is or is not a hero. Both he and the bystander must wait for the occasion to arise, and the opportunities for exhibiting heroism are as rare and perilous as those for exhibiting patriotism are common and safe. To Thomas Andrews the supreme test came--came in circumstances demanding almost superhuman fortitude and self-control. Here was not the wild excitement of battle to sustain him; death had to be faced calmly in order that others--to whom he must not even bid farewell--might live. And so in his last hour we see this brave, strong, capable and lovable man displaying, not only heroism, but every quality which had exalted him in the regard of his fellows and endeared him to all who had worked and lived with him. This is the verdict of his countrymen now that the facts of that terrible disaster are fully known. Yet it was far from our purpose to have the tragedy of the Titanic written with Thomas Andrews as the hero. We deemed it better to place the bare facts before some writer of repute, not one of his personal friends, and ask him to tell in simple language the plain tale of his life so far as it could be gleaned from printed and written records, from his family, friends, and employers; above all, from those fellow-workers--his "pals" as he liked to call them--to whom this book is most fittingly dedicated. The story thus pieced together would be chiefly concerned with his work, for his work was his life.

To Thomas Andrews the hero, then, we did not propose to raise a monument. To his memory a fine memorial hall is to be built and endowed in his native Comber by the inhabitants of the town and district and his friends, while he will be associated in memorials elsewhere with those who died nobly in the wreck. [1] These tributes will serve to remind us how he died, but will not tell us how he lived. It is the purpose of this short memoir to give a fairly complete record of his life--his parentage, his home, his education, his pleasures, his tastes and his thoughts, so far as they are known, upon things which count in the lives of peoples. The family, and all from whom information was sought, responded most cordially to our wishes. There remained the difficulty of finding a writer who could tell the story of Thomas Andrews the man, as we wished it to be told.

For such a task it was decided that, if he could be induced to undertake it, the right man was Shan Bullock. He is an Ulsterman, a writer of tales of Ulster life, distinguished among other Irish books by their sincerity and unequalled understanding of the Ulster character. While other Irish writers of imagination and genius have used Irish life to express their own temperament, Shan Bullock has devoted his great literary ability almost entirely to the patient, living and sincere study of what Ulster really is in itself as a community of men and women. It is true that his stories are of rural and agricultural communities, while the scene is now laid chiefly in a great centre of manufacturing industry. But in Mr. Bullock's studies it is always the human factor that predominates. One feels while reading one of his tales that he loves to look upon a man, especially an Ulster man. Here was the ideal historian of the life of Thomas Andrews.

It fell to me to approach Mr. Bullock. I induced him to go and see the family, having arranged with them to bring him into touch with the authorities at the Island Works, who were to show him round and introduce him to many who knew our friend. He promised me that he would look over all the material out of which the story could be pieced together, and that if he found that it "gripped " him and became a labour of love he would undertake it. The story did, as the reader will see, grip him, and grip him hard, and in telling it Mr. Bullock has rendered the greatest of all his services to lovers of truth told about Ireland by Irish writers.

It will now, I think, be clear why Thomas Andrews has, notwithstanding his noble end, been represented as the plain, hard-working Ulster boy, growing into the exemplary and finally the heroic Ulster man that we knew. We see him ever doing what his hand found to do, and doing it with his might. Our author, rightly as I think, makes no attempt to present him as a public man; for this captain of industry in the making was wholly absorbed in his duties to the great Firm he served. None the less I am convinced that the public side of the man would not long have remained undeveloped--who knows but that this very year would have called him forth?--because he had to my personal knowledge the right public spirit. Concentration upon the work in hand prevented his active participation in public affairs, but his mastery over complicated mechanical problems--his power to use materials--and to organise bodies of men in their use, would not, I believe, have failed him if he had come to deal with the mechanics of the nation.

These may be fruitless speculations now, and Mr. Bullock wisely leaves us to draw our own conclusions as to the eminence to which Thomas Andrews might have attained had his life been spared. Abundant proof of the immense influence he might have exercised is furnished in the eloquently sincere grief which pervades the letters of condolence that poured into the home of the parents at Comber when it was known that they had lost their distinguished son. They came--over seven hundred of them--from all sorts and conditions of men, ranging from a duke to a pauper in a workhouse. In one of these letters, too intimate to publish, a near relative pays to the dead shipbuilder a pathetically simple tribute with which I may well leave to the reader Mr Bullock's tale of a noble life and heroic death. "There is not," ran this fine epitaph, "a better boy in heaven."

HORACE PLUNKETT.

Chapter One

FOR six generations the Andrews family has been prominent in the life of Comber: that historic and prospering village, near Strangford Lough, on the road from Belfast to Downpatrick: and in almost every generation some one or other of the family has attained distinction. During the eventful times of 1779-82, John Andrews raised and commanded a company of Volunteers, in which his youngest son, James, served as Lieutenant. Later, another John Andrews was High Sheriff of Down in 1857; and he also it was who founded the firm of John Andrews & Co., which to-day gives employment to some six hundred of the villagers. The present head of the family, William Drennan Andrews, LL.D., was a Judge of the High Court, Ireland, from 1882, and has been a Privy Councillor since 1897. His brother, Thomas Andrews, is a man whose outstanding merits and sterling character have won[2] him an honoured place among Ulstermen. One of the famous Recess Committee of 1895, he is President of the Ulster Liberal Unionist Association, Chairman of the Belfast and County Down Railway Company, a Privy Councillor, a Deputy Lieutenant of Down, High Sheriff of the same county, and Chairman of its County Council. Two more brothers, James and John, were Justices of the Peace. In 1870 Thomas Andrews married Eliza Pirrie, a descendant of the Scotch Hamiltons, Lord Pirrie's sister, and herself a woman of the noblest type.

To these, and of such excellent stock, was born, on February 7th, 1873, a son, named after his father, and described in the family record as Thomas Andrews of Dunallan. His eldest brother, John Miller, born in 1871, and his youngest brother, William, born in 1886, are now Managing Directors of John Andrews & Co., Ltd., under the Chairmanship of their father. A third brother, James, born in 1877, adopted the profession of his distinguished uncle, and is now a barrister-at-law. His only sister, Eliza Montgomery, married in 1906, Lawrence Arthur, the third son of Jesse Hind, Esq., J.P., of Edwalton, Notts, and a solicitor of the Supreme Court.

ARDARA, COMBER

Tom was, we are told, "a healthy, energetic,[3] bonny child, and grew into a handsome, plucky and lovable boy." His home training was of the wisest, and of a kind, one thinks, not commonly given to Ulster boys in those more austere times of his youth. "No one," writes his brother John, "knew better than Tom how much he owed to that healthy home life in which we were brought up. We were never otherwise treated than with more than kindness and devotion, and we learned the difference between right and wrong rather by example than by precept." To Tom, his father, then and always, was as an elder brother, full of understanding and sympathy; nor did his mother, even to the end, seem to him other than a sister whose life was as his own. He and his elder brother, John, were inseparable comrades, there among the fields of Comber and in their beautiful home, with its old lawn and gardens, its avenue winding past banks of rhododendrons, the farm behind, outside the great mill humming busily, and in front the gleam of Strangford Lough. Both father and mother being advocates of temperance, encouraged their lads to abstain from tobacco and strong drink; and to this end their good mother offered to give a tempting prize to such of her sons as could on their twenty-first birthday[4] say they had so abstained. Tom, and each of his brothers, not only claimed his prize but continued throughout life to act upon the principles it signalised. Doubtless at times, being human boys, they fell into mischief: but only once, their father states, was bodily punishment given to either, and then, as fate willed it, he boxed the ear of the wrong boy!

Quite early, young Tom, like many another lad, developed a fondness for boats, and because of his manifest skill in the making of these he gained among his friends the nickname of "Admiral." In other respects also the man who was to be showed himself in the boy. He had a beautiful way with children. He loved animals of every kind and had over them such influence that they would follow him and come to his call. Still at Ardara, in shelter of the hedge, you may see his nine hives of bees, among which he used to spend many happy hours, and to which in later times he devoted much of his hard-won leisure: once, his mother will tell you, spending a whole winter's day—and a hunting day too!—carrying his half-famished workers to and fro between hive and kitchen in his cap. For horses he had a passion, and particularly for the Shetland pony given[5] to him one birthday. The fiercest brute yielded to his quiet mastery; he never used whip or spur; and in time he was known as one of the straightest and most fearless riders to hounds in County Down.

Until the age of eleven he was educated privately by a tutor, but in September, 1884, he became a student at the Royal Academical Institution, Belfast—the same institution through which, some years previously, his father and his uncle, then Mr. Pirrie, had passed. There he showed no special aptitudes, being fonder apparently of games than of study, and not yet having developed those powers of industry for which, soon, he became notable. In the Institution, however, was no more popular boy, both with masters and schoolfellows. He excelled at cricket, one is glad to know, and at all manly sports. Even then, we are told, generosity and a fine sympathy were prominent traits in his character. "He was always happy," writes a playmate, "even-tempered, and showed a developing power of impressing everyone with his honesty and simplicity of purpose." Wherever he went Tom carried his own sunshine. All were fond of him. One can see him returning with his brother from school, big, strong, well-favored,[6] and perhaps with some premonition of what the future had in store, lingering sometimes near the station doorway to watch the great ships rising above the Island Yard close by and to listen for a minute to the hammers beating some great vessel into shape: and whilst he stands there, grave and thoughtful for a minute, one may write here the judgment of his parents upon him, "He never caused us a moment's anxiety in his life."

Chapter Two

WHEN he was sixteen, on the 1st May, 1889, Tom left school, and as a premium apprentice entered the shipyard of Messrs. Harland & Wolff. In one important respect the date of his entry may be accounted fortunate, for about that time, chiefly through the enterprise of the White Star Company in the matter of constructing a fleet of giant ships for the Atlantic service, great developments were imminent, if not already begun, in the shipping world. To a boy of sixteen, however, the change from the comforts of home and the comparative freedom of school-life to the stern discipline of the yards must have been exacting. It was work now, and plenty of it, summer and winter, day in day out, the hardest he could do at the hardest could be given him. He was to be tested to the full. With characteristic wisdom, Mr. Pirrie had decided that no favour whatever was to be shown the boy on the score of relationship. By his own efforts and abilities he must make his way, profiting by no more than the inspiration of his uncle's example: and if he failed,[8] well, that too was a way many another had gone before him.

But Tom was not of the breed that fails. He took to his work instantly and with enthusiasm. Distance from home necessitated his living through the workaday week in Belfast. Every morning he rose at ten minutes to five and was at work in the Yard punctually by six o'clock. His first three months were spent in the Joiner's shop, the next month with the Cabinet makers, the two following months working in ships. There followed two months in the Main store; then five with the Shipwrights, two in the Moulding loft, two with the Painters, eight with the iron Shipwrights, six with the Fitters, three with the Pattern-makers, eight with the Smiths. A long spell of eighteen months in the Drawing office completed his term of five years as an apprentice.

HARLAND AND WOLFF'S TURBINE ERECTING SHOP

Throughout that long ordeal Tom inspired everyone who saw him, workmen, foremen, managers, and those in higher authority, as much by the force of his personal character as by his qualities of industry. Without doubt here was one destined to success. He was thorough to the smallest detail. He mastered everything with the ease of one in love with his task. We have a picture of him drawn by a comrade, in his moleskin trousers and linen jacket, and instinctively regarded by his fellow-apprentices as their leader, friend and adviser in all matters of shipyard lore and tradition. "He was some steps ahead of me in his progress through the Yard," the account goes on, "so I saw him only at the breakfast and luncheon hours, but I can remember how encouraging his cheery optimism and unfailing friendship were to one who found the path at times far from easy and the demands on one's patience almost more than could be endured." Many a workman, too, with whom he wrought at that time will tell you to-day, and with a regret at his untimely loss as pathetic as it is sincere, how faithful he was, how upstanding, generous. He would work at full pressure in order to gain time to assist an old workman "in pulling up his job." He would share his lunch with a mate, toil half the night in relief of a fellow-apprentice who had been overcome by sickness, or would plunge gallantly into a flooded hold to stop a leakage. "It seemed his delight," writes a foreman, "to make those around him happy. His was ever the friendly greeting and the warm handshake and kind disposition." Such testimony is worth pages of outside eulogy, and testimony of its kind, from all sorts and conditions, exists in abundance.

The long day's work over at the Island, many a young man would have preferred, and naturally perhaps, to spend his evenings pleasurably: not so Tom Andrews. Knowing the necessity, if real success were to be attained, of perfecting himself on the technical as much as on the practical side of his profession, and perhaps having a desire also to make good what he considered wasted opportunities at school, he pursued, during the five years of his apprenticeship, and afterwards too, a rigid course of night studies: in this way gaining an excellent knowledge of Machine and Freehand drawing, of Applied mechanics, and the theory of Naval architecture. So assiduously did he study that seldom was he in bed before eleven o'clock; he read no novels, wasted no time over newspapers; and hardly could be persuaded by his friends to give them his company for an occasional evening. His weekly game of cricket or hockey, with a day's hunting now and then or an afternoon's yachting on the Lough, gave him all the relaxation he could permit himself; and by 1894, when his term of apprenticeship ended, the thrill of hitting a ball over the boundary (and Tom was a mighty hitter who felt the thrill often) was experienced with less and still less frequency, whilst sometimes now, and more frequently as time went on, the joy of spending Sunday with his dear folk at Comber had to be foregone. Even when the Presidency of the Northern Cricket Union was pressed upon him, such were the stern claims of duty that the pleasure of accepting it had ruthlessly to be sacrificed.

What grit, what zest and sense of duty, the boy—for he was no more—must have had, so to labour and yet to thrive gloriously! Perfect health, his sound physique, his sunny nature, and strict adherence to the principles of temperance encouraged by his mother, helped him to attain fine manhood. During the period of his apprenticeship he was up to time on every morning of the five years except one—and of his doings on that fateful morning a story is told which, better perhaps than any other, throws light upon his character.

It was a good custom of the firm to award a gold watch to every pupil who ended his term without being late once. That morning Tom's clock had failed to ring its alarm at the usual time, so despite every endeavour the boy could not reach the gates before ten minutes past six. He might, by losing the whole day and making some excuse, have escaped penalty: instead, he waited outside the gates until eight o'clock and went in to work at the breakfast hour.

One other story relating to this period is told by his mother. It too reveals distinctive points of character.

On an occasion Tom, with several fellow-pupils, went on a walking tour during the Easter holidays over the Ards peninsula. Crossing Strangford Lough at Portaferry, they visited St. John's Point, the most easterly part of Ireland; then, finding the tide favourable, crossed the sands from Ballykinler to Dundrum—Tom carrying the youngest of the party on his back through a deep intervening stretch of water—and thence, by way of Newcastle, proceeded across the mountains to Rostrevor.

In their hotel at Rostrevor the boys, during an excess of high spirits, broke the rail of a bedstead; whereupon Tom, assuming responsibility, told the landlady that he would bear the expense of repairing the break. She answered that in her hotel they did not keep patched beds, consequently would be troubling him for the cost of a new one.

"If so, the old one belongs to me," said Tom.

"Provided you'll be taking it away," countered the dame.

The boy argued no further, but finding presently, through a friendly chambermaid, an old charwoman who said her sick husband would rejoice in the luxury of the bedstead, he offered to mend it and give it to her.

"Ah, but wouldn't it be more than my place is worth, child dear," she answered, "for the like of me to be taking it from the hotel."

"Never mind that," said Tom. "Give me your address, borrow a screw driver, and I'll see to it."

So he and his companions, having roughly repaired the rail, took the bedstead to pieces, and, applauded by the visitors, carried it to the street. A good-natured tram conductor allowed them to load their burden on an end of his car. Soon they reached the woman's home, bore in the bedstead, set it up in the humble room, raised the old man and his straw mattress upon it from the floor, made him comfortable, and dowered with all the blessings the old couple could invoke upon them, went away happy.

Chapter Three

So much impressed was the firm with Tom's industry and capacity that, soon after the time of his entering the Drawing Office in November, 1892, he was entrusted with the discharge of responsible duties. It is on record that in February, 1893, he was given the supervision of construction work on the *Mystic*; that in November of the same year he represented the firm, to its entire satisfaction and his own credit, on the trials of the White Star Liner *Gothic*; whilst, immediately following the end of his apprenticeship in May, 1894, he helped the Shipyard Manager to examine the *Coptic*, went to Liverpool and reported on the damage done to the *Lycia*, and in November discussed with the General Manager and Shipyard Manager the Notes in connection with the renovation of the *Germanic*—that famous Liner, still capable after twenty-five years on the Atlantic Service of making record passages, but now crippled through being overladen with ice at New York.

In 1894 he was twenty-one years old: a man and well launched on his great career.

It is not necessary, and scarcely possible, to follow Andrews with any closeness as rapidly, step by step, he climbed the ladder already scaled, with such amazing success, by Mr. Pirrie. The record of his career is written in the wonderful story of the Queen's Island Yard through all its developments onward from 1894, and in the story of the many famous ships repaired and built during the period.

The remarkable engineering feat of lengthening the *Scot* and the *Augusta Victoria*, by dividing the vessels and inserting a section amidships; the reconstruction of the *China* after its disaster at Perim and of the *Paris* following its wreck on the Manacles: in these operations, covering roughly the years 1896-1900, Andrews, first as an outside Manager and subsequently as Head of the Repair department, took a distinguished part. He was growing, widening knowledge, maturing capacity, and both by the Staff, and by those in touch with the Yard, he became recognised as what the watching crowd terms, not unhappily, a coming man.

Having made his mark in the Repair Department, Andrews was next to prove himself on construction work. Prior to the launch of the *Oceanic* in 1899, and whilst engaged in the[16] reconstruction operations already mentioned, he had also rendered good service at the building of ships for many of the great steamship lines; but it was perhaps with the building of the *Celtic* (1899-1901), when he became Manager of Construction Work, that the path of his career took him swiftly up into prominence. The duty of supervising all the structural details of the vessel brought him into close practical touch with the Drawing office, the Moulding loft, the Platers' shops, and all the other Departments through which he had passed as an apprentice; imposed upon his young shoulders great responsibilities; tested his capacity for handling men; put him in constant and intimate view of his employers; widened his relations with owners, contractors, directors, managers; opened to him not only the life of the Yard, but the vast outer life of the Shipping and Commercial world, and in a hundred other respects helped towards his development as a shipbuilder and a man. Now he had opportunity to apply his knowledge and experience, to express in tangible form his genius. The great ship rising there below the gantries to the accompaniment of such clang and turmoil—she was his, part of him. To the task, one of the noblest surely done by men, he gave himself unsparingly, every bit of him, might and main: and his success, great as it was, had the greater acclaim because in achieving it he worked not for personal success but for success in his work. That was the man's way. His job, first and last and always.

The names alone of all the ships in whose building Andrews had a hand, more or less, as Designer, Constructor, Supervisor and Adviser, would fill this page. The *Cedric*, the *Baltic*, the *Adriatic*, the *Oceanic*, the *Amerika*, the *President Lincoln* and *President Grant*, the *Nieuw Amsterdam*, the *Rotterdam*, the *Lapland* (of which recently we have heard so much): those are a few of them. The *Olympic* and the *Titanic*: those are two more. Their names are as familiar to us as those of our friends. We have, some of us, seen the great ships on whose bows they are inscribed, perhaps sailed in them, or watched anxiously for their arrival at some port of the world; well, wherever they sail now, or lie, they have upon them the impress of Tom Andrews' hand and brain, and with one of them, the last and finest of all, he himself gloriously perished.

There are many others, less known perhaps, but carrying the flag no less proudly upon the Seven seas, for whose design and construction Andrews was in some measure, often in great measure responsible: the *Aragon*, the *Amazon*, the *Avon*, the *Asturias*, the *Arlanza*, the *Herefordshire*, the *Leicestershire*, the *Gloucestershire*, the *Oxfordshire*, the *Pericles*, the *Themistocles*, the *Demosthenes*, the *Laurentic*, the *Megantic*, and the rest. It is a splendid record. Lord Pirrie may well be proud of it, and Ulster too: both we know are proud of the man who so devotedly helped to make it.

The work of building all those ships, and so many more, from the *Celtic* to the *Titanic*, covered a period of some thirteen years, 1899-1912, and in that period Andrews gained such advancement as his services to the Firm deserved. In 1904 he became Assistant Chief Designer, and in the year following was promoted to be Head of the Designing department under Lord Pirrie. His age then was thirty-two, an age at which most men are beginning their career; but he already had behind him what may seem the work and experience of a strenuous lifetime.

"When first I knew Mr. Andrews," writes one who knew him intimately, and later was closely associated with him in his work, "he was a young man, but young as he was to him were entrusted the most important and responsible duties—the direct supervision of constructing the largest ships built in the Yard from the laying of their keels until their sailing from Belfast. Such a training eminently fitted him for the important position to which he succeeded in 1905, that of Chief of the Designing department. For one so young the position involved duties that taxed him to the full. To superintend the construction of ships like the *Baltic* and *Oceanic* was a great achievement, but at the age of thirty-two to be Chief of a department designing leviathans like the *Olympic* was a greater one still. How well he rose to the call everyone knows. No task was too heavy, and none too light, for him to grapple with successfully. He seemed endowed with boundless energy, and his interest in his work was unceasing."

Others who knew him well during this important period of his career testify in the like manner.

"Diligent to the point of strenuousness," wrote one of them, "thinking whilst others slept, reading while others played, through sheer toil and ability he made for himself a position that few of his years attain"; and then the writer, whose ideal of life is character, notes approvingly and justly that Andrews worked not as a hireling, but in the spirit of an artist whose work must satisfy his own exacting conscience.

Those boundless energies soon were given wider scope. Early in 1907 the *Adriatic* was finished, and in March of that same year he was made a Managing Director of the Firm, the Right Hon. A. M. Carlisle being at this time Chairman of the Board. Everyone knows, or can judge for himself, what were the duties of this new position—this additional position, rather, for he still remained Chief of the Designing department—and what, in such a huge and complicated concern as the Island works, the duties involved. Briefly we may summarise them.

A knowledge of its fifty-three branches equal to that of any of the fifty-three men in charge of them; the supervising these, combining and managing them so that all might, smoothly and efficiently, work to the one great end assigned, the keeping abreast with the latest devices in labour-saving appliances, with the newest means of securing economical fitness, with the most modern discoveries in electrical, mechanical and marine engineering—in short, everything relative to the construction and equipment of modern steamships; and in addition all the numerous and delicate duties devolving upon him as Lord Pirrie's Assistant. Furthermore, the many voyages of discovery, so to speak, which he made as representative of the Firm, thereby, we are told by one with whom he sailed often, "gaining a knowledge of sea life and the art of working a ship unequalled in my experience by anyone not by profession a seafarer"; and, lastly, his many inspections of, and elaborate reports upon, ships and business works, together with his survey, at Lord Pirrie's instance, of the Harbours of Ireland, Canada, Germany, and elsewhere.

It seems a giant's task. Even to us poor humdrum mortals, toiling meanly on office stools at our twopenny enterprises, it seems more than a giant's task. Yet Andrews shouldered it, unweariedly, cheerily, joyfully, for pure love of the task.

One sees him, big and strong, a paint-smeared bowler hat on his crown, grease on his boots and the pockets of his blue jacket stuffed with plans, making his daily round of the Yards, now consulting his Chief, now conferring with a foreman, now interviewing an owner, now poring over intricate calculations in the Drawing office, now in company with his warm friend, old schoolfellow, and co-director, Mr. George Cumming of the Engineering department, superintending the hoisting of a boiler by the two hundred ton crane into some newly launched ship by a wharf. Or he runs amok through a gang—to their admiration, be it said—found heating their tea-cans before horn-blow; or comes unawares upon a party enjoying a stolen smoke below a tunnel-shaft, and, having spoken his mind forcibly, accepts with a smile the dismayed sentinel's excuse that "'twasn't fair to catch him by coming like that into the tunnel instead of by the way he was expected."

Or he kicks a red hot rivet, which has fallen fifty feet from an upper deck, missing his head by inches, and strides on laughing at his escape. Or he calls some laggard to stern account, promising him the gate double quick without any talk next time. Or he lends a ready hand to one in difficulties; or just in time saves another from falling down a hold; or saying that married men's lives are precious, orders back a third from some dangerous place and himself takes the risk. Or he runs into the Drawing office with a hospital note and a gift of flowers and fruit for the sick wife of a draughtsman. Or at horn-blow he stands by a ship's gangway, down which four thousand hungry men, with a ninety feet drop below them, are rushing for home and supper, and with voice and eye controls them ... a guard rope breaks ... another instant and there may be grim panic on the gangway ... but his great voice rings out, "Stand back, men," and he holds them as in a leash until the rope is made good again.

All in the day's work, those and a thousand other incidents which men treasure to-day in the Island, and, if you are tactful, will reveal to you in their slow laconic Northern way. He has been in the Yard perhaps since four or five o'clock—since six for a certainty. At seven or so he will trudge home, or ride in a tramcar with the other workers, to sit over his plans or his books well into the night.

One recalls a day, not long ago, spent most of it in tramping over the Island Works, guided by two men who had worked for many years with Andrews and who, like others we saw and thousands we did not see, held his memory almost in reverence. In and out, up and down we went, through heat and rain, over cobble stones and tram lines; now stepping on planks right down the double bottom, three hundred yards long, from which was soon to rise the *Titanic's* successor; now crouching amongst the shores sustaining the huge bulk of another half-plated giant; now passing in silent wonder along the huge cradles and ways above which another monster stood ready for launching. Then into shop after shop in endless succession, each needing a day's journey to traverse, each wonderfully clean and ordered, and all full of wonders. Boilers as tall as houses, shafts a boy's height in diameter, enormous propellers hanging like some monstrous sea animal in chains, turbine motors on which workmen clambered as upon a cliff, huge lathes, pneumatic hammers, and quiet slow-moving machines that dealt with cold steel, shearing it, punching it, planing it, as if it had been so much dinner cheese. Then up into the Moulding Loft, large enough for a football ground, and its floor a beautiful maze of frame lines; on through the Joiners' shops, with their tools that can do everything but speak; through the Smiths' shops, with their long rows of helmet-capped hearths, and on into the great airy building, so full of interest that one could linger in it for a week, where an army of Cabinetmakers are fashioning all kinds of ship's furniture. Then across into the Central power station, daily generating enough electricity to light Belfast. On through the fine arched Drawing hall, where the spirit of Tom Andrews seemed still to linger, and into his office where often he sat drafting those reports, so exhaustively minute, so methodical and neatly penned, which now have such pathetic and revealing interest. Lastly, after such long journeying, out to a wharf and over a great ship, full of stir and clamour, and as thronged with workmen as soon it would be with passengers.

THE TURNING SHOP

And often, as one went, hour after hour, one kept asking, "Had Mr. Andrews knowledge of this, and this, and that?"

"Yes, of everything—he knew everything," would be the patient answer.

"And could he do this, and this, and this?" one kept on.

"He could do anything," would be the answer.

"Even how to drive an engine?"

"Surely."

"And how to rivet a plate?"

"He could have built a ship himself, and fitted her—yes, and sailed her too"—was the answer we got; and then as one dragged wearily towards the gateway (outside which, you will remember, young Tom waited one bitter morning, disappointed but staunch) the guide, noting one's plight, said, "You will sleep well to-night?"

Why, yes, one felt like sleeping for a week!

"Ah, well," was the quiet comment, "Mr. Andrews would do all that and more three times maybe every day."

All in the day's work, you see. And when it was done, then home in a tramcar, to have his dinner, a talk with his mother over the telephone, and so to work again until eleven.

In 1901 Andrews became a Member of the Institution of Naval Architects, and in the year following a Member of the Institution of Mechanical Engineers. He was also a Member of the Society of Naval Architects and Marine Engineers (New York), and an Honorary Member of the Belfast Association of Engineers.

In 1908 he made a home for himself at Dunallan, Windsor Avenue, Belfast, marrying, on June 24th, Helen Reilly, younger daughter of the late John Doherty Barbour, of Conway, Dunmurry, County Antrim, D.L.—worthiest and most loyal of helpmates.

Concerning his married life, so woefully restricted in point of years as it was rich in bounty of happiness, it is perhaps sufficient to say here that, just before he sailed from Southampton, in April last, on that final tragic voyage, he made occasion, one evening whilst[27] talking with a friend, to contrast his own lot with the lot of some husbands he knew; saying, amongst other things, that in the whole time since his marriage, no matter how often he had been away or how late he had stayed at the Yard, never had Mrs. Andrews made a complaint.

She would not. With Jane Eyre she could say, "I am my husband's life as fully as he is mine."

In 1910 a child was born to them and named Elizabeth Law Barbour.

Chapter Four

ALL this is important, vital a great deal of it; but after all what concerns us chiefly, in this brief record, is the kind of man Thomas Andrews was—that and the fine end he made. Everything, one supposes, in this workaday world, must eventually be expressed in terms of character. Though a man build the Atlantic fleet, himself with superhuman vigour of hand and brain, and have not character, what profiteth it him, and how much the less profiteth it the fleets maybe, at last?

Perhaps of all the manual professions that of shipbuilding is the one demanding from those engaged in it, masters and men, the sternest rectitude. Good enough in the shipyard is never enough. Think what scamped work, a flawed shaft, a badly laid plate, an error in calculation, may mean some wild night out in the Atlantic; and when next you are in Belfast go to Queen's Island and see there, in the shops, on the slips, how everyone is striving, or being made to strive, on your behalf and that of all who voyage, for the absolute best—everything to a hair's breadth, all as strong and sound as hands can achieve, each rivet of all the millions in a liner (perhaps the most impressive thing one saw) tested separately and certified with its own chalk mark.

Well, Andrews, to the extent of his powers and position, was responsible for that absolute best, and the fact that he was proves his character—but does not of itself establish his claim to a place high and apart. Many others assuredly have succeeded as speedily and notably as he, taking success at its material valuation, and their names are written, or one day will be written in the sand; but irrespective of the great work he did and the great success he achieved, Andrews was a man, in the opinion of all who knew him, whose name deserves to be graven in enduring characters: and why that is so has yet, to some extent at least, to be shown.

In appearance he made a fine figure, standing nearly six feet high, weighing some two hundred pounds, well-built, straight, with broad shoulders and great physical development. He had dark brown hair, sharp clean-shaven features; you would call him handsome; his brown eyes met yours with a look of the frankest kindliness, and when he gripped your hand he took you, as it were, to himself. Even as you see him in a portrait you feel constrained to exclaim, as many did at first sight of him, "Well, *that's* a man!" He had a wonderful ringing laugh, an easy way with him, an Irishman's appreciation of humour. He was sunny, big-hearted, full of gaiety. He loved to hear a good story, and could tell you one as well as another. He had the luck to be simple in his habits and pleasures, his food, his dress, his tastes. Give him health, plenty of friends, plenty of work, and occasionally some spare hours in which to enjoy a good book (Maeterlinck's *Life of the Bee* for preference) and some good music, to go yachting on Strangford Lough, or picnicking at the family bungalow on Braddock Island, or for a long jolly ride with Mrs. Andrews in their little Renault round the Ards Peninsula, and he was thoroughly content. When of a Saturday evening he opened the door, so the servants at Ardara used to say, they like all the rest waiting expectantly for his coming, it was as though a wind from the sea swept into the house. All was astir. His presence filled the place. Soon you would hear his father's greeting, "Well, my big son, how are you?" and thereafter, for one more week's end, it was in Ardara as though the schoolboy was home for a holiday. You would hear Tom's voice and laugh through the house and his step on the stairs; you would see him, gloved and veiled, out working among his bees, scampering on the lawn with the children, or playing with the dog, or telling many a good story to the family circle. Everyone loved him—everyone.

A distinguished writer, Mr. Erskine Childers, in an estimate of Andrews, judges that the charm of the man lay in a combination of power and simplicity. Others tell how unassertive he was, and modest in the finest sense; "one of nature's gentlemen," says a foreman who owed him much, no pride at all, ready always to take a suggestion from anyone, always expressing his views quietly and considerately; "having of himself," writes Mrs. Andrews, "the humblest opinion of anyone I ever knew." And then she quotes some lines he liked and wrote in her album:

"Do what you can, being what you are,
Shine like a glow-worm, if you cannot as a star,
Work like a pulley, if you cannot as a crane,
Be a wheel-greaser, if you cannot drive a train";

and goes on to say how much Judge Payne's familiar lines express the spirit and motive of his actions throughout life, and how always he had such a love for humanity that everyone with whom he came in contact felt the tremendous influence of his unselfish nature. He was never so happy as when giving and helping. Many a faltering youth on the threshold of the world he took by the arm and led forward. A shipwright testifies "to his frequent acknowledgment of what others, not so high as himself, tried to do." Another calls him "a kind and considerate chief and a good friend always." A third, in a letter full of heartbreak at his loss, pays him fine tribute: "In the twenty years I have known him I never saw in him a single crooked turn. He was always the same, one of the most even-tempered men I ever worked with."

Such spontaneous testimony to character is perhaps sufficient; but one may crown it by repeating a story told, with full appreciation of its value, by his mother. When King Edward and Queen Alexandra made their memorable visit to Belfast in July, 1903, the line of route passed through the street in which Andrews lived; and to witness the procession he invited to his rooms, all decorated for the occasion and plentifully supplied with dainties, a large party of children. "Well, my dear," one was asked afterwards, "and what did you think of the King?" "The King," answered the child—"oh, cousin Tommy was *our* King."

Regarding his remarkable powers of application and industry, enough too has perhaps already been written; but what must be made clear, even at the cost of repetition, for therein lay the man's strength, was the spirit in which he approached the great business of work.

It has been said, and doubtless will be said again, that for one to labour as Andrews did, whatever the incentive or object, is an inhuman process making for narrowness of manhood and a condition of drudgery. Perhaps so. Herbert Spencer once expressed some

27

such opinion. It is largely a question of one's point of view, to a lesser extent perhaps a matter of aptitude or circumstance. At all events, in this respect, it seems wise to distinguish as between man and man, and work and work; for with the example of Andrews before them even cavillers must admit that what they call drudgery can be well justified.

How he would have laughed had someone, even a Herbert Spencer, called him a drudge! Anyone less the creature, however you regarded him, you could not easily find. Work was his nature, his life; he throve upon it, lived for it, loved it. And think what a work it was! The noblest, one repeats, done by men.

In his dressing room was hung a framed copy of Henry Van Dyke's well-known sonnet.

It is worth quoting:

"Let me but do my work from day to day
In field or forest, at the desk or loom,
In roaring market-place, or tranquil room;
Let me but find it in my heart to say,
When vagrant wishes beckon me astray,
This is my work, my blessing, not my doom;
Of all who live, I am the one by whom
This work can best be done in my own way.
Then shall I see it not too great nor small,
To suit my spirit and to prove my powers;
Then shall I cheerfully greet the labouring hours,
And cheerful turn, when the long shadows fall
At eventide, to play, and love, and rest,
Because I know for me my work is best."

"This is my work, my blessing, not my doom ... because I know for me my work is best": can it be said that the man who worked in the spirit of those words, having them before him like a prayer each morning and each night, was not fulfilling destiny in a noble way? No mean thought of self, no small striving after worldly success, but always the endeavour to work in his own way to suit his spirit and to prove his powers. If that way be narrow—well, so is the way narrow that leads to eternal life.

But, it might be said, Andrews had such opportunity and the rare good fortune also to have his spirit suited with work that proved his powers. It was so. Yet one knows certainly that had his opportunity been different he would still have seized it; have been the best engine driver in Ulster or have greased wheels contentedly and with all diligence. One remembers the sentence from Ruskin which he had printed on his Christmas card for 1910: "What we think, or what we know, or what we believe, is in the end of little consequence. The only thing of consequence is what we do."

The best doing, always and every way, one knows how that aspiration would appeal to Andrews, good Unitarian that he was; just as one knows how Ruskin, he who made roads and had such burning sympathy always with honest workers, would have appreciated Andrews and agreed that the name of such a man should not perish as have the names of most other of the world's great Architects and Builders. "To-day I commence my twenty-first year at the works, all interesting and happy days. I would go right back over them again if I could": one feels that the spirit of those words, written by Andrews to his wife on May 1st, 1909, would have appealed to Ruskin; and had he known the man would he not have noted, as did another observer—Professor W. G. S. Adams,[2] of Oxford—"how it was to the human question the man's mind always turned," and been eager to judge, "that here was one who had in him the true stuff of the best kind of captain of industry"?

A captain of industry: the phrase is happy, and convincing too is the passage wherein Mr. Erskine Childers gives his impression of Andrews as, towards the close of 1911, he saw him one day working in the Island Yard.

"It was bracing to be near him," writes Mr. Childers, and then goes on: "His mind seemed to revel in its mastery, both of the details and of the *ensemble*, both of the technical and the human side of a great science, while restlessly seeking to enlarge its outlook, conquer new problems, and achieve an ever fresh perfection. Whether it was about the pitch of a propeller or the higher problems of design, speed, and mercantile competition, one felt the same grip and enthusiasm and, above all perhaps, the same delight in frank self-revelation."

Chapter Five

WE come back, then, to Andrews as Mr. Childers saw him on that day in the Yard—big, strong, inspiriting, full of enthusiasm and mastery—a genuine captain of industry there on the scene of his triumphs, yet revealing himself as modestly, we know, as any of the great army of workers under his direction.

Before attempting to give some further and completer account of the relations which existed between him and the Islanders, it may be well to give a letter written by Andrews in 1905 to a young relative then beginning work as an engineer:—

"I am sorry I did not get a shake of your fist, old chap, before leaving, just to wish you good luck at your business and a good time at ——

"Please accept from me the enclosed small gift to go towards a little pocket-money.

"You are such a sensible boy I know that you require no advice from me, but as an old hand who has come through the mill myself I would just like to say how important it is for you to endeavour to give your employers full confidence in you from the start. This can best be gained:

"(1) By punctuality and close attention to your work at all times—but don't allow your health to suffer through overwork.

"(2) Always carry out instructions given by those above you, whether you agree with them or not—and try to get instructions in writing if you are not sure of your man.

"(3) Always treat those above you with respect, no matter whether they are fools or know less than yourself.

"(4) Never give information unless you are perfectly sure, better to say you are not sure, but will look the matter up.

"(5) Never be anxious to show how quick you are by being the first out of the shop when the horn blows. It is better on these occasions to be a bit slow.

"Now this is a sermon by Thomas, but not one of your father's—only that of an old cousin who has high expectations of you and is interested in your welfare.

"Goodbye and good luck."

That little sermon by Thomas, with its admixture of shrewdness, wisdom, and kind-heartedness, may be taken as embodying the workaday rules of duty perfected by Andrews through a varied experience of sixteen years—rules doubtless as faithfully observed by himself as they were commended for the guidance of others. What may be called its horse sense, its blunt avowal of how to play the game, helps us towards a fuller understanding of the man, puts him in the plain light through which, every day in view of everyone, he passed. It shows us why he succeeded, why in any circumstances and irrespective almost of his higher qualities, he was bound to succeed. It explains, to some extent, what a workman meant in calling him "a born leader of men." It helps us to understand why some called him a hard man and why he made a few enemies; helps us also to understand why the Islander who threatened to drop a bag of rivets on his head was treated with laughing amenity. What Andrews demanded of others he exacted in greater measure of himself. If at times he enforced his code of conduct with sternness, in that, as all who felt the weight of his hand would eventually acknowledge, he was but doing his plain duty. Did men skulk or scamp their job, they must be shown decisively that a shipyard was no place for them. Someone discovered asleep on a nine inch plank spanning an open ventilator must be taught discretion. But no bullying, no unfairness—above all, no show of malice.

If in Andrews' nature was no trace of maliciousness, neither did there lurk in it any meanness. Not once, but a thousand times, during the past black months, has his character been summed with characteristic terseness by the Island shipwrights:

"Just as a judge.... Straight as a die.... There wasn't a crooked turn in him": simple phrases conveying a magnificent tribute. For what better in anyone can you have than the straightness of a die, whether you regard him as man or master? And such straightness in a shipbuilder is not that the supreme quality?

At all events this quality of absolute rectitude, so indispensable in other respects, was the main quality which, in their personal relations with him, won for Andrews the admiration and esteem of the Islanders. They could trust him. He would see fair play. "If he caught you doing wrong he wasn't afraid to tell you so." "If he found you breaking a rule he wouldn't fire you straight away, but would give you the rough side of his tongue and a friendly caution." "So long as one reported a mistake honestly he had consideration, but try to hide it away and he blazed at you." "He had a grand eye for good work and a good man, and the man who did good work, no matter who he was, got a clap on the shoulder." So the Islanders, this man and that; and then once more comes the crowning judgment on the tongue of so many, "He was straight as a die."

But not that one quality alone gained for Andrews his great, one might say his unique, popularity in the Yard. His vast knowledge, his mastery of detail, his assiduity, his zest: all these merits had their due effect upon the men: and effective too was the desire he showed always to get the best possible out of every worker. It was not enough to *do* your job, he expected you to *think* about it: and if from your thinking resulted a suggestion it got his best consideration. It might be worthless—never mind, better luck next time; if it were worth a cent, he would make it shine in your eyes like a dollar.

In addition, were those more personal qualities—emanations, so to speak, of the man's character: his generosity, kindliness, patience, geniality, humour, humility, courage, that great laugh of his, the winning smile, the fine breezy presence: of those also the men had constant and intimate experience. Anyone in trouble might be sure of his sympathy. After a spell of sickness his handshake and hearty greeting stirred new life in your blood. Once he found a great fellow ill-treating a small foreman who, for sufficient reason, had docked his wages; whereupon Andrews took off his coat and hammered the bully. During labour and party troubles, he several times, at risk of his life, saved men from the mob. One day, in a gale, he climbed an eighty foot staging, rescued the terrified man who had gone up to secure the loose boards, and himself did the work. Another day, he lent a hand to a shipwright toiling across the yard under a heavy beam, and as they went Andrews asked, "How is it, M'Ilwaine, you always like to be beside me?" "Ah, sir," was the reply, "it is because you carry up well."

These incidents, chosen from so many, enable us to see why, in the words of the Island poet, "though Andrews was our master we loved him to a man." He always carried up well, "stood four-square to all the winds that blow." Too often, those in authority rule as tyrants, using power like some Juggernaut crushing under the beasts of burden. But Andrews, following the example of his uncle, preferred to rule beneficently as a man among his fellows.

"One evening," writes Mrs. Andrews, "my husband and I were in the vicinity of Queen's Island, and noticing a long file of men going home from work, he turned to me and said, 'There go my pals, Nellie.' I can never forget the tone in his voice as he said that, it was as though the men were as dear to him as his own brothers. Afterwards, on a similar occasion, I reminded him of the words, and he said, 'Yes, and they are real pals too.'"

You see now why a colleague, Mr. Saxon Payne, secretary to Lord Pirrie, could write, "It was not a case of liking him, we all loved him"; and why during those awful days in April, when hope of good news at last had gone, the Yard was shrouded in gloom and rough men cried like women. They had lost a pal. And not they only. On both sides of the Atlantic, wherever men resort whose business is in the great waters, owners, commanders, directors, managers, architects, engineers, ships officers, stewards, sailors, the name Tom Andrews is honoured to-day as that of one whose remarkable combination of gifts claimed not only their admiration, but their affection.

"What we are to do without Andrews," said a Belfast ship-owner, "I don't know. He was probably the best man in the world for his job—knew everything—was ready for anything—could manage everyone—and what a friend! It's irreparable. Surely of all men worth saving he ought to have been saved. Yes, saved by force, for only in that way could it have been done."

Here, too, it may be mentioned that during his business career Andrews received many acknowledgements of a gratifying description from those whom in various ways he had served—amongst others from the White Star Company, the Hamburg American Company and, what I daresay he valued as much, from the stewards of the *Olympic*. Following the announcement of his marriage, a Committee was organised at the Yard for the purpose of showing him in a tangible way the esteem of the Islanders, but for business reasons, or perhaps feeling a delicacy in accepting a compliment without parallel in the history of the Yard, he whilst making it plain how much the kindly thought had moved him, felt constrained to ask the Committee to desist.

One may end this imperfect chapter with two more tributes, themselves without any great literary merit perhaps, yet testifying sincerely, one thinks, to the love which Andrews inspired in everyone.

THE "TITANIC" AND THE "OLYMPIC" BUILDING
IN THE LARGEST GANTRY IN THE WORLD

Long ago, poor Doctor O'Loughlin wrote in collaboration with the Purser of the *Oceanic* some verses to be sung to the air *Tommy Atkins*. Doubtless they have been sung at ship's mess on many a voyage, and perhaps have elsewhere been printed. One verse is given here:

"Neath a gantry high and mighty she had birth.
And she'd bulk and length and height and mighty beam.
And the world was only larger in its girth
And she seemed to be a living moving dream.
Then she rode so grandly o'er the sea
That she seemed a beauty decked in bright array.
And the whistle sounded loudly
As she sailed along so proudly,
That we all cried out 'She must be quite O.K.'

The second tribute is taken from a *Lament*, written by the Island poet in the ballad form so popular in Ireland, and circulated widely in the Yard:

"A Queen's Island Trojan, he worked to the last;
Very proud we all feel of him here in Belfast;
Our working-men knew him, as one of the best
He stuck to his duty, and God gave him rest."

Chapter Six.

It remains, before giving account of the finest action of his life, to consider briefly, by way of rounding his portrait, what we may call Andrews' outside aspect—the side, that is, he might turn to some Committee of Experts sitting in solemn judgment upon him as a possible candidate for political honours.

That side, it may be said at once, is singularly unpretentious; and indeed when we think of his absorption, heart and soul, in what he knew for him was best, who could expect, or wish, it to be otherwise? In Ulster, heaven knows, are publicists galore, and sufficient men too willing to down tools at any outside horn-blow, that we should the less admire one who spoke only once in public, took no open part in politics, and was not even a strong party-man. He was, however, a member of the Ulster Reform Club. Twice he was pressed to accept the presidency of Unionist Clubs. Frequently he was urged to permit his nomination for election to the City Council. The Belfast Harbour Board shared the opinion of one of its leading members that "his youthful vigour, his undoubted ability, and his genial personality, would have made him an acquisition to this important Board." His fellow-directors, in a resolution of condolence, expressed their feeling that "not only had the Firm lost a valued and promising leader, but the city an upright and capable citizen, who, had he lived, would have taken a still more conspicuous place in the industrial and commercial world." Even in the south, where admiration of Northerners is not commonly fervent, it was admitted by many that in Andrews Ulster had at last found the makings of a leader.

From such straws, blown in so prevailing a wind, we may determine the estimation in which Andrews, as a prospective citizen, stood amongst those who knew him and their own needs the best; and also perhaps may roughly calculate the possibilities of that future which he himself, in stray minutes of leisure, may have anticipated. But some there will be doubtless whose admiration of Andrews is the finer because he kept the path of his career straight to its course without any deviation to enticing havens.

Such a man, however, the son of such a father, could not fail to have views on the burning topics of his time, and no estimate of him would be complete which gave these no heed.

He was, we are told, an Imperialist, loving peace and consequently in favour of an unchallengeable Navy. He was a firm Unionist, being convinced that Home Rule would spell financial ruin to Ireland, through the partial loss of British credit, and of the security derived from connection with a strong and prosperous partner. At times he was known to express disapproval of the policy adopted by those Irish Unionists who strove to influence British electors by appeals to passion rather than by means of reasoned argument. Also he felt that Ireland would never be happy and prosperous until agitation ceased and promise of security were offered to the investing capitalist.

Though no believer in modern cities, he was of opinion that an effort should be made to expand and stimulate Irish village life, it seeming to him that a country dependent solely on agriculture was like a man fighting the battle of life with one hand. Were, however, an approved system of agriculture, such as that advocated by Sir Horace Plunkett, joined with a considered scheme of town and village industries, he believed that emigration would cease and Ireland find prosperity.

To the practical application of Tariff Reform he saw many difficulties, but thought them not insuperable. In view of the needs of a world-wide and growing Empire, "the necessity of preserving British work for British people," and the injury done to home trade by the unfair competition of protected countries, he judged that the duties upon imported necessities should be materially reduced and a counterbalancing tax levied on all articles of foreign manufacture.

He advocated moderate Social reform on lines carefully designed to encourage thrift, temperance and endeavour; and as one prime means towards improving the condition, both moral and physical, of the workers he would have the State, either directly or through local authorities, provide them with decent homes.

To the consideration of Labour problems, particularly those coming within the scope of his own experience, he gave much thought; and when it is considered that his great popularity with all classes held steady through the recent period of industrial unrest, we may judge that his attitude towards Labour, in the mass as in the unit, was no mere personal expression of friendliness. As his real pals he wanted to help the workers, educate and lift[52] them. Other things being equal, he always favoured the men who used their heads as well as their hands; and if in the management of their own affairs they used their heads, then also, so much the better for all concerned. He considered that both in the interests of men and masters, it was well for Labour to be organized under capable leaders; but honest agreements should, he thought, be binding on both sides and not liable to governmental interference. Politicians and others should in their public utterances, he felt, endeavour to educate the workers in the principles of economics relative to trade, wages and the relations between capital and labour; but publicists who, for party or like reasons, strove to foster class hatreds and strifes he would hang by the heels from a gantry.

Where economically possible, the working day should, he thought, be shortened, especially the day of all toiling in arduous and unwholesome conditions. Similarly he was disposed to favour, when economically possible, encouragement of the workers by means of a system of profit sharing. He would, furthermore, give them every facility for technical education, but such he knew from experience was of little value unless supplemented by thorough practical knowledge gained in the workshop.

These views and opinions, whatever their intrinsic value in the eyes of experts, are at least interesting. Sooner or later, had Andrews lived, he would perhaps have made them the basis of public pronouncements; and then indeed might his abounding energy, applied in new and luring directions, have carried him to heights of citizenship.

Chapter Seven.

HAPPILY, there is no need in these pages to attempt any minute estimate of the share Andrews had in building the *Titanic*. Such a task, were it feasible, would offer difficulties no less testing than those met courageously by half the world's journalists when attempting to describe the wonders of that ill-fated vessel—her length that of a suburban street, her height the equivalent of a seventeen story building, her elevator cars coursing up and down as through a city hotel, her millionaire suites, her luxuries of squash racquet courts, Turkish and electric bath establishments, salt water swimming pools, glass enclosed sun parlours, verandah cafés, and all. Probably no one man, was solely responsible for the beautiful thing. She was an evolution rather than a creation, triumphant product of numberless experiments, a perfection embodying who knows what endeavour, from this a little, from that a little more, of human brain and hand and imagination. How many ships were built, how many lost; how many men lived, wrought, and died that the *Titanic* might be?

So much being said, it may however be said further, that to her building Andrews gave as much of himself as did any other man. All his experience of ships, gained in the yards, on voyages, by long study, was in her; all his deep knowledge, too, gathered during twenty years and now applied in a crowning effort with an ardour that never flagged. It was by the *Titanic*, "her vast shape slowly assuming the beauty and symmetry which are but a memory to-day," that Mr. Childers met Andrews and noted in him those qualities of zest, vigour, power and simplicity, which impressed him deeply. Yet Andrews then was no whit more enthusiastic, we feel sure, than on any other day of the great ship's fashioning, from the time of her conception slowly down through the long process of calculating, planning, designing, building, fitting, until at last she sailed proudly away to the applause of half the world. Whatever share others had in her, his at least cannot be gainsaid. As Lord Pirrie's Assistant he had done his part by way of shaping into tangible form the projects of her owners. As Chief Designer and Naval Architect he planned her complete. As Managing Director he saw her grow up, frame by frame, plate by plate, day after day throughout more than two[56] years; watched her grow as a father watches his child grow, assiduously, minutely, and with much the same feelings of parental pride and affection. For Andrews this was *his* ship, whatever his hand in her: and in that she was "efficiently designed and constructed" as is now established[3] his fame as a Shipbuilder may well rest. As surely none other did, he knew her inside and out, her every turn and art, the power and beauty of her, from keel to truck—knew her to the last rivet. And because he knew the great ship so well, as a father knows the child born to him, therefore to lose her was heartbreak.

THE "TITANIC" LEAVING BELFAST

On Tuesday morning, April 2nd, 1912, at 6 a.m., the *Titanic* left Belfast, in ideal weather, and was towed down Channel to complete her trials. On board was Andrews, representing the Firm. Her compasses being adjusted, the ship steamed towards the Isle of Man, and after a satisfactory run returned to the Lough about 6 p.m. Throughout the whole day Andrews was busy, receiving representatives of the owners, inspecting and superintending the work of internal completion, and taking notes. "Just a line," he wrote to Mrs. Andrews, "to let you know that we got away this morning in fine style and have had a very satisfactory trial. We are getting more ship-shape every hour, but there is still a great deal to be done."

Having received letters and transferred workmen, the ship left immediately for Southampton, Andrews still on board and with him, amongst others, the eight brave men from the Island Yard who perished with him. They were:

- William Henry Marsh Parr, Assistant Manager Electrical Department.
- Roderick Chisholm, Ships' Draughtsman.
- Anthony W. Frost, Outside Foreman Engineer.
- Robert Knight, Leading Hand Engineer.
- William Campbell, Joiner Apprentice.
- Alfred Fleming Cunningham, Fitter Apprentice.
- Frank Parkes, Plumber Apprentice.
- Ennis Hastings Watson, Electrician Apprentice.

During the whole of Wednesday, the 3rd, until midnight, when the ship arrived at Southampton, Andrews was ceaselessly employed going round with representatives of the owners and of the Firm, in taking notes and preparing reports of work still to be done. All the next day, from an early hour, he spent with managers and foremen putting work in hand.[58]

In the evening he wrote to Mrs. Andrews: "I wired you this morning of our safe arrival after a very satisfactory trip. The weather was good and everyone most pleasant. I think the ship will clean up all right before sailing on Wednesday": and then he mentions that the doctors refused to allow Lord Pirrie to make the maiden voyage.

Thereafter from day to day, until the date of sailing, he was always busy, taking the owners round ship, interviewing engineers, officials, agents, managers, sub-contractors, discussing with principals the plans of new ships, and superintending generally the work of completion.

"Through the various days that the vessel lay at Southampton," writes his Secretary, Mr. Thompson Hamilton, "Mr. Andrews was never for a moment idle. He generally left his hotel about 8.30 for the offices, where he dealt with his correspondence, then went on board until 6.30, when he would return to the offices to sign letters. During the day I took to the ship any urgent papers and he always dealt with them no matter what his business." Nothing he allowed to interfere with duty. He was conscientious to the minutest detail. "He would himself put in their place such things as racks, tables, chairs, berth ladders, electric fans, saving that except he saw everything right he could not be satisfied."

One of the last letters he wrote records serious trouble with the restaurant galley hot press, and directs attention to a design for reducing the number of screws in stateroom hat hooks.

Another of earlier date, in the midst of technicalities about cofferdams and submerged cylinders on the propeller boss, expresses agreement with the owner that the colouring of the pebble dashing on the private promenade decks was too dark, and notes a plan for staining green the wicker furniture on one side of the vessel.

Withal, his thought for others never failed. Now he is arranging for a party to view the ship; now writing to a colleague, "I have always in mind a week's holiday due to you from last summer and shall be glad if you will make arrangements to take these on my return, as, although you may not desire to have them, I feel sure that a week's rest will do you good."

On the evening of Sunday, the 7th, he wrote to Mrs. Andrews giving her news of his movements and dwelling upon the plans he had in mind for the future.

On the 9th he wrote: "The *Titanic* is now about complete and will I think do the old Firm credit to-morrow when we sail."

On the 10th he was aboard at 6 o'clock, and thence until the hour of sailing he spent in a long final inspection of the ship. She pleased him. The old Firm was sure of its credit.

Just before the moorings were cast off he bade goodbye to Mr. Hamilton and the other officials. He seemed in excellent health and spirits. His last words were, "Remember now and keep Mrs. Andrews informed of any news of the vessel."

The *Titanic*, carrying 2,201 souls, left Southampton punctually at noon on April 10th. There was no departure ceremony. On her way from dock she passed the *Majestic* and the *Philadelphia*, both giants of twenty years ago and now by contrast with Leviathan humbled to the stature of dwarfs. About a mile down the water she passed Test Quay, where the *Oceanic* and the *New York* lay berthed. Her wash caused the *New York* to break her moorings and drift into the Channel. As the *Titanic* was going dead slow danger of a collision was soon averted, "but," as Andrews wrote that evening, "the situation was decidedly unpleasant."

From Cherbourg he wrote again to Mrs. Andrews: "We reached here in nice time and took on board quite a number of passengers. The two little tenders looked well, you will remember we built them about a year ago. We expect to arrive at Queenstown about 10.30 a.m. to-morrow. The weather is fine and everything shaping for a good voyage. I have a seat at the Doctor's table."

One more letter was received from him by Mrs. Andrews, and only one, this time from Queenstown, and dated April 11th. Everything on board was going splendidly, he said, and he expressed his satisfaction at receiving so much kindness from everyone.

Here all direct testimony ceases. Proudly, in eye of the world, the *Titanic* sailed Westward from the Irish coast; then for a while disappeared; only to reappear in a brief scene of woefullest tragedy round which the world stayed mute. If, as is almost certain, a chronicle of the voyage was made by Andrews, both it and the family letters he wrote now are gone with him. But fortunately, we have other evidence, plentiful and well-attested, and on such our story henceforward runs.

The steward, Henry E. Etches, who attended him says, that during the voyage, right to the moment of disaster, Andrews was constantly busy. With his workmen he went about the boat all day long, putting things right and making note of every suggestion of an imperfection. Afterwards in his stateroom, which is described as being full of charts, he would sit for hours, making calculations and drawings for future use.

Others speak of his great popularity with both passengers and crew. "I was proud of him," writes the brave stewardess, Miss May Sloan, of Belfast, whose testimony is so invaluable. "He came from home and he made you feel on the ship that all was right." And then she adds how because of his big, gentle, kindly nature everyone loved him. "It was good to hear his laugh and have him near you. If anything went wrong it was always to Mr. Andrews one went. Even when a fan stuck in a stateroom, one would say, 'Wait for Mr. Andrews, he'll soon see to it,' and you would find him settling even the little quarrels that arose between ourselves. Nothing came amiss to him, nothing at all. And he was always the same, a nod and a smile or a hearty word whenever he saw you and no matter what he was at."

Two of his table companions, Mr. and Mrs. Albert A. Dick, of Calgary, Alberta, also tell how much they came to love Andrews because of his character, and how good it was to see his pride in the ship, "but upon every occasion, and especially at dinner on Sunday evening, he talked almost constantly about his wife, little girl, mother and family, as well as of his home."

This pre-occupation with home and all there, was noticed too by Miss Sloan. Sometimes, between laughs, he would suddenly fall grave and glance, you might say, back over a shoulder towards Dunallan and Ardara far off near Strangford Lough.

"I was talking to him on the Friday night as he was going into dinner," writes Miss Sloan, in a letter dated from the *Lapland* on April 27th. "The dear old Doctor[4] was waiting for him on the stair-landing, and calling him by his Christian name, Tommy. Mr. Andrews seemed loth to go, he wanted to talk about home; he was telling me his father was ill and Mrs. Andrews not so well. I was congratulating him on the beauty and perfection of the ship; he said the part he did not like was that the *Titanic* was taking us further away from home every hour. I looked at him and his face struck me as having a very sad expression."

One other glimpse we have of him, then in that brief time of triumph, whilst yet the good ship of his which everyone praised was speeding Westwards, "in perfectly clear and fine weather," towards the place where "was no moon, the stars were out, and there was not a cloud in the sky."[5] For more than a week he had been working at such pressure, that by the Friday evening many saw how tired as well as sad he looked: but by the Sunday evening, when his ship was as perfect, so he said, as brains could make her, he was himself again. "I saw him go in to dinner," said Miss Sloan, "he was in good spirits, and I thought he looked splendid."

An hour or two afterwards he went aft to thank the baker for some special bread he had made for him; then back to his stateroom, where apparently he changed into working clothes, and sat down to write.

He was still writing, it would seem, when the Captain called him.

Chapter Eight

ON the night of Sunday, 14th April, at 11 40 ship's time, in clear fine weather, near Latitude 41° 46′ N., Longitude 50° 14′ W., the *Titanic* collided with the submerged spur of an iceberg and ripped her starboard side ten feet above the level of the keel for a length of about three hundred feet, thereby giving access to the sea in six of her forward compartments.

The calamity came with dreadful swiftness. In the vivid words of a stoker, on duty at the time of collision some two hundred and fifty feet from the stem: "All of a sudden the starboard side of the ship came in upon us; it burst like a big gun going off; the water came pouring in and swilled our legs." Within ten minutes the water rose fourteen feet above the keel in five of the compartments; afterwards it rose steadily in all six; and by midnight had submerged the lower deck in the foremost hold. Yet so gentle apparently was the shock of contact that among the passengers, and probably among most of the crew as well, it was only the stopping of the engines that warned them of some happening; whilst for a considerable time, so quietly the great ship lay on the flat sea, such confidence had all in her strength, and so orderly was everything, that to many, almost to the last, it seemed impossible that disaster had come.[6]

"At first we did not realise," says Mr. Albert Dick,[7] "that the *Titanic* was mortally wounded.... I do not believe that anyone on her realised she was going to sink." Mr. Dick goes on to record that, in his view, nothing deserved more praise than the conduct of Andrews after the ship had struck. "He was on hand at once and said that he was going below to investigate. We begged him not to go, but he insisted, saying he knew the ship as no one else did and that he might be able to allay the fears of the passengers. He went.

"As the minutes flew by we did not know what to do or which way to turn.... Captain Smith was everywhere doing his best to calm the rising tide of fear.... But in the minds of most of us there was ... the feeling that something was going to happen, and we waited for Mr. Andrews to come back.

"When he came we hung upon his words, and they were these: 'There is no cause for any excitement. All of you get what you can in the way of clothes and come on deck as soon as you can. She is torn to bits below, but she will not sink if her after bulkheads hold.'

"It seemed almost impossible that this could be true ... and many in the crowd smiled, thinking this was merely a little extra knowledge that Mr. Andrews saw fit to impart...."

It is almost certain that Andrews, who knew the ship as no one else did, realised at his first sight of her wounds—a three hundred feet gash, six compartments open to the sea and perhaps twenty feet of water in one or more of them—that she was doomed. Possibly with some of his faithful assistants, probably with Captain Smith, he had made a thorough examination of the damaged side, reporting to the Captain as result of his examination that the ship could not live more than an hour and a half, and advising him to clear away the boats.

42

How this order was carried out, with what skill and unselfishness on the part of Captain Smith and his officers, has been told elsewhere[8] in full detail; nor is it necessary to record further here than that eventually, after two hours of heroic work, a total of 652 lives left the *Titanic* in eighteen boats. Subsequently 60 more were rescued from the sea, or transferred from the collapsibles, making a sum total of 712 rescued by the *Carpathia*. 712 out of 2,201: it seems tragically few! Yet at midnight it may have seemed to Andrews that fewer still could be saved, for not even he hoped that his ship could live for two hours and twenty minutes more.

As he came up from the grim work of investigation he saw Miss Sloan and told her that as an accident had happened it would be well, just by way of precaution, to get her passengers to put on warm clothing and their life belts and assemble on the Boat deck. But she read his face, "which had a look as though he were heart broken," and asked him if the accident were not serious. He said it was very serious; then, bidding her keep the bad news quiet for fear of panic, he hurried away to the work of warning and rescue.

Another stewardess gives an account of Andrews, bareheaded and insufficiently clad against the icy cold, going quietly about bidding the attendants to rouse all passengers and get them up to the boats.

Overhearing him say to Captain Smith on the Upper deck, "Well, three have gone already, Captain," she ran to the lower stairway and to her surprise found water within six steps of her feet. Whereupon she hurried above to summon help, and returning met Andrews, who told her to advise passengers to leave the Upper deck.

Ten minutes went. The water had crept further up the stairway. Again Andrews came to her and said, "Tell them to put on warm clothing, see that everyone has a lifebelt and get them all up to the Boat deck."

Another fifteen minutes went. The top of the stairway was now nearly awash. A second time Andrews came. "Open up all the spare rooms," he ordered. "Take out all lifebelts and spare blankets and distribute them."

This was done. Attendants and passengers went above to the Boat deck. But returning for more belts, the stewardess again met Andrews. He asked her whether all the ladies had left their rooms. She answered "Yes, but would make sure."

"Go round again," said he; and then, "Did I not tell you to put on your lifebelt. Surely you have one?"

She answered "Yes, but I thought it means to wear it."

"Never mind that," said he. "Now, if you value your life, put on your coat and belt, then walk round the deck and let the passengers see you."

"He left me then," writes the stewardess, "and that was the last I saw of what I consider a true hero and one of whom his country has cause to be proud."

In how far Andrews' efforts and example were the means of averting what might well have been an awful panic, cannot be said; but sure it is that all one man could do in such service, both personally and by way of assisting the ship's officers, was done by him. "He was here, there and everywhere," says Miss Sloan, "looking after everybody, telling the women to put on lifebelts, telling the stewardesses to hurry the women up to the boats, all about everywhere, thinking of everyone but himself."

Others tell a similar story, how calm and unselfish he was, now pausing on his way to the engine-room to reassure some passengers, now earnestly begging women to be quick, now helping one to put on her lifebelt—"all about everywhere, thinking of everybody but himself."

It is certain also that on the Boat deck he gave invaluable help to the officers and men engaged in the work of rescue. Being familiar with the boats' tackle and arrangement he was able to aid effectively at their launching; and it was whilst going quietly from boat to boat, probably in those tragic intervals during which the stewardess watched the water creep up the stairway, that he was heard to say: "Now, men, remember you are Englishmen. Women and children first."

Some twenty minutes before the end, when the last distress signal had been fired in vain, when all that Upper deck and the Fore deck as well were ravaged by the sea, there was a crush and a little confusion near the place where the few remaining boats were being lowered, women and children shrinking back, some afraid to venture, some preferring to stay with their husbands, a few perhaps in the grip of cold and terror. Then Andrews came and waving his arms gave loud command:

"Ladies, you must get in at once. There is not a minute to lose. You cannot pick and choose your boat. Don't hesitate. Get in, get in!"

They obeyed him. Do they remember to-day, any of them, that to him they, as so many more, may owe their lives?

A little way back from that scene, Miss Sloan stood calmly waiting and seeing Andrews for the last time. She herself was not very anxious to leave the ship, for all her friends were staying behind and she felt it was mean to go. But the command of the man, who for nearly two hours she had seen doing as splendidly as now he was doing, came imperatively. "Don't hesitate! There's not a moment to lose. Get in!" So she stepped into the last boat and was saved.

It was then five minutes past two. The *Titanic* had fifteen minutes more to live.

Well, all was done now that could be done, and the time remaining was short. The Forecastle head was under water. All around, out on the sea, so calm under those wonderful stars, the boats were scattered, some near, some a mile away or more, the eyes of most in them turned back upon the doomed ship as one by one her port lights, that still burnt row above row in dreadful sloping lines, sank slowly into darkness. Soon the lines would tilt upright, then flash out and flash bright again; then, as the engines crashed down through the bulkheads, go out once more, and leave that awful form standing up against the sky, motionless, black, preparing for the final plunge.

But that time was not yet. Some fifteen minutes were left: and in those minutes we still have sight of Andrews.

One met him, bareheaded and carrying a lifebelt, on his way to the bridge perhaps to bid the Captain goodbye.

Later, an assistant steward saw him standing alone in the smoking-room, his arms folded over his breast and the belt lying on a table near him. The steward asked him, "Aren't you going to have a try for it, Mr. Andrews?"

He never answered or moved, "just stood like one stunned."

What did he see as he stood there, alone, rapt? We who know the man and his record can believe that before him was home and all the loved ones there, wife and child, father and mother, brothers and sister, relatives, friends—that picture and all it meant to him then and there; and besides, just for a moment maybe, and as background to all that, swift realisation of the awful tragedy ending his life, ending his ship.

But whatever he saw, in that quiet lonely minute, it did not hold or unman him. Work—work—he must work to the bitter end.

Some saw him for the last time, down in the Engine-room, with Chief engineer Bell and Archie Frost and the other heroes, all toiling like men to keep the lights going and the pumps at work.

Others saw him, a few minutes before the end, on the Boat deck, our final and grandest sight of him, throwing deck chairs overboard to the unfortunates struggling in the water below.

Then, with a slow long slanting dive, the *Titanic* went down, giving to the sea her short-spanned life and with it the life of Thomas Andrews.

So died this noble man. We may hope that he lies, as indeed he might be proud to lie, in the great ship he had helped to fashion.

Appendix.

AT the request of the Family the publishers have inserted the following cables (telegrams) and letters which were received when the news of the disaster first became public.

Cable dated New York, 19th April, 1912, addressed to Mr. James Moore, Belfast.

Interview Titanic's officers. All unanimous Andrews heroic unto death, thinking only safety others. Extend heartfelt sympathy to all.

JAMES MONTGOMERY.

Cable dated 21st April, 1912, received by the White Star Line in Liverpool from their Office in New York.

After accident Andrews ascertained damage, advised passengers to put on heavy clothing and prepare to leave vessel. Many were sceptical about the seriousness of the damage, but impressed by Andrews' knowledge and personality, followed his advice, and so saved their lives. He assisted many women and children to lifeboats. When last seen, officers say, he was throwing overboard deck chairs and other objects to people in the water, his chief concern the safety of everyone but himself.

Extract from letter written by Lord Pirrie to his sister, Mrs. Thomas Andrews, Sen.

"A finer fellow than Tommie never lived, and by his death--unselfishly beautiful to the last--we are bereft of the strong young life upon which such reliance had come to be placed by us elders who loved and needed him."

Copy of Letter received by Mrs. Thomas Andrews, Jun. from Mr. Bruce Ismay.

30 JAMES STREET,

LIVERPOOL, 31st May, 1912.

DEAR MRS. ANDREWS,

Forgive me for intruding upon your grief, but I feel I must send you a line to convey my most deep and sincere sympathy with you in the terrible loss you have suffered. It is impossible for me to express in words all I feel, or make you realise how truly sorry I am for you, or how my heart goes out to you. I knew your husband for many years, and had the highest regard for him, and looked upon him as a true friend. No one who had the pleasure of knowing him could fail to realise and appreciate his numerous good qualities and he will be sadly missed in his profession. Nobody did more for the White Star Line, or was more loyal to its interests than your good husband, and I always placed the utmost reliance on his judgment.

If we miss him and feel his loss so keenly, what your feelings must be I cannot think. Words at such a time are useless, but I could not help writing to you to tell you how truly deeply I feel for you in your grief and sorrow.

Yours sincerely,

BRUCE ISMAY.

Letter from Sir Horace Plunkett to Right Hon. Thomas Andrews.

THE PLUNKETT HOUSE,

DUBLIN, 19th April, 1912.

MY DEAR ANDREWS,

No act of friendship is so difficult as the letter of condolence upon the loss of one who is near and dear. Strive as we may to avoid vapid conventionality, we find ourselves drifting into reflections upon the course of nature, the cessation of suffering, the worse that might have been, and such offers of comfort to others which we are conscious would be of little help to ourselves. In writing to you and your wife on the sorrow of two worlds, which has fallen so heavily upon your home and family, I feel no such difficulty. There is no temptation to be conventional, but it is hard to express in words the very real consolation which will long be cherished by the wide circle of those now bitterly deploring the early death of one who was clearly marked out for a great career in the chief doing part of Irish life.

Of the worth of your son I need not speak to you--nothing I could say of his character or capacity could add to your pride in him. But you ought to know that we all feel how entirely to his own merits was due the extraordinary rapidity of his rise and the acknowledged certainty of his leadership in what Ulster stands for before the world. When I first saw him in the shipyard he was in a humble position, enjoying no advantage on account of your relationship to one of his employers. Even then, as on many subsequent occasions, I learned, or heard from my Irish fellow-workers, that this splendid son of yours had the best kind of public spirit--that which made you and Sinclair save the Recess Committee at its crisis.

It may be that the story of your poor boy's death will never be told, but I seem to see it all. I have just come off the sister ship, whose captain was a personal friend, as was the old doctor who went with him to the Titanic. I have been often in the fog among the icebergs. I have heard, in over sixty voyages, many of those awful tales of the sea. I know enough to be aware that your son might easily have saved himself on grounds of public duty none could gainsay. What better witness could be found to tell the millions who would want and had a right to know why the great ship failed, and how her successors could be made, as she was believed to be, unsinkable? None of his breed could listen to such promptings of the lower self when the call came to show to what height the real man in him could rise. I think of him displaying the very highest quality of courage--the true heroism--without any of the stimulants which the glamour and prizes of battle supply-- doing all he could for the women and children--and then going grimly and silently to his glorious grave.

So there is a bright side to the picture which you of his blood and his widow must try to share with his and your friends--with the thousands who will treasure his memory. It will help you in your bereavement, and that is why I intrude upon your sorrow with a longer letter than would suffice to tender to you and Mrs. Andrews and to all your family circle a tribute of heartfelt sympathy.

Pray accept this as coming not only from myself but also from those intimately associated with me in the Irish work which brought me, among other blessings, the friendship of men like yourself.

Believe me,
Yours always,

HORACE PLUNKETT.

(THE END OF THE 1912 TEXT)

FOOTNOTES:

[1] In Belfast a memorial to Thomas Andrews and the other Belfast men who died in the wreck has been generously subscribed to by the citizens, and by the Queen's Island workers. He is also included amongst those to whom a similar memorial is to be erected in Southampton. The Reform Club in Belfast is honouring his memory with a tablet.

[2] It is interesting to note the circumstances which brought these two men together. Mr. Adams, who is now Professor of Political Theory and Institutions at Oxford, was then Superintendent of Statistics and Intelligence in the Irish Department of Agriculture and Technical Instruction. He went to Andrews as the man most likely to give him reliable information and sound opinions upon certain industrial questions of interest to the Department. A peculiar value attaches to the high regard in which Thomas Andrews was held by this distinguished political and economic thinker.

[3] Report of Mersey Commission, pp. 61 and 71.

[4] Dr. W. F. N. O'Loughlin, Senior Surgeon of the White Star Line, a close friend of Andrews and his companion on many voyages. Some lines which he helped to write have been quoted. Soon after the ship struck he said to Miss Sloan—"child, things are very bad," and went to his death bravely. His Assistant, Dr. T. E. Simpson, son of an eminent Belfast physician, and himself a physician of much promise, died with him.

[5] Report of Mersey Commission, p. 29.

[6] Mersey Commission Report; Sir William White's letter to the *Times*, dated May 14th.

[7] *New York Herald*, April 20th, 1912.

[8] *E.g.*, Mersey Commission Report, pp. 39-41.

ADDITIONAL PHOTOS

-firstly the ones from the book enlarged to do them justice ……..

Ardara, Comber – the house where Tommy was born

Harland and Wolff's Turbine Erecting Shop – men in the centre distance give an impression of its huge size

Harland and Wolff's Turning Shop

The 'Titanic' and 'Olympic' Building – in the largest gantry in the world at the time

The 'Titanic' leaving Belfast Lough.

Secondly, some additional photos ………

North Down Cricket Club 1895 –the Andrews IX Team

Tommy is at the top of the photo – moustached at that time - with his uncle and two of his brothers and his cousins of whom my great grandfather Arthur is at the bottom right..

24th June 2008 Wedding Day

Nellie Elba and Tommy –probably taken in 1911

The house where the couple lived - Dunallan 12 Windsor Avenue, Belfast

Andrews Family group –Tommy second in from the right with his mother and father, his sister and his three brothers.